AN AMERICAN IN CHINA

THIRTY YEARS IN THE PEOPLE'S REPUBLIC

BY

SIDNEY SHAPIRO

A MERIDIAN BOOK

NEW AMERICAN LIBRARY

TIMES MIRROR

NEW YORK AND SCARBOROUGH, ONTARIO

Published by arrangement with the author

MERIDIAN TRADEMARK REG. U.S. PAT. OFF. AND FOREIGN COUNTRIES
REGISTERED TRADEMARK—MARCA REGISTRADA
HECHO EN FORGE VILLAGE, MASS., U.S.A.

SIGNET, SIGNET CLASSICS, MENTOR, PLUME, MERIDIAN and NAL BOOKS
are published *in the United States* by The New American Library, Inc.,
1633 Broadway, New York, New York 10019, *in Canada* by The New American
Library of Canada Limited, 81 Mack Avenue, Scarborough, Ontario M1L 1M8.

First Meridian Printing, October, 1980

1 2 3 4 5 6 7 8 9

PRINTED IN THE UNITED STATES OF AMERICA

CONTENTS

I

AN END AND A BEGINNING

1947-1948

He was running along the shore, his long black gown flapping in the wind. I stared from the rail of the freighter moving slowly up the Whangpoo River toward Shanghai. A medieval monk? It was my first view of the *chang pao*, the long gown worn by Chinese men, if they could afford one, in lieu of an overcoat. He was no monk, but the medieval impression was prophetic, for China in April 1947 was something very much out of the Dark Ages.

I had come a long way. What had brought me, a thirty-two-year-old-American, member of the bar of the state of New York, army veteran, to these distant shores? It had started six years before.

In 1941 I was one of a crew of nursemaids to a 40 mm. Bofors anti-aircraft gun. We were stationed in a swamp euphemistically known as the Jersey Meadow, guarding Westinghouse and General Electric plants from attack by German bombers. There were about a dozen of us. We served in shifts — two hours on, four hours off, around the clock — waiting for the raids which fortunately, considering our marksmanship, never came.

It was a lonely job, though we had plenty of rats and mosquitoes for company. When the smog wasn't too thick, we could see the Empire State Building and the New York skyline. Another reminder of civilization was the fragrance of Secaucus, famed pig slaughtering center, wafted to us by the breeze.

Then, word spread that an Army Specialized Training Program had been established. Men were being sent to the universities, in uniform, to learn foreign languages for possible future assignment abroad.

Why not? I had had a few years of French in high school and college. At least it would get me out of the swamp. I applied.

1

Some weeks later I was sent to the City College of New York, ASTP testing center for the military region.

I had forgotten a lot of French but managed to scrape through the written exams. Next came the oral. My spoken French was virtually non-existent, but the army grapevine was operating with its usual efficiency, and we all were quickly informed of the pattern of the oral tests. "What is your name? Where are you from? What did you do before the war? . . ." I prepared accordingly.

My inquisitor was an old City College professor, a Frenchman. Sure enough, he put forward the routine questions. I answered smoothly, my Flatbush accent impeccable.

"What were you before the war?"

"*Un avocat, monsieur.*"

He looked at me with interest. Switching to English, he confided that he too had been *un avocat*, when a young man in France. And what was my opinion of *Les Freres Coudert*?

Coudert Brothers, one of the largest French law firms in New York? I had just been reading about them in the papers. They were the attorneys for the Vichy French government. Though somewhat mystified, I gave a candid reply.

"I think they stink."

The old professor's eyes glowed. It turned out that we were in complete accord. Not for political reasons, but because *Les Freres Coudert* had ruined his life. Forty years ago he had landed in New York with dreams of making his fortune as a French lawyer and applied to Coudert Brothers for a job. Since he was not from a rich family and couldn't introduce any wealthy clients, they turned him down. He was forced to take up the teaching of French, a profession he loathed. For this, Coudert Brothers were responsible. He had never forgiven them.

I had uttered sentiments very close to his heart. He smiled amiably, and passed me on the oral.

There seemed little doubt I'd soon be studying French again. I relaxed.

But it wasn't that simple. The last step was to appear before a board of army brass and college professors who formally announced your assignment. A few days later, spruce and polished, I stood smartly at attention before the board.

They informed me I had passed the French tests. However, they said, they had more French students than they could use. How would I like to study Chinese?

I stood goggle-eyed, gaping like a cod.

A major oiled in smoothly with a soft sell.

"You live in New York City, don't you?"

"Yes sir."

"Well, while I'm not at liberty to divulge the details, I can tell you this — the college we are planning to send you to is in New York State. You'll be able to get home fairly often."

I still hesitated. Chinese? I'd never given it a thought. The major moved in with the clincher.

"It's co-ed!"

"I'll take it!"

The next week I was at Cornell, ensconced in a fraternity house with a well-equipped bar in the basement. It was wartime, and most of the male student population was gone. The girls seemed glad to see us.

Nine months later we finished our course. We could carry on simple conversations, read a bit, write practically not at all. We had a smattering of Chinese history, geography and current affairs. By US Army standards that made us experts. We went to Chinese restaurants whenever possible and practiced using chopsticks. We were, we thought, ready to go.

Again, forces mightier than ourselves were at work. The rumored allied landing in China, if it had ever been seriously contemplated, was called off, and with it the need for Chinese interpreters.

What to do with us? The army had spent thousands training men in Chinese at half a dozen different universities. With typical genius, some brain in the Pentagon made a brilliant decision — we would translate Japanese, and not just the ordinary kind, but Japanese in code. The fact that there is hardly any resemblance between the two languages bothered no one.

A few weeks quickie course at a school for cryptanalysts, with a perfunctory nod at Japanese grammar, and we were whisked off to MIDPAC — Middle Pacific Headquarters — in Honolulu.

We spent the next six months till the end of the war deciphering low priority intercepted messages, mostly between Japanese pilots and their control towers regarding the state of the weather. It was just another army boondoggle and everyone was bored stiff.

To keep ourselves busy and because we were interested, a few of us sat in on Chinese language courses at the University of Hawaii when we were off duty. We studied and practiced on chow lines and during our work shifts whenever the officer on duty goofed off. By that time I was really hooked on Chinese.

The end of 1946 found me back in New York, a civilian again. I had been a lawyer, a junior partner of my father, but he had died during the war. I couldn't afford to keep up our office in the Paramount Building and I didn't want to work for any of the big law firms.

Under the GI Bill a veteran was entitled to paid tuition in a university plus subsistence allowance for roughly as many years as he had served in the armed force. I decided to use some of that time studying Chinese, until I could make up my mind what I wanted to do with my life. I enrolled at Columbia, taking nothing but Chinese language courses. I did two terms there, then transferred to Yale where I did a third.

At Yale I roomed with Julian Schuman, whom I had met in Hawaii. He had studied Chinese in the ASTP at Harvard and, like me, had also been made a Japanese cryptanalyst. A New Yorker, Julian was still in his early twenties, while I was already past thirty.

Wandering amid Yale's ivy-clad towers was pleasant enough, but I couldn't go on being a schoolboy indefinitely. To what use could I put the Chinese which so intrigued me?

A few Chinese students whom I had met studying at Columbia and Yale suggested that I go to China. They said an American lawyer who spoke Chinese would certainly do well.

I wasn't so sure, but the idea appealed to me. I was unmarried. My mother had a job which could sustain her. I was fed up with the rat race, the money grubbing, the wheeling and dealing which was the milieu of the average lawyer. Commercial law was the only field I knew, but I hoped that in the glamorous East business might somehow be different. Although a certain amount of risk was involved, it didn't worry me. I had hitchhiked and ridden freight during the depression and still had a craving for adventure.

My total finances consisted of $500 — my army discharge bonus. I spent $300 of it for a ticket on a small freighter which had passenger accommodations for four, traveling from New York to Shanghai via the Panama Canal. The only commercial possibilities I could line up before leaving were a couple of small exporters who gave me samples of army surplus clothing and a promise of commission if I sold anything, and a stringer arrangement with *Variety* for coverage of Chinese stage and screen events. I never wrote a line for *Variety,* but the clothing came in handy when my own suits began wearing out.

Julian Schuman said he might join me later, depending on what I found. I promised my mother I would come back soon if I couldn't make a go of things.

I was not to see New York again for twenty-five years.

We set sail one dreary day early in March, 1947. My cabin mate was a French Canadian Catholic priest on his way to one of his order's numerous missions in north China. He spoke no English, but was generous with bottles of excellent brandy he had brought along for *le mal de mer,* and we were soon on good drinking, if not speaking, terms.

The passengers sharing the other cabin were a young husband and wife, she very pregnant. He had been with the US Marines in south China during the war and discovered that the Chinese had no milk to drink. He was going to set up a dairy farm somewhere in Fukien province and make his fortune. He didn't know, nor for that matter did I, that cow's milk was never part of China's diet. They had got along without it for centuries, subsisting on a "milk" of dried powdered soybean mixed with hot water, which was a lot simpler to make and had nearly the same nourishment. Though his scheme was highly impractical, he had obviously been smitten by the charm of China, and his enthusiastic descriptions of lush southern scenery was good for my morale.

I needed all the morale boosting I could get, for I was sick as a dog from the time we passed Cape Hatteras, off the Carolinas. What is it they say about sea-sickness? "First you're afraid you'll die, then you're afraid you won't."

Miraculously, from the Panama Canal on, I was cured. I began to enjoy the beauty of the sea, its changing shades of blue and gray and green. We saw porpoises and whales. We came quite close to one great cow of a mother whale and her baby. They lay meditating, placidly unconcerned.

We stopped for a day in Honolulu, and I wandered around. The colors were so bright, the flowers so fragrant. It looked cleaner and more spacious without the thousands of men in uniform who had filled the streets only two years before.

We started the last lap of our journey. Chinese stations were coming in loudly over my radio. I could understand quite a lot. I was thrilled. What would I do when we actually got there? My mind was vague. I had about $200 in my pocket, a duffle bag full of army surplus clothing samples, a few letters and gifts from Chinese students in America to their families in Shanghai, some things of my own, and that was all.

I suppose what I wanted most was to improve my Chinese until I was really fluent, then see what the job opportunities were. It seemed to me I would have to go to Peking for language training, since Shanghai dialect is very different from the "national speech" used north of the Yangtze. But first I would spend some time in Shanghai and get the feel of things.

The ocean began turning yellow when we were still three days from land. We were approaching the estuary of the Yangtze, the great river running west to east across China's middle, past Chungking, Wuhan and Nanking to the bustling port of Shanghai, which means, literally, "on the sea".

The yellow tinge deepened to brown. A hazy blur grew on the horizon. China! I slept like a log that night, worn out by the excitement.

When I awakened the following morning we were already steaming slowly up the Whangpoo, which leads from the Yangtze to the center of the city.

It was then I saw on the distant bank that strange figure in the flapping black gown. Soon he was joined by another man, similarly clad. They both kept trotting along, in the opposite direction, until they were out of sight. I could see squat houses, with thatched roofs and walls of daubed wattle. Cars and trucks tooled along dirt roads, trailing clouds of dust. Tall modern buildings appeared. Wharves and docks lined the river. Beside them ferries and ocean-going passenger ships were berthed. Foreign warships rode at anchor.

A launch pulled alongside, and we were boarded by customs and immigration officers. They made a perfunctory examination of our luggage. One of them, a smartly dressed fellow who spoke good English, took me aside and asked if I wanted to exchange any US dollars.

"I'll give you the top rate," he said.

It seemed there were two rates for foreign currency. One was official, a prestige form of wishful thinking and an opportunity for manipulation of public funds by crooked bureaucrats. The other was the black market rate, which was quite open, and changed from day to day in keeping with supply and demand. Chinese *yuan* rolling off the printing presses of the Kuomintang — Chiang Kai-shek's ruling party — was worth very little, and inflation was rapid.

I handed the gentleman $50 and he counted out what looked to me like a large sum of *yuan* in crisp new bills. I discovered later, when I became familiar with the rates, that he cheated me handsomely.

On landing I was met by the family of Nancy Yang, a girl with whom I had exchanged English for Chinese lessons at Yale. I brought them gifts — mostly men's clothing, which I was able to bring through Customs as my personal belongings. The Yangs insisted I stay with them temporarily, and I gladly agreed, for I hadn't the slightest idea where I was going to live or what I was going to do, and Shanghai was like no place I had ever seen.

Everyone was in a great hurry, and there were tall buildings and busses and trolleys. That, at least, was like New York.

But there the resemblance ended. Many people rode in pedicabs or rickshaws. The first was a tricycle with the driver pedaling in front while a passenger, or two in the larger types, sat in the rear. Rickshaws were two-wheeled carts with long shafts gripped by the runners, usually thin to the point of emaciation, who pulled the vehicle. They ran or plodded, depending on their age and physical condition, and were very dexterous at weaving in and out of traffic. Later, I often rode in pedicabs, but after one ride in a rickshaw I could never bring myself to do it again. Being hauled along by a sweating panting fellow man was too repugnant.

The busses and trolleys seemed to be in a perpetual rush-hour state. They were packed with people who, for the most part, managed to maintain their good humor in spite of their obvious discomfort.

Hawkers and pedlars of every variety thronged the streets, crying their wares. A lot of the merchandise bore US Army or UNRRA labels, evidence that "free trade" was being conducted by enterprising individuals of both countries who had discovered a simple way of getting American taxpayers to finance their business.

Beggars were everywhere, people in patched and tattered clothes, old folks, women with babes in arms, wide-eyed older children clutching the edges of their tunics. Most of them came from the impoverished countryside, and swarmed after the more smartly dressed, who occasionally tossed them a few coppers or simply ignored them.

Affluence was also visible among the chosen few. Sleek limousines, horns insolently blaring, nosed relentlessly through narrow streets choked with pedestrians, carts, rickshaws, pedicabs and vehicles of every description. The refugees, not used to big city traffic, scattered wildly when automobiles bore down. But the blasé Shanghai natives stolidly proceeded at their own pace until the creeping vehicles virtually pushed them out of the way.

Clothes were a mixture of East and West. Some of the men wore European style business suits, but most were dressed in tunic and trousers, over which was a long cotton or quilted gown in the cold weather.

For the country women it was mainly tunics and slacks. Their city sisters tended more to the *chi pao*, a kind of sheath dress slit up the sides. These, for the richer ladies, were made of flowered silk or satin and tailored to hug the contours of the body.

The noise was incredible. Loudspeakers roared Chinese opera or whined saccharine love songs from innumerable store fronts in a wild effort to attract customers. Drivers used their horns instead of brakes. People had to shout to be heard above the din. Others had to yell still louder to be heard above them. The endless hopeless competition went on and on.

And of course there were the smells, so characteristic of the exotic colonial Orient. Intermingled with the fumes of cars and busses was the odor of thousands of sweat-stained bodies, the fragrance of the tidbits cooking in the many street stalls for consumption on the spot, and over all, when the wind was right, the smell of the "honey boats" — barges laden with human excrement being hauled to outlying farms for use as fertilizer.

The sudden combination of these assaults on the senses was overwhelming. I tottered dizzily to the car which the Yangs had provided and drove off with them to their home.

They lived in the Bubbling Well section of the city, not the poshest area in Shanghai, but definitely upper middle class. The house was a slightly run-down three-storey building, identical with dozens of others arranged in rows along paved lanes, and all enclosed within a high wall to form an estate.

The house was dimly lit and had creaky wooden floors. There was no steam heat or even coal stoves, Shanghai people being under the illusion that they are southerners, and that it doesn't get really cold till you go north a few miles across the Yangtze. As a sop to the elderly and infirm they may light a charcoal brazier, which provides some warmth to whichever part of your anatomy is facing it, while your opposite area freezes.

As a result, you're compelled to wear the same clothes indoors as out, either padded or fur-lined. In this way, the winters are fairly tolerable. Even in north China where homes and offices are heated, the warmth is so slight that you must wear long woolen underwear from autumn to spring, plus as much padded clothing as you can navigate in.

It took me about three years to get this principle through my skull, during which I suffered perpetual colds every winter, plus an occasional bout of flu. Finally I climbed out of my fashionable threads into more practical Chinese garb, and I was alright.

I was ushered to my room, which was large, high-ceilinged and had a big four-poster bed, canopied over with a thick mosquito netting, an indispensable piece of equipment. While not as large as the New Jersey variety, Shanghai mosquitoes move in fast and hit hard, like dive bombers.

The bed was a wooden platform on which a thin mattress was laid. Most Chinese prefer a hard bed. After I got used to it, I liked it too.

I slept well that first night in China. The next morning a servant led me to the bathroom. It had the usual Western style equipment, but there was no hot water. This was supplied in thermos flasks, freshly filled.

Breakfast was "foreign" in my honor and consisted of toast, butter, jam and a cocomalt drink mixed from powder out of an American can. Later, I was to eat more conventional Shanghai breakfasts — rice gruel, bits of pickled vegetable and tasty little steamed dumplings stuffed with meat or fish or shrimp.

I spent the next few days delivering gifts to relatives of Chinese students I had met at Yale. Each time the recipients expressed their thanks with an invitation to lunch or dinner. The food was fabulous and had little resemblance to the Chinese fare I had eaten in New York.

That's a delightful thing about the Chinese. Any occasion is an excuse for a feast. When you visit someone they always try to get you to stay for a meal. Holidays, send offs, welcome backs, birthdays, anniversaries — they're not considered properly celebrated without a

banquet. Even what they throw together on short notice seems sumptuous to a foreigner. When you see their simple kitchens — sans refrigerators, master mix blenders and electric ovens — you wonder how
they do it.

I also called on a few people I had been asked to look up by mutual
friends in the States. The first was Phoenix, a pal of Nancy Yang.
Nancy had said that Phoenix was studying English and probably would
also be interested in exchanging English lessons for Chinese. I telephoned and arranged to call on her in the afternoon.

It was a sunny day and I walked down the Bund toward Garden
Bridge. The Bund, a broad thoroughfare along the Whangpoo River,
was fringed with old-fashioned granite edifices which then housed many
of the foreign companies extracting huge profits from modest investments. The Japanese, having lost the war, had been driven out. But
the French still controlled the electricity supply and trolley lines, the
British ran most of the shipping and banking, and American interests
were expanding fast.

I crossed Garden Bridge into the Hongkew section where Phoenix
lived. Most of Shanghai had been divided into foreign concessions before the Second World War — Japanese, French and British. In these
concessions the foreigners levied taxes, had their own courts, their own
police, and owned the public utilities. The Chinese had sovereignty in
only one part of Shanghai — the section known as the "Chinese City",
and even this was actually run by the Shanghai Municipal Council, on
which the foreign representatives outnumbered the Chinese. There were
similar foreign concessions in other major cities such as Tientsin and
Hankow. After World War II the concessions were "surrendered" to
China, but foreign interests continued to dominate.

Hongkew, part of the Japanese concession, had been the scene of
heavy fighting during the war. Now the Japanese were out, their
holdings confiscated by the ruling Kuomintang Party of Chiang Kai-
shek, an inefficient gang of crooked politicians. The area was very run
down. Whole streets were lined with bars. There were many prostitutes, catering mainly to foreign sailors and merchant seamen.

Phoenix lived on the top floor of a dilapidated five-storey apartment
building. The elevator hadn't worked for years. As I trudged up the
stairs, I was enveloped in smoke. The flats had no kitchens, and everyone cooked in the hallways on stoves burning coalballs — a mixture of
coal dust, lime and mud.

I knocked on the door. It was opened by a pretty woman in her thirties. She was wearing a simple *chi pao* sheath dress, high heels, and very little make-up. I had noticed this lack of cosmetics on Chinese girls. They used only powder and a faint touch of lipstick. That was alright with me. Since Chinese women have about the best skin in the world — smooth, hairless, small-pored — the application of cosmetics was only gilding the lily.

With a rather worried expression, Phoenix ushered me in. I was wearing a raglan sleeve topcoat, and years later she told me the lack of shoulders struck her as odd. She asked me to be seated and immediately poured the inevitable cup of tea. There is a large variety of teas, and different regions have different favorites. People in north China prefer jasmine, but south of the Yangtze they go in mostly for green teas which are "heat removing", particularly the Dragon Well brand. There are about a dozen grades of this, ranging in price accordingly. It comes from the tea plantations on the hills outside of Hangchow, whose beauties Marco Polo extolled seven centuries before. The most expensive kind is made from buds picked at dawn in early spring with the dew still on them. In the old days it was thought best if the girls who did the picking were virgins, but this is now generally considered an exploded theory.

Phoenix and I began hacking our way through our first attempt at conversation. I knew a bit of Chinese sentence structure, but hadn't nearly enough vocabulary. She, to my surprise, had a fairly large vocabulary, but her approach to English tenses and grammar was highly original and creative.

Meanwhile, I looked around the apartment. There was a small room to the left as you came in, piled high with copies of a magazine she was editing. A short hall led directly into a large combination parlor and bedroom, with a small sofa and a couple of big chairs grouped around a low glass-topped table. Four large windows faced a view of the river and, beyond that, lowlands running down to the sea. It gave the impression of being on the bridge of a ship. On stormy days, when gales lashed rain against the glass, the building swayed slightly, and you almost expected to see spume-capped billows breaking against the wall. There was also a small bathroom with the usual plumbing, but no heat or hot water.

I told Phoenix something of my earlier life. She was interested in the fact that I had represented young theater people when I was a lawyer in New York. She herself had been an actress for over ten years, on the stage and on the screen. Though she had become a newspaper correspondent during the war and was now an editor of a magazine, she was still devoted to the theater. She promised to introduce me to her friends, most of whom were connected with the arts.

We arranged to meet at her place three afternoons a week and exchange an hour of English for an hour of Chinese, starting the following week. When we parted later that evening I felt pleased and comforted. I had met someone intelligent, attractive and interested in my welfare. A friend — that was how I thought of her then. I rode back to the Yangs in a pedicab and watched the moon through the clouds above the roofs of Shanghai. Already, China was beginning to lose some of its strangeness.

The weeks slipped by, and with them what remained of my $200. No one was interested in my army surplus clothing. Shanghai warehouses were full of merchandise, part of the billions worth of goods and equipment left over in the Pacific by the US armed forces after the war and "sold" to the Kuomintang — in exchange for more rights and concessions. It was supposed to be used in the "fight against communism", but most of it wound up as the private property of the high officials running the country..

Chiang Kai-shek, T. V. Soong, H. H. Kung and the Chen brothers — the "Big Four" — were the top dogs. Through various government banks and organizations they owned or controlled the best land, skimmed the cream off the rural usury network, and had a tight grip on all industry and commerce. At the same time, for suitable cuts and bribes, they gave away rich plums to foreign investors. They fronted for dummy Chinese corporations actually owned by Europeans or Americans, or received large blocs of stock in foreign corporations which were then legally permitted to operate on Chinese soil. On behalf of the government they entered into treaties of the most servile nature with the imperialist powers.

In 1946 they had signed an agreement with the United States called "Treaty of Friendship, Commerce and Navigation" which allowed both countries to export their products without limit to their opposite number, tax free. Since Chinese industry was still in its infancy, it was promptly crushed by the deluge of technologically superior American goods. The US could sell cars and trucks and tractors in China. All the Chinese were capable of manufacturing was bicycles and pedicabs. Not much market for that in America.

The Big Four didn't mind. They bathed in the stream of gold, from whatever direction it flowed. The only problem was that real business was practically dead. There were few ultimate consumers. The handful who could afford cars already had several. Ninety percent of the population considered themselves lucky if they had enough to eat. I saw piles of trucks and tractors rusting on islands in the river. Brand new automobiles gathered dust in warehouses. A great deal of commerce consisted of paper speculations in warehouse receipts and bills of lading. That was about all that moved for domestic consumption by way of foreign trade.

Export-wise, it was a different matter. Silks, cotton goods, soybeans, tobacco, coal, tin, bristles, hog casings, were siphoned out of bleeding China smoothly and efficiently, at rock-bottom prices. Wages paid by foreign companies were delightfully low. "After all, the Chinese aren't like us. They can live on a bowl of rice a day!"

Unemployment was very high. There were no statistics. Many of the "employed" received such pitiful stipends that they were barely able to feed themselves.

Among the foreigners there was also some unemployment. Jewish refugees from Hitler Germany, many of them distinguished scientists, doctors and professors, were living in fetid slums in Hongkew, waiting endlessly for visas to America. White Russians, who had fled the Bolshevik revolution and ended up in the big cities of China — Harbin, Tientsin, Shanghai — had long since reached the end of their financial tether, but had difficulty in finding work suitable to their gentlemanly background. Some of their ladies did better, and were among the highest paid in their chosen profession.

Jobs for Anglo-Americans were no problem at all. Any idiot could pull down fifty US dollars a week for doing next to nothing. At that salary he could have a nice flat, keep a servant who also cooked delicious Chinese meals, and drive his own car. After all, it wouldn't do to have one of the supporters of the White Man's Burden panhandling in public.

But I had rather special requirements. I wanted to work for an American firm in Peking, where I could combine business with perfecting my Chinese. I decided to make the rounds of the American law firms in Shanghai (there were only three or four), and see whether they had any clients in Peking who could use a young American attorney.

The first lawyer I visited was a man I shall call "Harding". (From here on, all names used in quotation marks the first time mentioned are fictitious.) He was then about fifty, ruddy complexioned, with a gray clipped moustache. Harding had got his law degree through a correspondence course. By a stroke of luck, he won a sweepstakes at the Shanghai racecourse, which brought him enough money to open a law office. Later, he found himself a smart partner who did most of the research and paper work. Harding was the business getter, the back-slapping hail-fellow-well-met who threw dice for drinks on mahogany-topped bars with leading members of the commercial community.

Harding explained that very little business was conducted in Peking, and that any American firms operating there had their main offices in Shanghai. But, he said, he'd like to offer me a proposition. His partner had gone to America when the war broke out and had never returned. He needed someone badly. If I would become his partner he would pay me a third of the profits or $500 a month, whichever was greater.

With about $20 left in my pocket, this sounded pretty good, particularly since for $10 a day in Shanghai you could live in luxury. Still, it wouldn't get me to Peking, which was my main objective. I told Harding I'd think it over and let him know in a day or so.

I discussed the matter with my Chinese friends. They said it was a marvellous deal and that I should grab it. After I accumulated a decent reserve I could always quit and head north. I accepted their advice and closed a contract with Harding.

Perhaps it sounds a little wild for a lawyer to take on a partner he'd never seen before. But the poor guy really was on the spot. He hardly knew any law. Besides, for foreigners, Shanghai was a wide-open free-swinging place. It wasn't known as "The Paradise of Adventurers" for nothing. Quick fortunes were made, and lost. It had the casual atmosphere of an old frontier town.

So no one was particularly surprised when Harding introduced me around as his partner at the bar of the American Club a few days later. I had moved to the Club, after thanking the Yangs warmly for their hospitality. It was dull institutional missionary in decor, but the food and service were good, and the costs, if you went easy on the booze, were fairly reasonable. It also had the advantage of being centrally located, and was just around the corner from my office.

Harding had the entire eleventh floor in the Development Building, a 15-storey "skyscraper", one of Shanghai's few tall buildings. Several of the lower floors housed the US Consulate. The building got its name from some "Development Project" or other on the ground floor, another Kuomintang racket.

A lot of our business consisted of organizing and filing the annual reports of what were known as "China Trade Act Corporations". These were US federal companies. Their president and treasurer had to be US citizens, and Americans in Shanghai earned annual fees for serving in a nominal capacity. Actual ownership was in the hands of Chinese, usually import-export people, who felt this gave them added prestige in dealing with American firms. Some Americans also formed and operated such firms, since judicious filing of the annual reports exempted them from all US taxation.

Harding had a number of interesting clients. One was a certain Spanish religious order which had sold real estate to the Japanese during the occupation for a considerable sum. Now, along with all other Japanese-held property, this parcel of land and buildings (tenanted by brothels, gambling dens and warehouses), had been taken over by the Alien Property Custodian of the Kuomintang. The gentle fathers had suddenly come up with a claim that they had been forced to deliver title to the Japanese, that they hadn't been paid a cent, and they wanted the property back.

No one was particularly deceived by this, but business was business. Harding went to Nanking several times a month to negotiate with the Kuomintang officials, each time upping a bit the size of the proposed bribe.

I was left to handle the more prosaic matters of wills, contracts and assignments. Still, it was a far cry from the Paramount Building. One of the duties of the clerks was to keep you supplied with tea and, in summer, hot towels. Chinese businessmen, while every bit as sharp as their American counterparts, had to be treated more ceremoniously. Tea had to be poured, polite small talk had to be made. Only then could you come to grips with the matter at hand.

One of Shanghai's more imaginative con men honored me with a visit. Mr. Ionin was a White Russian who dressed neatly in a quiet business suit and whose eyes were slightly out of alignment. He told a fascinating story about kegs of gold Napoleons which had been retrieved from a sunken freighter and were stored in an abbey under the label of nails. He had the papers for them and needed only a buyer who could take delivery. He showed me the documents and entrusted me with a few of the coins, but said under no circumstances was I to mention his name to the customer. I was to be paid a large commission, Ionin a small one.

Madder things had happened in Shanghai. I said I would see what I could do. I discussed the matter with some European gentlemen who dealt in currency. They examined the Napoleons and said they were genuine enough. But when, at their urgent persuasion, I told them who my client was, they laughed. They said because I was new to Shanghai and hadn't yet heard of Mr. Ionin's reputation, he no doubt was trying to work me for a few dollars. The touch would come soon, they predicted.

Sure enough, a few days later Ionin dropped in again. He said he needed twenty-five dollars to pay the monk who was keeping an eye on the nails. It was to be a loan, of course, which I could deduct from his commission. I said I was sorry, that I had no ready cash at the moment. He said ten might do. I shook my head.

That was the last I saw of Mr. Ionin.

Phoenix took me to a dinner given by some of Shanghai's intellectuals for a prominent archeologist. Most of them were writers and newspaper people. All, including the archeologist, were having a hard time making ends meet. Publishers didn't pay much, there was only a small reading public since the majority of the population was illiterate, and the cost of living kept increasing with the rising inflation. The Kuomintang, Chiang Kai-shek's ruling party, offered sinecures and well-paying jobs to anyone who would write for their periodicals or do public relations work for them. Only a tiny fraction responded. China's literati scorned and hated the Kuomintang, which had run when the Japanese invaded. Corrupt and venal, it was creating new spheres of influence for foreign capital, and was content to see the country slide into ruin while it lined its own pockets. Few of China's writers were members of the Communist Party, but most were patriots and they were infuriated by what the Kuomintang was doing in China. They spoke out against it as best they could, using indirection and historical analogy. Everything had to pass the ferret eyes of the Kuomintang censors, and writers' manuscripts were always being sent back with deletions and demands for revision, or rejected out of hand. But the literati I met were seldom depressed. In addition to their considerable charm, they were possessed of a wit and gayety which warmed my American heart.

At the dinner that night we were drinking Shaohsing wine, a honey-colored rice liquor which tastes something like sherry when cold and something like ambrosia when heated, which is the customary way to serve it. At banquets, you start drinking before the food is served, and continue right through to the end of the meal, when anyone who still hasn't had enough is brought bowls of rice to fill the remaining crevices. As the toasts go round, the hilarity grows, with wisecracks and puns. I'm afraid I missed most of them that night, since my limping Chinese couldn't possibly keep up with the racing humor.

Thanks to my language inadequacies I provided a bit of humor myself. During the course of the meal I observed various people getting up and going out, obviously to answer calls of nature. I too rose and strolled unsteadily from the banquet room.

"Where is the bathroom?" I asked a passing waiter in my best Yale Chinese.

"Bathroom?" He looked puzzled.

"I want to wash my hands," I said.

"Ah, wash your hands. This way please." He led me to a room where there was a basin and water, and nothing else.

I made my way dejectedly back to the table. Phoenix noticed my expression.

"What's the matter?"

I explained.

"This gentleman wants to go to the toilet," she called to a waiter on the far side of the room.

"Big convenience or small convenience?"

All eyes turned to me expectantly.

"Small," I said, bravely.

"Come along," said the waiter.

Everyone went on with their conversation, smiling a bit at my obvious embarrassment as I left the room.

I was to be frequently reminded that Chinese customs are free in many ways of the prudery and cant which pervade the West. The facts of life are discussed freely in front of children, women nurse their infants in public, toddlers wear split pants until they are housebroken. It is thought better for them to wet the floor than wet their clothes.

At the same time, China in the forties had a prudery and hypocrisy of its own. Boys and girls never dared to show any interest in each other. To be seen even speaking to a girl usually let the boy in for a lot of snide ribbing, which I always found irritatingly puerile and mawkish. As a result, they could never get to know one another, and had to rely on the old feudal matchmakers.

Yet if they did meet on their own and live together there was never any particular onus attached to them. In the old days people were pretty casual about registering their marriage, anyway. You lived together, so you were married. If you had children you had to support them, with or without a marriage registration. You didn't need a licence. You simply registered as a *fait accompli*, usually in the county magistrate's office, that your marriage had occurred.

People were still talking about the war, which had only recently ended, and whose ravages were still felt. When the Japanese had invaded China, Chiang Kai-shek's armies gave ground, mostly without a fight. The capitol moved from Nanking to Chungking, deep in Szechuan. The rich, the bureaucrats, the big operators, devoted themselves to money-making and high life while the rest of the country staggered under the blows of the virtually unopposed foe. Only the Communist forces fought back, but they were constantly harrassed by the Chiang gang, who showed more ardor against them than against the Japanese, in spite of the fact that they were supposed to be joined in a "united front".

Americans in China had nothing but contempt for the Kuomintang. "Peanut!" was the epithet for Chiang Kai-shek of "Vinegar Joe" Stillwell, Commanding General of the US Armed Forces in the China-Burma-India Theater. State Department advisers like John S. Service recommended close cooperation with the Communists, who were leading the fight against the Japanese. This was never done. In fact men like Service were subsequently hounded for their honesty by the McCarthy committee.

When the Japanese surrendered, the Kuomintang moved into the cities like a swarm of locusts, seizing the best apartment houses, the best office buildings, handing out spoils to their friends, imposing the same dirty regime they had before. Whoever had harbored any hopes the government would improve was quickly disillusioned.

In many parts of the country only Communist-led armed forces were present to accept surrender from the defeated Japanese. Chiang Kai-shek had pulled his armies so far back from the battlefronts, they were hundreds of miles away. This was a source of considerable disturbance to the reactionaries on both sides of the Pacific, who were terrified lest the Communists consolidate the excellent relations they had established with the local people and strengthen themselves militarily with surrendered Japanese arms.

An "Armistice Commission" was hastily whipped together, composed of American, Kuomintang and Communist representatives, with an "executive headquarters" in Peking. Teams of one of each were sent to restore peace wherever clashes broke out between Communist and Kuomintang troops. In the meantime, US ships and planes were secretly rushing Chiang Kai-shek armies back from the hinterlands. They shifted forty-one Kuomintang divisions and eight military police regiments — half a million men — into the Communist-controlled Liberated Areas. The moment these were in position, they attacked. Ninety thousand US Marines were landed in Shanghai, Tientsin, Peking and Chinwangtao to guard Kuomintang lines of communication.

People were thoroughly sick of the Chiang Kai-shek gang, and resistance grew. Fighting spread in the Liberated Areas. A revolutionary movement also developed in the cities, in which workers, students and intellectuals joined.

I began meeting members of the American community. The business and diplomatic crowd led a closed ingrown social life, remote from the ordinary Chinese. What mixing they did was more with the rich merchants and the government officials, which categories frequently overlapped.

There were other kinds of Americans, as well. "Harry", for example, worked for the China Welfare Fund, a society devoted to giving educational opportunities to poor and underprivileged children. Headed by Madame Sun Yat-sen, widow of the hero of the 1911 bourgeois revolution, the organization enjoyed the undying hatred of the wealthy ruling class and the officialdom, who had always monopolized education as their private prerogative. But Madame Sun was too prominent to be attacked openly, even more so since CWF was known and supported by prominent figures abroad.

Then there was Bill Powell Jr., editor of *China Weekly Review*, a magazine founded by his father. The elder Powell had been one of those old-fashioned Americans who told the truth as he saw it and let the chips fall where they may. He adhered to this policy even after the

Japanese occupied Shanghai, and he wound up in a Japanese-run prison, where ill treatment caused injuries which led to his death. Bill junior carried on his father's tradition. Not only was the magazine widely circulated abroad but, as one of the few reliable sources of information, it was avidly read by Chinese who knew English. Since many of its articles flatly contradicted the lies of the Chiang Kai-shek gang and exposed their scandals, the magazine aroused the fury of the Kuomintang. But it would have been awkward for them to interfere with an American enterprise at a time when they were using American arms to slaughter Chinese suspected of communist sympathies, so they let Bill alone.

By then Julian Schuman had come out, at my suggestion, and he went to work for *China Weekly Review*. He stayed on until 1955, as Bill's assistant editor. Julian roomed with me in the American Club. He took to Shanghai like a duck to water, wandering around, eating local delicacies in little hole-in-the-wall restaurants, chatting with Chinese and American friends far into the night. He became a first-rate newspaperman, and broadcast live the last days of the Kuomintang for ABC. His book *Assignment China* is the best thing written by an American on that period.

By then, Phoenix and I knew each other pretty well. She was the last child of a large family, born when her father was already forty. They lived in Hankow, a bustling river port on the Yangtze, though their ancestral home was in the province of Kwangsi, far to the south, bordering Vietnam. Father was a well-known classical poet, and later became Kwangsi's provincial historian. He was very fond of the baby of the family and taught her to read and appreciate the classics, an indispensable attribute in a truly educated Chinese. It was mainly on the strength of this knowledge, since her acquaintance with subjects like chemistry and math was remote, that she was able to gain entrance to Futan University in Shanghai while still in her teens.

Well brought-up girls from proper feudal families were rarely permitted to leave home to attend universities, but times were changing. People were looking for new attitudes, new solutions, to save China from its rapidly accelerating decay. Education of the younger generation, even girls, in the methods of the West, was one approach.

At Futan she became quickly involved in student unrest and protests against the persecution of liberals by the Chiang Kai-shek government and its supineness in the face of exploitation by foreign imperialist powers. She also discovered an aptitude for acting and took part in student performances of some of the new plays. These were so successful that they were tried out in a Shanghai theater. Audience response was enthusiastic, and Phoenix quit school and became a professional actress.

She starred in the dramas of Tsao Yu, a young writer strongly influenced by Eugene O'Neill, and whose vehicles exposed the corruption and decadence of Chinese society. She played also in a few films. Drama consisting solely of spoken dialogue without musical accompaniment and singing was a new art form in China, as were motion pictures, and both dealt with contemporary themes. Traditional theater was mainly historical costume opera.

After the Japanese invasion in 1937 Phoenix worked as an editor and war correspondent. In 1945 when the Japanese surrendered she returned to Shanghai where she became the editor of a left-wing magazine. At the same time she performed in several plays.

Though she had never known any foreigners personally, they were not as strange to her as they would be, say, to a peasant. She had seen them in Hankow, Kweilin and Chungking. Shanghai, a big seaport, was full of them. She had read extensively about foreign lands in novels and plays translated from the English, French, Russian and German. She saw the best and worst Hollywood had to offer in Shanghai cinemas named "The Palace", "The Granada" and "The Roxy". Among the educated classes Western dress was popular, as were restaurants which cooked Western style. Western music could be heard at concerts, on the radio, on phonograph records.

Phoenix, like many of her contemporaries, was influenced by the romantic aspects of Western culture. In some ways they were comfortably similar to feudal chivalry and sentimentality, and yet seemed to be a step forward in that they called for the emancipation of women and such shining goals as liberty and democracy.

By the time I met her in 1947 she had come under much stronger influences. During the war she had encountered leaders of the Communist Party and worked under their guidance. Though not herself a member, she felt that what they advocated and practiced was much more suited to the realities of China than the political approaches of the West. In fact the magazine she was editing was being directed by the Communist underground in Shanghai. Chiang Kai-shek's Kuomintang party and government were hopelessly venal and corrupt. They hadn't fought the Japanese invaders, they attacked the Communist forces who did, they oppressed the people. As a patriot, she could only support the Communists.

These aspects of her personality I came to know gradually over the coming months. What struck me first were the outward things, her animation and expressiveness. I couldn't tell whether this was something she was born with, or whether the projection of emotion which she had learned as an actress had become second nature. When indignant, her eyes would flash fire, when happy she would laugh unrestrainedly like a child. I quickly changed my preconceived notions about the "inscruta-bleness" of Orientals.

She had few questions about life in America. Perhaps she thought the films she saw presented the true picture. She did, in typical Chinese fashion, want to know all about my family — what my sister did, how many children she had, who looked after my widowed mother. . . .

About herself she spoke freely. She was a rebel in an age of rebel-lion. China was still very feudal. In Hankow she had nearly been arrested for walking arm in arm with a schoolmate along the riverbank in broad daylight, until it was discovered that "he" was actually another girl with a boyish bob. People were sick of outmoded strictures. Phoenix had been deeply impressed by two literary creations, one Chinese, one foreign — the novel "The Family" by Pa Chin, and Ibsen's play "The Doll's House". The first is the story of a young man who runs away from his wealthy feudal family after a hopeless affair with a young servant girl ends in her suicide. In the second, Nora leaves her pompous husband because he treats her more like a cherished plaything than a person.

Phoenix herself had broken many of the rules. She had gone to college, she had become an actress (what respectable girl would ever take up such a career?), she had traveled around, alone, as a newspaper correspondent. She had also divorced a young professor when she discovered that he expected her role in their marriage to be primarily that of a housewife and hostess to his guests. "I wasn't going to be a Chinese Nora," Phoenix said firmly. She had not remarried because she had not found anyone for whom she could care enough and who would respect her independence.

Not, at least, till I came along. Our physical attraction was immedi-ate and mutual. But more than that, we shared an identity of interests and found pleasure in each other's company. We went to the theater together and saw new Chinese plays and old Chinese operas. Explaining these to me meant interpreting not only plot, but also the thinking, motivation, customs and cultural background. I, in turn, tried to make sense of the American films we saw and the translated fiction she read. On the way home after an evening out we walked through the streets and stopped at one of the all-night stands for a bowl of fragrant *huntun* or a few crisp oil fritters. We might ride the rest of the way in a pedicab — a big tricycle pedaled by the driver in front and two seats in the rear, with a folding awning, like a baby carriage cover, for shelter against the rain.

We sat in tea gardens amid flowering shrubs and fanciful pavilions and sipped green "Dragon Well" tea and cracked watermelon seeds. We wended through the City God Temple, with its many shops of marvellous handicrafts connected by a zigzag bridge around a lotus pond.

And we met in Phoenix's flat with a few other Chinese friends and talked in low voices, with the radio turned on loud against possible eavesdroppers, about who had just been arrested, or what bookstores had been raided, or whether more revolutionaries had been executed, and what the news from the Liberated Areas was. Sometimes we could pick up Yenan on my short-wave set.

Phoenix had no doubt about our compatibleness, and if our future was unsure, so was the future of everyone in China. Nor did my "foreignness" seem to present any problems. She had got used to my appearance, and recovered from the initial shock of seeing me in a raglan sleeve topcoat on finding, when I took it off, that I had shoulders after all. In fact she had become bemused to such an extent that she thought I was quite nice-looking. No one stared when we appeared in public together, nor did I, for some reason, attract the crowds which often trailed other foreigners, awestruck by their outlandish garb and, by Chinese standards, huge noses. Her family offered no objections whatever.

Absence of racial or religious prejudice is traditional in China. For two thousand years foreigners had been encouraged to settle in the Middle Kingdom and practice their religions and retain their customs. There was some talk among the rustics that all foreigners had red hair and blue eyes and walked without bending their knees. But those who had actually seen them knew better. None of Phoenix's compatriots was shocked, though some perhaps wondered why she chose a foreigner when there were so many Chinese around.

As for me, I was finally ready for marriage. In 1948 I was thirty-three, earning a good living and confident I could fend for myself as a lawyer. China intrigued me, and China was where I wanted to remain. Though I had no anticipation that Chiang Kai-shek would be over-thrown so quickly, I thought that even with a change of government there surely would be a use for an American lawyer with a knowledge of Chinese. I wanted only to live in modest comfort and be able to pursue my studies of Chinese language and culture.

For that, Phoenix would be an ideal wife. Charming, with a host of intellectual friends, she was a guarantee that I would never lack for an interesting life. She knew a great deal about Chinese classics and history, and was an invaluable interpreter of current politics. And she mixed well with my foreign acquaintances, who were clearly enchanted by her.

I was a little concerned about what my mother's reaction might be but, as she often did, she surprised me. Whether it was the absence of any historical conflict between Chinese and Jews, or seeing them in America as another discriminated-against minority that won her favor, I don't know. In any event, she fully approved the match, and that made it unanimous.

Phoenix and I were married in May of 1948. We signed a simple statement of marriage in Chinese, to which a Master of Ceremonies, an Introducer and a Witness also affixed their signatures. That was it, simple, quiet and dignified.

We found a small apartment at a reasonable rent at the far end of the old French concession. But we had to pay a stiff fee, known as "key money", in U.S. dollars to the departing tenant. This was the custom, and the only way you could get an apartment in Shanghai. We were much better off than the bulk of the population, who lived in crowded run-down tenements, and the thousands whose only shelters from the elements were flimsy mat sheds.

By current standards I was a success. I had left Harding and opened my own law office. I was earning more money than I could use, sending half of it back to my mother. I had a wife, an apartment, a fluid-drive Chrysler, good clothes. What more could I want?

For one thing, I wanted life to have more meaning. I had traveled twelve thousand miles because I had the romantic illusion that physical distance would enable me to escape the environment of the market place. But Shanghai was just another market, if anything more sordid and openly corrupt than the one I had left. I spent most of my waking hours with people who were trying to think up improved means of screwing their fellow man, and I was supposed to help them make it legal. Not a very inspiring existence.

Also I felt uncomfortable living it up surrounded by such utter poverty and degradation. You couldn't walk along Tibet Road near the race-course without being mobbed by hundreds of prostitutes, many pitifully young, whose hard-faced "mothers" would grab your arm and hang on with a grip of iron.

If my Chrysler had to stop for a red light at Nanking Road, beggars would swarm all over it, climbing on the running board, thrusting grimy hands in through the open window. In winter these poor people died like flies. Garbage trucks went around every morning to collect the frozen corpses off the sidewalks.

The whole regime was dying, but it struggled desperately, striking out hysterically, viciously, at the mounting opposition. People were arrested in the middle of the night, tortured, murdered. Sirens howled incessantly on police wagons racing through the streets.

One night a young woman, a friend of Phoenix's, asked us to hide her in our apartment. She was a newspaper reporter. The Kuomintang was after her. Arrangements were being made for her to escape to Hongkong. A few days later she left.

Not long after, we gave shelter to a boy who rushed in, pale and sweating. He was active in the student movement in one of the universities, and had been tipped off that the police were looking for him. His father finally managed to buy them off with a substantial bribe.

A round-up of non-cooperative intellectuals had also begun. Friends in the underground said that the Kuomintang was taking an unhealthy interest in Phoenix and the magazine she was running. They suggested this might be a good time for her to go.

Go where? For some time we had been closely following the Communist-led revolution, listening to short-wave broadcasts from the Liberated Areas, reading secretly articles that had been made available to us, and talking with men in the underground.

I too had become involved to a certain extent. I had helped a student group edit a magazine in English which favored land reform. The Kuomintang, representative of the big landlords, didn't like that at all, and the magazine had been forced to close down. My fancy office in the Development Building had been used as a meeting place for discussions with emissaries from the Liberated Areas seeking to get medicines through the Kuomintang blockade. Everything we heard about these areas sounded positive, exciting. Why not go there?

Phoenix was all for immediately agreeing on a permanent change. I was more cautious. I didn't want to commit myself finally, but was willing to have a look, and then decide.

A message was sent in to the Liberated Areas asking whether it was alright for me, a foreigner, to go. Two weeks later word came back: Yes.

We started making arrangements. I told everyone we were going to Tientsin on a business trip. Taking Harry into my confidence, I gave him the keys to my law office, and asked him to return all my files to the people concerned as soon as he heard we had got across. I left him enough money to refund the annual retainers I had received from certain clients, pay off my secretary and close down the office. I also arranged for him to sell my car, home and office furniture, and dispose of my apartment.

Phoenix put her affairs in order.

Harry asked if we could take "Helen", an American girl, who wanted to join her fiance, a Vermont agronomist, already in the Liberated Areas. We checked with the Chinese. Agreed.

We packed only absolute essentials, having been advised that we might have to do a lot of walking, and carry our belongings ourselves.

Then, on November 11, 1948 — I remember because it was Armistice Day — we boarded a plane and flew to Peking. It had snowed the night before, and when we landed we could see nothing but an expanse of white. We took a taxi to the city, where we had reservations at the Peking Hotel.

It was comfortable and old fashioned, with large high-ceilinged rooms. I had a rotten cold, but the radiators were sizzling. I sweated buckets, and felt much better in the morning. We had a big breakfast and waited for the contact we knew would call.

At about ten o'clock a courteous Chinese man dressed in Western clothes knocked at our door. He greeted us warmly, like old friends, until the floor attendant who had escorted him to our room was gone, then entered, shut the door and strolled around, his eyes taking in every detail. We invited him to be seated, served tea. He asked whether our

journey had been pleasant, inquired after our health. He said a friend
of his, a prominent movie director, had a large house and garden on
the north shore of Rear Lake. Since we were interested in the arts, we
might find staying there more enjoyable than living in a hotel. Other
guests, some of whom we knew, were also visiting there. He was sure
it would be a convivial gathering.

Politely protesting we would be putting our host to too much trouble,
we let ourselves be persuaded. Late that afternoon, Phoenix, Helen
and I moved over.

The house was large, with well over a dozen rooms, but had a
homey atmosphere. There were gardens front and back, a high retaining
wall closed out any curious eyes. Our host was indeed a film director,
but he and his wife, an actress, plus their permanent house guest, a
composer, were all working for the Communist underground, and the
house was a way station for people headed for the Liberated Areas.
Several other "visitors" were already there, waiting like ourselves to be
escorted through the Kuomintang lines.

We were delighted to see a few old friends from Shanghai. They too
had kept their plans secret, but now we all relaxed, and there was much
banter and laughter.

Every few nights, someone would drop in, garbed as a peasant, or
merchant, or pedlar. This would be the escort, and he would discuss
plans and routes and disguises with the next to go. The following day,
or night, they would slip off together. New guests would arrive, and the
same type of routine would follow.

Our problem was considered more complicated, since Helen and
I were undisguisable foreigners, at least nobody would ever mistake us
for Chinese. We were told to wait while the details were being worked
out.

"You're rich American tourists," the film director reminded us.
"Get around. Go sight-seeing, take pictures, go shopping, eat in the
big restaurants. Then you won't be noticed."

We followed instructions, wining and dining and doing the town. A
week passed. Two. We were growing impatient. Why the delay?

At last late one night, our escort arrived. He was a young man
wearing a long dark gown and a snapbrim felt hat. A Peking University
student, he had been doing these jobs for about two years. He said
the plan was this: Helen and I would pose as husband and wife, using
our own names and identification. I was to claim that I was an American

lawyer going to Tsinan, in Shantung Province, to help other Americans, still there, wind up their business interests and bring them back. Tsinan was already in Communist hands, in fact once you crossed a small river about fifty miles north of the Yellow River, you were in a Liberated Area.

Phoenix would play the role of a widow from the Northeast whose husband had just died and who was joining relatives in Tsinan. We would pretend not to know each other. The guide would be a traveling merchant who, naturally, didn't know us either. He ostensibly would pay no attention to us, but we were to follow him wherever he went. We would go via Tientsin.

Two possible routes had been considered. The first was to take a train south from Tientsin, which was quick and would get us all the way to the Shantung border. But this method had been rejected because on the train papers were checked very carefully. The second alternative, which had been the one adopted, was to go by bus. This was slower and not so comfortable, but in the heavy traffic which flowed regularly along this route check-ups were inclined to be more hasty, and sometimes skipped altogether.

In any event, said our guide, the Kuomintang treated Americans very gingerly. If questions arose, we were to pretend not to understand Chinese, and browbeat our way through with foreign arrogance. It was highly unlikely that any petty functionary would dare to stop us.

Phoenix's case might be more awkward. Being small and petite, she didn't look much like a woman from the Northeast, and her accent was all wrong. But if she didn't say much and remained as inconspicuous as possible, she would probably get by in the crowd.

If, for some reason, we should be separated during the journey, we were to go back to Tientsin and meet at the underground way station from which we would start.

We left Peking for Tientsin by train the next day. Helen and I were checked at both ends of the line by Kuomintang security men and our passport numbers noted. Tientsin seemed drab after Peking. It was more like Shanghai, nothing particularly Chinese about its architecture, most of the better buildings standing in what had been the various foreign concessions. There were long rows of gray three-storey houses, their front yards separated by high stone walls.

It was to one of these that our guide led us. We mounted the creaking stairs and were greeted by our host. He was a thin esthetic-looking man about forty, with wild unkempt hair and dressed in a long quilted gown. Dusk was falling and he lit a few oil lamps. The electricity had been turned off because he had refused to pay his bill. I gathered this was part of some long feud he was waging with the municipal authorities.

Or maybe he was just poor and too proud to admit it. Obviously he hadn't always been in this condition. The house was full of beautiful mahogany furniture in classic Ming style, scrolls of calligraphy, old traditional paintings, bowls, vases, bronzes — remnants of a treasured family collection. He had been selling them off, reluctantly, piece by piece, and living on the proceeds. In ordinary times, he could have gone on doing this for years. But a revolution was raging, and the type of Chinese who went in for antiques was cutting down on his collection rather than adding to it, while the foreign connoiseurs were leaving China. I was to encounter quite a few decaying scholar-gentry families in later times. Some of them owned fine works of art.

There wasn't any heat in the house either, and this was the coldest late November in living memory. Or so it seemed to us, sitting around in our overcoats, hatted and gloved, barely able to see each other through our icy breaths, which spread in clouds whenever we could rouse ourselves sufficiently from our torpor to speak.

The greatest nuisance was going to the john. It was on the second floor of a rear building which you got to by crossing a kind of flying bridge, as the gale tried to knock you off into the yard below. Wind whistled through every crack in the well-ventilated walls of the chamber itself, so that by the time you finally returned to the chill living room you were thoroughly frozen.

Strangely enough, we had an excellent dinner, which our host somehow managed to prepare in another dim recess of the house. He even served wine, warmed well above room temperature. The place seemed a bit brighter after the meal, and we chatted with him for a while. He talked mostly of his battle against the electric company, and of antiques, about which he was clearly very knowledgeable. But why he was running this underground station and what his connection with the Communist Party was he said not a word, and we didn't feel it diplomatic to ask.

We slept that night in our army surplus sleeping bags, weighted down with whatever clothing we could muster from our luggage. It was still bitterly cold, and that, plus the fact that we were excited wondering what tomorrow would bring, kept any of us from getting much rest. We staggered wearily to our feet when our guide called us shortly before dawn.

Without pausing for breakfast, we got our gear together. Helen and I had a duffle bag each. I also had a portable typewriter. Phoenix, as befitted a peasant woman, carried a kerchief-wrapped bundle. I, the big lawyer, wore a large overcoat to cover my padded clothes, and was topped off with a smart fur hat. Helen, never very fashion-conscious, dressed in sensible padded slacks and tunic. Phoenix wore a long padded *chi pao* over tunic and trousers.

The sky was just brightening and there wasn't a pedicab in sight. We had to tote our heavy luggage to the nearest trolley stop, which seemed miles away. We were all in a sweat by the time we got there, in spite of the north wind screaming around our ears. We boarded a trolley full of morning shift factory workers, who gazed at us curiously.

Arriving at the station, we examined our "bus". It was an old two-and-a-half-ton army truck, completely open, without even a canvas cover. Passengers, mostly peasants, were already throwing their bundles in the back and climbing in after them. I persuaded the driver to let Helen ride up front in the cab with him. Then I too clambered into the back to watch our luggage. Phoenix and our guide were seated on their respective bundles. We studiously ignored each other.

The "bus" started. Ten minutes later, it stopped. We had reached a Kuomintang military police inspection post in the outskirts of the city. All papers had to be checked, all luggage examined.

We were in trouble the moment a soldier began going through Helen's duffle bag. Half of its contents were bottles of medicine. Helen was recovering from sprue and the doctor had prescribed an assortment of pills and liquids. She had taken enough to last for several months. Although we didn't know it, there was a thriving business going on of smuggling medications into the Liberated Areas. The smaller Kuomintang officials cooperated readily enough, given suitable bribes.

The soldier examining my bag found nothing exceptionable, but my portable typewriter worried him.

"What's that?" he asked, with a puzzled frown.

"A '*ta tzu chi*', a word-writing machine," I explained.

"Can you send telegram messages on it?"

I laughed. "No, of course not."

He wasn't convinced. He walked off and five minutes later came back with his superior, a military police officer.

"May I see your papers?" the officer asked politely.

I showed him my American passport and a letter I had written on that same portable typewriter, at the suggestion of our guide, only two nights before.

"What does it say?"

"The United States Embassy requests that every courtesy be shown to Mr. Sidney Shapiro, American attorney, and his wife, who are going to Tsinan on temporary business."

"And is it signed?"

"Oh, yes," I pointed to the flourishing scrawl at the end. "Leighton Stuart."

"Ah." He smiled sceptically. "Why doesn't it have a red seal?"

"The US Embassy doesn't go in for that sort of thing," I said haughtily.

"I see. Will you wait, please?" He was gone for about twenty minutes, telephoning, no doubt. When he returned, he said: "Why don't you go back to the city and come tomorrow with a note from the US Consulate in Tientsin? Then you won't have to ride in this old bus. We'll send you through in a car."

I argued that it would be too much of a nuisance. Since we had already come this far, we insisted on going through.

"Those wretched foreigners are delaying us too long," Phoenix grumbled aloud. She was trying to signal me to drop the whole thing. Clearly our little device had failed. An important American lawyer, with a letter of introduction from the embassy, certainly wouldn't be riding in a local peasant bus. We had been naively optimistic.

But a peasant woman didn't voice dissatisfaction before a high and mighty Kuomintang officer. He strode toward Phoenix menacingly.

"What's that you said?"

The other passengers closed around her quickly in a protective phalanx.

"Don't pay any attention to her. She's upset because she just lost her husband."

The officer glared at Phoenix, then turned back to us. "See you tomorrow," he said, with a tinge of sarcasm.

There was nothing we could do. I got two pedicabs, and Helen and I started back for town, our bulky duffle bags between our knees.

Phoenix watched us as we left the MP check point, her face expressionless. I knew she was worried.

"What are you going to do?" said Helen. "We can't return to the house in broad daylight." It was only nine in the morning.

"Let's go to a hotel and rest till dark. I'll slip back quietly this evening. You stay at the hotel till someone calls for you."

The arrangement was that if any of us couldn't get through, the others would leave the bus at the nearest railway station and return by train to Tientsin. We all would meet that night in the house of our underground friend.

Our pedicabs jolted along the pitted road, past hovels and grimy factory buildings. Gradually these gave way to the more pompous Victorian structures of the old foreign concessions.

"Where to?" demanded one of the drivers.

"The Astor House," I replied, after a moment's thought.

It was the best hotel in town. If we were going to bluff, we'd do it in style. The Chiang Kai-shek gang worshipped wealth and position. They were pretty jumpy now, as the fortunes of the revolution improved, and made frequent raids, usually late at night, to check the identity of visitors in homes and hotels. But they stayed away from the posh places, afraid of offending someone important. We rolled up to the entrance of the Astor House. I paid off the pedicabs, hailed a hotel porter in a lordly manner for our bags, and strolled up to the desk.

"A double room for my wife and myself." I pulled out my passport and a wallet of greenbacks.

"Certainly, sir. For how long?" the registration clerk asked obsequiously, eyeing my money. He barely glanced at my passport.

"One day. I'm not sure of my plans yet."

We were ushered in to a large double room. Helen and I looked at each other. She grinned.

"You should see yourself."

I laughed. "You wouldn't win any beauty prizes either."

Our ears and noses were still red from the cold, and both of us were covered with dust.

"I don't know about you," said Helen, "but I'm going to take a bath and go to bed."

"After you, madame."

Half an hour later, we were both much cleaner and fast asleep, I on the floor in my sleeping bag, having gallantly relinquished the large double bed to Helen.

We awakened at about four and had a substantial meal served in the room. By five it was already dusk. I waited another hour, then went back to our agreed rendezvous. I had some difficulty locating the house in the dark, they all looked so much alike. Both the gate and the front door were unlocked.

I went in and climbed the stairs. Not a glimmer of light showed anywhere, and there was no sign of our host. As before, the rooms were very cold. I groped my way to a chair and sat down, my mind in a whirl. I would just have to wait.

Not long after, I heard footsteps on the stairs. Phoenix and the guide must have returned.

"Who's there?" I called softly, so as not to startle them.

"Me," a voice replied. A man entered. It was our host, with bags of food in his hand. "What are you doing, sitting in the dark?" He lit a lamp. "Have you eaten?" His manner was casual.

I told him what had happened. He merely nodded.

"Why aren't they back yet?" I fretted.

"Don't worry," he said. "They'll be back. They're just being careful."

But I was worried. I had seen the brutality of Kuomintang police. They thought nothing of punching or kicking anyone of the poorer classes who displeased them. Suppose they began pushing someone around at the next check point? Suppose they got rough with Phoenix? She was hot-tempered and impetuous. She didn't act like a peasant woman. There would be real trouble if she blew up. She might be questioned, tortured.

Time dragged on. Eight o'clock, nine. I kept looking at my watch, my anxiety growing. Then, more footsteps on the stairs, and Phoenix and the guide were in the room. I rushed up and threw my arms around her, speechless with relief.

Phoenix was a bit embarrassed. Chinese don't indulge much in public demonstration of their emotions. But there were tears in her eyes. Shortly after Helen and I left them, she and the guide had climbed back on the truck and gone on. At the next town the railroad and the highway met. Many people went off in various directions to relieve themselves. The guide ambled into a grove of trees. Phoenix followed slowly at a distance. The guide continued through the grove and kept walking for about half a mile till he came to a small village. He went into the only restaurant, sat down and ordered a bowl of noodles. He was calmly eating when Phoenix joined him. He urged her to have something, too. Food was the last thing she wanted, but she forced herself to consume half a bowl.

Then they returned to the town. The bus was gone. They had to wait about an hour for a train. It brought them to Tientsin fairly quickly, so they wandered around for a few more hours, stopping in little restaurants from time to time to warm up. When it was good and dark, they came back to the house.

I told my story. The guide went to pick up Helen. Soon we were all sitting around the lamp-lit table again, cold and tired and depressed. But the guide's spirits were unflagging.

"Get some rest," he urged. "I may have news for you tomorrow." He said goodnight and left.

We didn't see him until the following evening, and when he returned another man was with him. He introduced us to "Comrade Li". Li said the underground group had talked over our problem. They had considered sending us by small boat along the network of waterways that connected with our destination. But this was rejected as too dangerous. The boats were often checked as they neared the Liberated Areas. Another alternative was to go via the Western Hills outside Peking. But this region was the scene of clashes between the guerrillas and Kuomintang forces, and was already under Communist artillery bombardment. Therefore, the best thing for us to do was return to Peking and wait for "liberation".

Comrade Li must have seen the disappointment on our faces, for he added with a smile: "It's coming very soon."

We thought he was only consoling us, but we were to learn that he wasn't exaggerating in the least. Two months later the Kuomintang was gone from the ancient city for good.

Late the next afternoon we arrived in Peking. We decided against going back to the hotel and put up for the night in the house of a friend. But we couldn't remain long. By now the Kuomintang was alerted to what we had been up to, and while they couldn't do much to Helen and me, they probably would be very nasty to any Chinese caught giving us shelter.

An underground contact recommended that we find some prominent American residents and move in with them. This would keep the Kuomintang off our tails.

Whom did I know? I remembered that a few of the teachers in the College of Chinese Studies had been my professors at Yale, in the Chinese department — George Kennedy, Gardiner Tewksbury. I dropped in at the College. My friends were gone, as were all of the teachers and students. Only Henry Fenn, the dean, remained, in the process of closing down.

I said I would like to rent one of the foreign style houses. He said I could have the whole place, campus and all, if I would keep an eye on it for them. I said I couldn't do that, since I wasn't sure of my plans, but that I would find a custodian for him and keep an eye on the custodian.

And so it was arranged. I dug up a certain Hungarian gentleman, who took over the actual maintenance but lived off the grounds, while Phoenix and Helen and I moved into a rather old fashioned steam-heated three-storey house. Fenn left for the States.

We were fairly safe. From time to time officers of General Fu Tso-yi's Kuomintang army would appear at the compound entrance and demand that they be allowed to quarter troops inside. The gatekeeper would stall them off with a tale that this was the residence of a high American dignitary, and advise that they take the matter up with the US Consulate. They never did, of course. To make sure that we could maintain our privacy, we usually kept the front gate bolted with a foot-thick beam.

We weren't exactly alone, however. Several hundred students and teachers from the high school in Paoting, where a battle was raging, were living in the College dorms. They were well behaved and kept pretty much to themselves.

Our life was quiet, peaceful. On the recommendation of one of the local Americans, we hired a "Western style" cook who had experience working for foreigners. He must have been a magician in his spare time. For while he provided us with excellent apple pies, he managed to make enough flour and sugar disappear to feed ten times our number.

The boom of artillery grew louder and more frequent. Tientsin had been taken in a brief but bloody fight. The Communist-led People's Liberation Army was closing in on Peking. Soon they were lobbing shells just outside the crenellated city walls. There was a growing undercurrent of excited anticipation. Groups of Chinese literati began dropping in "for tea" — actually to discuss how they should coordinate with the impending take-over.

Kuomintang frenzy mounted to fever pitch. They murdered political prisoners and arrested hundreds of innocuous people in a paranoic hysteria. One girl — a devout Christian and member of the YWCA — we had to conceal in our house for several weeks until Liberation because someone or other had said something or other to some idiot in the police.

Fu Tso-yi, the general holding the city, was stubbornly refusing to capitulate. The Communists didn't want to take Peking by storm, though their strength was overwhelming, out of consideration for the lives of its citizenry and to save the city's priceless art treasures from damage. They sent emissaries to negotiate with Fu — including, according to one account, his daughter, a revolutionary who was correspondent for the Tientsin newspaper *Ta Kung Pao*. They said if he surrendered he and his men would be treated honorably, and Fu would be given a post in the new government commensurate with his rank.

After hesitating for several days, he agreed. On January 31, 1949 the artillery barrages ceased. A hush fell on the city. I rode my bike to Hsi Chih Men, Peking's northwest gate. The People's Liberation Army began marching in, clean, smartly stepping, smiling young men. Contingents of jeeps, trucks, artillery caissons — all made in the USA — rolled through the streets. No wonder the Communists referred to Chiang Kai-shek ironically as their "Quartermaster General". Eventually, most of the equipment which Washington gave him ended up in Liberation Army hands.

The people cheered and applauded. Parents held their kids higher on their shoulders for a better view. Pleasure and relief were universal. No doubt there were some who wondered whether to give any credence to the horror stories the Kuomintang had spread about the newcomers. But good news travels fast, and many had also heard how correctly this army had behaved in other, already liberated, parts of the province. In any event the fighting was over, and this was something welcomed by all. The streets were gay with flags and buntings.

II

EARLY REFORMS

1949-1952

In the next few days representatives of several organizations called on me to request that we lease them the College premises. I put them in touch with an American who was on the College board, an administrator of PUMC, the Peking Union Medical College, a Rockefeller foundation. He entered into a contract with the unit which later became the Ministry of Culture. The Ministry paid rent, plus the wages of the old staff, who were kept on. Only when the US pulled their diplomatic personnel out of China and sent the Seventh Fleet into the Taiwan Straits were rent payments suspended.

Administrative organizations were set up, a government was functioning — though it was characteristic of the new regime that it wasn't formally proclaimed until October first, when most of China had been liberated, and more experience had been gained in governing a large country.

We stood that day with hundreds of thousands in the square before Tien An Men — the Gate of Heavenly Peace — massive entrance to what had once been called the Forbidden City, the palace where for five hundred years China's emperors had ruled. Now, on the magnificent gate house, topped with tiles of imperial yellow, Mao Tsetung and his staunchest colleagues had gathered. Mao, the philosopher, poet and historian, was surely profoundly conscious of the significance of that day as he ringingly proclaimed the establishment of the People's Republic of China.

Phoenix was in tears, and I was deeply moved. It wasn't my country, I was a foreigner. But in that sea of humanity I could feel the emotions sweeping through like an electric current. People in shabby patched clothes. Army men and women, sprucer, but whose uniforms showed signs of hard wear. The crowd had been silent at first, recalling years of suffering and fierce fighting. But now, at last, victory. A roar welled from thousands of throats, a heart-cry of triumph and resolve.

We began to see changes almost immediately. Hills of uncollected refuse were removed — in Peking, 200,000 tons in ninety days. Court-yards were swept, housewives organized to keep the lanes clean. Streets had their foreign names converted into Chinese.

On Wangfuching, formerly Morrison Street, the main shopping thoroughfare, for a time the black market dealers in currency continued to stand openly on street corners, jingling piles of silver dollars. Security police informed them that this was no longer allowed. A few days later, those still at it had their money confiscated. If, after another week, they persisted, they were arrested.

A new currency was issued, pegged to the value of a few essential commodities like grain, edible oil and cotton goods, whose prices were kept strictly controlled. Gradually the inflation subsided and prices stabilized.

There was a crackdown on crime. Phoenix took part in closing down the brothels. Peking's houses of joy were anything but. The girls were mostly peasant children who had been sold, often for a pittance, by their desperately poor parents to professional collectors who, in turn, resold them to the brothels. Theoretically, if the girl earned enough, she could pay off her purchase price and regain her freedom. This, in fact, rarely happened. The girls told the raiders some shocking stories. They had been beaten, ill-fed, and treated with the most callous brutality by the owners of the establishment. A dying girl was nailed into a coffin even before she drew her last breath, because she was "no longer of any use". . . .

The worst of the monsters were arrested and tried, with the girls giving testimony. A few, after the details of their crimes had received full publicity, were shot, in the presence of their victims and the local citizenry.

Rehabilitation was not easy, at first. The girls couldn't conceive of anyone being genuinely interested in their welfare. But after several days of good food, rest, and medical treatment — nearly all had venereal disease — they relaxed and started talking openly with the women who had been sent to look after them. Then they aired their suffering at "Speak Bitterness" Meetings. The Women's Association and political workers helped them see that the root of their troubles, like the troubles of all of China's poor, was class oppression. The girls were impressed by the arrest and punishment of the brothel keepers. They were finally convinced that the old days were not going to return.

Training programs were set up. They were taught to operate sewing machines and other useful trades. Those who wished were sent home, all expenses paid. Those who preferred to start a new life were found jobs in other parts of the country, and their pasts were kept secret from the general public. Many of them subsequently married and had children.

Phoenix went to work as an editor of *Peking Literature and Art* — a monthly magazine. She also wrote film and drama articles for newspapers and periodicals.

A thinnish foreigner in his forties, dressed in an army padded uniform, dropped in at the house. Big liquid brown eyes shone behind horn-rimmed glasses. He introduced himself as "Dr. Ma" in an American accent you could cut with a knife. Orginally George Hatem, a doctor from North Carolina, he had gone to the Red Areas with Edgar Snow in 1937 and remained on with the Chinese revolution, dispensing medical treatment from the lowest to the highest.

He told Helen to pack her things, that she could leave tomorrow to join her fiancé on a dairy farm in Inner Mongolia. George chatted pleasantly for a few minutes, then said goodbye and left. We were to become close friends. Helen departed the next day. I didn't see her again for nearly ten years, when I visited her in a commune on the outskirts of Sian, where she and her husband, plus a couple of kids, were tending milk cows.

No one seemed to know quite what to do with me. There wasn't much use for an American lawyer. While waiting, I found a new novel which appealed to me called *Daughters and Sons*, and began translating it, hopefully for the American market. The story of guerrilla warfare against the Japanese amid the reedy marshes of southern Hopei province, it was fast-moving, hard-hitting, and full of peasant colloquialisms, which I'm afraid I rendered into rather Damon Runyonesque prose. Still, it was published in New York by a book club, and had the distinction of being the first novel of "Red" China to appear in the States.

If I could translate, why not make me a translator? I was taken on by the Bureau of Cultural Relations with Foreign Countries, where I worked on turning into English diverse books and pamphlets. We operated in a charming setting — a large traditional compound of one-storey tile-roofed buildings in a hollow square around a garden. The head was Hung Shen, a well-known dramatist who had once startled a movie audience in Shanghai by leaping on the stage and denouncing the film for its imperialist content. He was a colorful, emotional fellow, another living refutation of the canard about the "inscrutable Oriental".

A year or two later an assistant head was appointed, a short mild-mannered man with glasses. It turned out that this innocent-looking fellow had done extremely dangerous work in the Communist under-ground during World War II, posing as a Kuomintang army officer. He managed to work himself into the position of staff officer to Hu Tsung-nan, warlord of Shensi province. One day he was tipped off that he was under suspicion, and had to leave quickly. The Communist Party sent him clear out of the country. He spent the next few years as a student — at Columbia University.

I once asked him about the risks he took in the old days. "They weren't much," he said with a smile. I had the feeling he really thought that, too. I met quite a few Chinese who had shown incredible courage at one time or another in their lives. But you only embarrassed them if you tried to discuss it.

Phoenix, sent to interview several women who had been called to Peking for a National Conference of Outstanding Workers, ran into this same modesty. It was difficult to get a story out of them. One woman she spoke to was puzzled. She said she didn't understand why she had been invited to Peking — she hadn't done anything special.

A modest demeanor is part of the Chinese way of life. Braggarts and blowhards are viewed with pitying scorn. But the modesty is not just superficial. When you live in a country where the prevailing motto in "Serve the People", one is not likely to get too big for one's britches.

In January 1950 our daughter was born. We called her "Ya-mei", the "Ya" standing for "Asia", the "Mei" representing "America". Ya-mei had also been Phoenix's baby name, but the meaning had been different. Her father, a feudal poet-scholar, was enormously fond of the little girl, the last in a long series of progeny. He wanted to express his adoration, but at the same time he had to be appropriately reticent and modest. He settled, at last, on "Ya-mei", since while "Mei" means "beauty", "Ya" can also mean "inferior". So Phoenix spent her early years hailed as a "Second-Rate Beauty".

Fortunately — we were both very new at being parents — Ya-mei was aggressively healthy right from the start. We hired a nursemaid, or *paomu* who picked the baby up every time she cried. Ya-mei quickly caught on and developed an excellent pair of lungs, bawling at all hours of the day and night. That was practically the only suffering we had to endure, for the *paomu* took care of all the messy details which infancy entails, besides cooking, washing, and cleaning the house.

In October of 1950 South Korean and US troops pierced the 38th Parallel, driving north. American planes bombed Antung, industrial city in China's Northeast. Douglas MacArthur, commanding general, boasted that his men would cross the Yalu River by Christmas. After repeated warnings from Peking were ignored, the Chinese People's Volunteers joined the fight.

They were indeed volunteers, men from villages only just recovering from the ravages of war — imposed first by the Japanese, then by the Chiang Kai-shek riffraff. Now the Americans were threatening another invasion. This the Chinese could not tolerate. They flocked to the colors and marched off to battle, in tennis sneakers, meagerly equipped, with no planes and not much by way of anti-aircraft guns, but grimly determined.

The whole country rose to back a massive war effort. This was the first of the Chinese "movements" I was to see — masterpieces of nation-wide education and organization which mobilize the entire population in support of major policies.

People in the arts also played an active role. One dramatist wrote a play about doctors in PUMC, the former Rockefeller medical center. A team is being formed to go to the front to treat the wounded and cope with germ warfare. One or two of the doctors cannot believe that the civilized Americans would actually indulge in such obscenities. But facts are uncovered which prove that some years previous in that same hospital a number of the American philanthropists had been experimenting on poor Chinese patients to discover which strains could make the most deadly bacteriological weapons. Their doubts resolved, the doctors join the team. As the play ends, they depart for Korea.

Adulation for the West, however, was still very strong. China, perhaps the most culturally and scientifically advanced country four or five hundred years before, had fallen behind by the turn of the twentieth century. There was an eagerness to learn — from Japan, from the Soviet Union and, more recently, from America. The rich sent their sons to universities in these countries, books were translated by the thousands and avidly read.

With America's growth as a world power, interest in the US grew. Many city-bred Chinese intellectuals before Liberation were attracted by the "absolute freedom", the "art for art's sake" philosophy which promised to free them from social commitment and responsibility to the downtrodden majority.   America's scientific and technological skills were undeniably of the highest order.   American affluence, as seen on the streets of China's big cities in flashy cars piloted by well-tailored drivers, had certainly been impressive.   There was a tendency to equate everything American with "desirable" and "good".   As one Chinese writer sarcastically put it, the USA worshippers thought "the American moon is brighter than the Chinese moon".

There was a sizable hang-over of this mentality after Liberation. Of course people were angry that the US had helped Chiang Kai-shek with billions of dollars in arms and equipment, and thus delayed the collapse of his hated regime.   But there had been little direct confrontation, and a reservoir of goodwill remained toward Americans for helping defeat the Japanese.

Now, however, US soldiers were shooting at Chinese boys in Korea, US planes were striking Chinese cities with conventional and bacteriological bombs. We saw newsreels of atrocities and devastation in Korea committed by American troops.   Children in the lanes of Peking, too young to have a concept of nations, who had formerly used the word "American" synonomously with "foreigner" in an interested and friendly sense, now shouted it at each other in swearing matches as the worst imprecation.

Yet all through the Korean war I was treated with complete amity and naturalness.   I carried on with my job as usual, I visited and was visited by Chinese friends as usual.   If my relation to the war was mentioned at all it was only to assure me that China makes a clear distinction between the American people and their government.

In spite of the kindly attitude of the Chinese, I was ashamed, probably because I wasn't much of a Marxist. What America was doing in Korea was disgraceful, indefensible.   I had a lot of pride in and affection for my country of origin.   I felt personally responsible.   And I was responsible, to the extent that every man is responsible who silently observes his government performing reprehensible acts and takes no measures to prevent them.   But the ultimate blame lay with the policy makers, whom Eisenhower described as the "military-industrial complex", the men who called the tune. The American people were only the suckers who did the dying.

Phoenix left for the front with a group of writers and artists to convey greetings from the folks back home. There was quite a bit of this by delegates representing different segments of Chinese society. They chatted with the young Volunteers, told them of the latest domestic developments, and in general reminded them that the people were interested and concerned. It was a great morale builder, typical of new China.

The writers and artists were bombed and napalmed. Phoenix told me how she lay on the earthen floor of a peasant's thatched hut while the ground trembled beneath her and heavy bombs burst all around. Two delegates were killed. Phoenix returned seething with fury. It added fire to the speeches she gave in a number of places, reporting what she encountered in Korea.

One of the incidental goods to come out of the war was the increased stress on environmental hygiene. China had been a filthy place for decades. Before Liberation, toilet facilities were primitive. Collectors who sold excrement to outlying farms came around and ladled it out of the privies every week or so. They were fairly regular because human manure had value as a fertilizer. But garbage was something else. It would accumulate for months, until the under-paid haphazard sanitation department men of the Kuomintang felt inclined to scrape a little off the top. The stink and flies and mosquitoes were a menace, and in the hot weather they were unbearable.

I remember visiting a small village not far from Shanghai in 1948. We had been walking for hours, and we were tired and hungry. We went into a local restaurant and ordered bowls of noodles. The swarms of flies that joined us the moment the noodles were served presented an intriguing problem. You had to hold the bowl in one hand and the chopsticks in the other while shoveling the noodles. But how could you shoo off the flies and avoid pushing them down your gullet? The more experienced members of our party had a simple solution, which I quickly emulated. They put their bowls on the table, leaned close and plied their chopsticks with their right hand, and kept the flies off with energetic waves of their left.

Now American planes were dropping canisters of insects which carried deadly infectious bacteria. We had all seen the newsreels of germ warfare raids on Chinese cities in the Northeast, saw how white-gowned figures rushed to the areas where the canisters had broken open on contact with the ground and sprayed the crawling lethal hosts, saw how thousands of people built walls of burning brush and flailed the insects with brooms. We had read the reports of the distinguished team of international scientists who had made investigations on the spot, both in Korea and in China. Everyone understood that it was vital to destroy potential disease spreaders and eliminate the kind of environment in which they thrived.

The whole population turned out in a huge campaign, disposing of garbage, improving sanitary facilities, killing flies, mosquitoes, lice, fleas, bedbugs and rats. They nullified the germ raids in Northeast China, and the nationwide clean-up resulted in a marked drop in the incidence of contagious disease.

Meanwhile the war raged on. The North Koreans forced the Americans back across the 38th Parallel, chased them all the way down to the southern tip of the peninsula, nearly drove them into the sea. US forces made a landing at Inohon on the west coast and counter-attacked almost to the border with China. The Chinese volunteers entered the war. Battles see-sawed furiously. Saturation bombing leveled every city and town in North Korea. The Chinese learned to dig deep caves in the mountainsides. They studied or entertained themselves while blockbusters ineffectually churned up the earth outside.

In July of 1951 armistice talks began at Panmunjom. They were not to be concluded for another two years. The fighting continued. Each time the Americans made a little military progress, they broke off the negotiations. Then the defenders would give them another drubbing, and they would rush back to the conference table crying: "Let's talk this over!"

We heard quite a bit about Panmunjom from a Western newsman who lived in Peking and attended the conference. The foreign correspondents were dissatisfied with the handouts they were receiving from the US press officer on the progress of the battles. These usually proved to be glowingly triumphant fabrications, or were so vague as to be useless. Our friend got the real news from the Chinese and passed it on to his brother gentlemen of the press, who incorporated it in their dispatches.

This included, at a time when the Pentagon was baldly claiming that there were no GIs in enemy hands, photos of thousands of US soldiers disporting themselves at baseball and other pleasant activities in Chinese camps for POWs.

Within China, major developments were taking place. Land Reform had reached almost every corner of the country. It was the most important economic measure to date, since eighty to ninety percent of the population lived on the land. What they wanted most at that time was to own their own plot of ground, free and clear, and to break the economic strangle-hold of the landlords. It was estimated that ninety percent of the tillers — the peasants — owned only thirty percent of the land. Seventy percent was owned by the landlords and rich peasants, who constituted only ten percent of the rural population.

Phoenix went off with a team heading for Kiangsi Province. These teams were composed of personnel from government organizations, and they worked with local cadres and PLA men stationed in the vicinity.

The first thing they did was call on and hold meetings with the poor tenant farmers and hired hands. They would get them to speak up and tell what the situation had been before Liberation. The story generally followed a simple dreadful pattern: A peasant leased a few fields from a landlord, paying rent in kind ranging from fifty to eighty percent of the harvest. He would need money for seed, or food grain to tide his family over till harvest time. The only place he could get it was from the village landlord. (Larger communities might have two or three, but ordinarily one big landlord controlled the entire village.) He would make the loan to the tenant at a usurious rate of interest. At harvest time he would weigh the rent grain in his own measure boxes, which invariably were rigged to cheat the tenant. The amount the tenant would be "short" would be added to his debt, also at compound interest. It was only a question of time until the tenant was so crushed that he couldn't make payment. The landlord would then confiscate his property and kick him and his family off, or keep them on as semi-serfs. The tenants' wives and daughters were, of course, always fair game.

In some places a few peasants at first were reluctant to talk. They had been oppressed by centuries of feudal rule. The landlords had been very powerful, the backbone of the Kuomintang. They were the magistrates and local officials, they collected the taxes, they ran the police, had private gangs of their own thugs. Their sons officered the army. It was commonplace for them to have people brutally beaten or murdered. Their military power had been broken, but they were still around, as were their families and their cronies. What would happen after the land reform team left? The gentry spread rumors that Chiang Kai-shek was going to make a landing very soon, and uttered dire threats against anyone who dared touch their property.

But the timid ones were definitely in the minority. There were plenty of people who spoke out. At the mass meetings they exposed in detail, from personal experience, the landlord's cruelty and oppression. Men and women wept as they testified. The audience yelled angrily, shouted political slogans, until the haughty or hypocritical landlord cringed abjectly. If he had committed shocking crimes, such as murder or rape, and the people demanded it, he was turned over to the judicial authorities for trial. A few of the particularly vicious types were executed. But only a very few.

The work teams helped in the formation of Poor Peasant Unions, Women's Associations and militias. The members of those were the most militant and most politically aware, and became the nucleus of government, security and education in the village. People were taught that the enemy was not so much this or that individual landlord, but the entire landlord class. They heard about landlords in other counties, in other provinces, and began to understand the meaning of "class struggle".

In a village in Kwangtung Province a landlord killed three members of a land reform team in their sleep with a knife. Some years later there was a famous case of an ex-landlord who got a job as a cook at a construction site and nearly slaughtered half a hundred workers by putting poison in their food. Luckily, they were treated in time. In the late sixties I heard accounts from people in a village not far from Peking of mysterious figures in white who howled like banshees night after night outside the homes of the more enthusiastic commune members. The "ghosts" when caught turned out to be ex-landlords who were trying to shake the villagers' confidence during the early stages of the Cultural Revolution.

The average person soon learned the meaning of Mao Tsetung's warning about the persistence of class struggle. And if it slipped his mind for a time, there were always class enemies to forcibly remind him.

Land Reform, because it was in the people's interest and had their support, succeeded. The majority of the landlords accepted it, however reluctantly, because they had to. Only their land, draft animals, farm implements and surplus grain were divided. None of their industrial or commercial interests were touched. Landlords lost their civil rights, but if they behaved themselves the villagers could restore them at the end of five years. This had no effect on the status of their children, who were treated the same as everyone else. The landlords received an equal share in the land along with their villagers.

Naturally, the situation didn't remain static. In the countryside, where the bulk of the Chinese population live, many involved struggles were yet to come.

At this time, we were still living in the former College of Chinese Studies, now Ministry of Culture compound, occupying an entire three-storey house. I had the Minister, in a similar house, on my right, and another high official on my left. Everyone was very polite, but I felt awkward living there. I wanted something homier and more relaxed, a place where my visitors didn't have to sign in at the gate. So I asked the Ministry to find me other quarters. Phoenix hadn't come back from Land Reform yet, and I thought it would be a nice surprise to be all set up in a new house before she returned.

I looked at a few prospects and finally settled on a traditional hollow-square compound, to be shared with three other families, Chinese, who occupied the wings. The rooms were smaller than what we'd had in the College, and the floors were stone flagging instead of wood, but we had our own little hollow-square garden in the rear of the large one. I liked the privacy, the tile roofs, the paper windows and having less exalted Chinese cadres for neighbors. The only concession to modernity were electric lights and flush toilets. Gone was our steam heat and gas range. We cooked with the popular coalballs and kept warm with old-fashioned pot-bellied stoves. But all the housekeeping was done by our *paomu*, who ate and slept in.

My new neighbors were very friendly. They helped us get settled. From various parts of the country, they had different characteristics. What they had in common was that they all, the men, that is, worked for a department under the Ministry of Culture, which collected and published folk songs. The wives stayed home and looked after the kids. Later, as more opportunities opened up and literacy spread, most of the younger women were absorbed into full or part-time jobs.

Our neighbor Ho was short, stocky, round-headed, with a shaven pate, and he had a short, stocky, roly-poly wife who laughed a lot. They had two kids, a little girl about a year old, very cute and cuddly, and a boy of about five, a holy terror who was always getting into scrapes. They seemed to be perpetually cooking and eating, and they looked it.

Wang, on the other hand, was a thin esthetic type, of peasant origin, but intellectual and bookish. While still in the Liberated Areas he had married a village girl, a doe-eyed beauty, slim and graceful. For some reason she was very jealous, and she often wept and raged over suspected infidelities. I'm sure they were imagined, for Wang was quiet and reserved and a little cross-eyed. Afterwards, they had a baby, which fortunately took after the mother, and she lavished on it all of her sensitive emotion.

Our third neighbor, the Tangs, were from Szechuan, which meant they liked hot spicy food and were great yarn-spinners. She was small and petite, but rounded. He was big and fleshy, and talked in a slow easy-going manner, in spite of the fact that he was really high-strung and suffered from high blood pressure. Of course they both spoke with a Szechuan accent, which evokes the same kind of pleasurable amusement among other Chinese as a southern drawl produces in New York. They had a daughter of two or three when we moved in, and were expecting another baby soon.

Phoenix returned from her Land Reform, very healthy and full of stories. Since she had been in Szechuan during World War II, she and the Tangs had a lot to talk about, and we became quite friendly. Our daughter Ya-mei greeted her mother politely as "aunty". Phoenix was stricken. She had been away from home so much the kid didn't recognize her.

I had become both father and mother to Ya-mei. In the evening she would climb into my lap and demand stories. Having exhausted what little I remembered of Grimm and Andersen, I was forced to resort to science-fiction of my own creation. This placed a considerable strain on my Chinese vocabulary. But evidently I got over pretty well, for Ya-mei would correct me if I told it any differently on fifteenth or sixteenth rendition. I think I placed first in her affections, followed as a close second by her kitten, which she clutched to her a good part of the day, when she wasn't dressing it in doll's clothes and trying to induce it to sleep in her crib.

What would it have been like if I had become a father in the States with both my wife and myself working? I certainly couldn't have afforded to pay a full-time nursemaid, or to put the baby in a nursery. Neither could most Chinese parents, for that matter. But usually there was a widowed grandma who was glad to take over the running of the household. Phoenix's mother was dead, and mine was twelve thousand miles away. Fortunately, our relatively high salaries enabled us to hire a *paomu*.

Ten years before, I would never in my wildest dreams have imagined that my offspring would be Chinese. Yet now that she had come she didn't look any different to me than any other baby — except that she was more beautiful, of course. Ya-mei was in turn capricious, sweet, ornery, inconsolable, sunny, pensive, and completely adorable. No Flatbush infant could have captivated me more.

One of our friends and frequent visitors was "Leng", a Chinese woman obstetrician from southeast Asia. She had been born in a wealthy overseas Chinese family and had studied piano as a girl. She must have been good at it, for she won some kind of British Empire scholarship to a music academy in London. A brilliant erratic person, she didn't actually care much for piano, and switched to medical school. She finished the course with honors, qualified, and returned home. There she quickly became bored with a social life alternating between sets of tennis and bouts of drinking. New China captured her imagination. She came and was given a post in one of the big hospitals. I understand that she was an excellent obstetrical surgeon. But she was too individualistic and temperamental to get along with her steadier, self-disciplined colleagues. For that same reason, although she was strikingly attractive, she scared off anyone who might have considered her as a marriage partner. When we met her, she was frustrated in her job and in her private life, and had taken to drinking again. A few years later, she returned to her own country where I hear that, professionally at any rate, she's doing well.

Leng came to dinner one spring night. At about nine o'clock we were chatting over our teacups when we heard wild shouts from the courtyard. Our neighbor Tang, his head bound in an aromatic compress to lower blood pressure, was milling about, uttering incomprehensible cries. When we calmed him down sufficiently, he sobbed that his wife had just given birth to a baby — in the house.

We left him, half-fainting on a chair in the yard, and ran inside. Sure enough, his panting wife was lying on the bed, a tiny infant, the umbilical cord still attached, there beside her. Leng swiftly took charge, sent me for a razor blade and matches, a basin of hot water, towels. . . . Feeling a bit faint myself, I did what I was told, and before long mother and child were in fine shape. It took somewhat more time to bring father around.

Gradually, we pieced together the story. The mother had been taking one of those breathing and painless childbirth courses. A reservation had been made for her at a maternity hospital, the telephone number of the taxi company had been written down. Perhaps the course hadn't been taught very well, or maybe she just didn't understand it correctly, but when her labor pains started she told herself firmly it was all psychological, and relaxed.

The Tangs decided that everything had turned out for the best. The baby, another girl, had indeed been born painlessly. She was pretty and healthy, and had been tended by one of the best obstetricians in Peking. They hadn't even had to pay for the taxi. What more could you ask?

They thanked Leng again and again. I was honored with the position of the child's godfather. For several years after, until they returned to Szechuan, they brought the little girl to pay her respects to godfather at Spring Festival, the Chinese lunar new year holiday.

This painless childbirth routine was something new to China, and was part of a spate of medical reforms. In the past there had been two kinds of medicine — traditional, for the vast majority, and Western, for a handful of rich in the cities. Even in the cities many of the well-to-do preferred the Chinese form of treatment. The Western-trained doctor tended to be scornful of the traditionalists, and considered them quacks, while many of the patients were cautious of the former's "new-fangled" ways. With the coming of Liberation, Mao called on both kinds of practitioners to learn from each other, especially for the Western type doctor to learn from China's vast store of ancient medical lore. Of course it was only the complete change in the social fabric that enabled the average Chinese to receive any medical treatment at all.

Western medicine advanced from being acceptable and available to a sort of panacea in the minds of some. There was a tendency to give children penicillin freely for the slightest touch of fever, until it was found they were building up a resistance against the drug, rendering it ineffectual at times when it was really needed. Geriatric injections according to a Romanian formula were popular, as was tissue therapy from the Soviet Union. These methods may be valid under certain conditions, but for a period they seemed to be used indiscriminately in China.

People were inclined to accept on faith almost anything coming out of the Soviet Union. This was the honeymoon period. The Soviet Union helped the Chinese build industrial and engineering projects, and sent experts and advisers. While the Chinese had to pay stiff prices and high salaries, they were pleased, for the most part, with what they got. Soviet prestige was never higher.

There were some reservations. A few of the big engineering projects did not come up to standard, or failed completely, because Soviet engineers insisted on mechanically transposing copies of their own projects in disregard of Chinese materials and conditions. While many of the experts were sincere, hard-working people, some were not. You used to see them tooling up to the Friendship Shop, that caters to foreigners, in big Zis and Zim limousines, and walking in with large suitcases, which they would cram with purchases of Chinese furs and silks. They could get several times the price back in Moscow. People began to suspect they were not really "selfless proletarian internationalists". Even the kids in the lanes had a jingle they use to recite while skipping rope:

> *Soviet big brother in a big car goes to town,*
> *Soviet big sister wears a fancy gown.*

Still, recognition of the nature of Soviet revisionism did not come in a day, nor was it as virulent in the beginning as it grew later, and a lot of the Soviet achievements were genuinely admirable. The Chinese wanted to learn from them. Russian was taught in the schools, lessons were broadcast over the radio. Soviet movies and dramas played in the Chinese theaters, Soviet directors showed how to put them on, taught the Stanislavsky method of acting.

A few Soviet films stressed the horrors and sufferings of war and said all wars are bad. Did that mean the Russians were not supposed to fight back when invaded by the nazi legions? Were people ground down under the heel of a foreign imperialist or a domestic dictator simply to bow their heads and take it? Was it immoral to fight a defensive war or war of liberation?

We saw a Chinese version of *Twelfth Night*, not exactly one of Shakespeare's most immortal dramas, put on with the aid of a Soviet *regisseur*. All I remember is large putty noses on the Chinese actors, yards of lace at the cuffs, and splendid plumed hats. I don't think the audiences took this opus too seriously. For weeks after it hit the boards irreverant Chinese teenagers were greeting each other on the street with deep curtsies on the part of the girls, and hat-flourishing bows by the boys.

What devastated Peking audiences was *La Traviata,* done by a Chinese opera company schooled by a Soviet impresario. They must have spent a fortune getting the costumes and scenery rigidly correct. Everything was sung, including the *recitative.* That tickled the Chinese. The night we went, when rich papa came to plead with Violetta to release his darling son from her wiles, even before he had time to come into the parlor, the maid began to warble.

"A gentleman here to see you."

"Who is it?" trilled Violetta.

"Monsieur So-and-so," in dainty staccato.

"Ask him to come in," Violetta chimed.

The audience collapsed into tears of helpless laughter. It was several minutes before the show could go on.

Yet much of the Soviet art that came to China was excellent — Oistrach, Richter, Ulanova, the Bolshoi. . . . Several new novels, translated into Chinese, reached millions of readers. The Soviet impact on Chinese culture was considerable.

If some of it was negative, ideologically wrong, the Chinese weren't worried. Mao's attitude to foreign arts, and to China's own cultural heritage, had always been one of critical appraisal. He felt it was good for the public to be exposed to a wide variety of fare. A certain amount of ugly or hostile material wouldn't hurt, in fact it would serve to immunize them and sharpen their political perceptions.

Economically and politically China was making progress. Land Reform was completed, and the peasants were organizing mutual-aid teams to help one another during the planting and harvest seasons. Many had gone further and formed farming cooperatives, working together all year round, and dividing the harvests according to their respective investments and the amount of work they did. This was more efficient than going it alone. People's incomes were growing, they were living better.

Consumer demand increased. In a country of hundreds of millions even a modest rise of consumer purchasing power takes an awful lot of satisfying. Suddenly there weren't enough thermos bottles, bicycles, sewing machines . . . and all the things poor Chinese families previously could never afford.

Industrial production — heavy and light — had to be stepped up.

When the Communists came to power in 1949, industry and commerce were in a sorry state. What heavy industry there was had been in the hands of the Four Families — the bureaucrat-capitalists. This — along with their holdings in fields like banking — the new government confiscated. But the rest of trade and manufacturing was conducted by relatively small and medium businessmen. Many were on the verge of bankruptcy, due to the fact that the big boys had scraped off all the cream, plus the disruption caused by years of fighting.

To get the wheels rolling again, the government entered into contracts with the manufacturers, whereby it supplied the raw materials or semi-finished goods, bought their entire output, and handled all sales and distribution. It also intervened in labor relations to ensure that the workers got a fair wage without putting too high a demand on the enterprise. In addition, the government began building industrial projects of its own.

This worked well. Machines were soon humming all over the country. The number of industrial workers increased. More goods appeared on the market, though they still couldn't meet the growing consumer demand.

Businessmen prospered. They redecorated their homes, took their cars out of storage, dressed well, and resumed their social life. For the new government they had nothing but praise. The more influential ones joined the Chinese People's Consultative Council which, while it had no power, cooperated with the elected National People's Congress, and served as a forum for discussion and study.

But the leopard hadn't changed its spots. The tricks began again, assuming they had ever stopped. The bourgeois gentlemen bribed government cadres, cheated on their taxes, swiped goods and materials they were working on under government contracts, substituted cheaper stuff and turned out shoddy merchandise, and stole economic information from government sources. On the government side, instances of graft, waste and bureaucracy helped provide a conducive environment for machinations of this sort.

A double-barrelled nationwide campaign was launched against these "peccadillos", starting at the end of 1952, known in typical Chinese shorthand as the "Five Antis" and the "Three Antis". It was conducted in a style people had learned to recognize — throw everything open to the public, get everyone involved. This is how the Chinese Communist Party operates, an aspect of what they call their "mass line". In every drive for or against something, up to and including the Cultural Revolution they have followed this pattern.

It didn't take long before the people working in the various enterprises, public and private, produced enough evidence to expose the gentlemen involved. Most of them cried loud *mea culpa*, or muttered they had only been engaging in what had been honorable business practice for centuries. Which brought the discussions to the crux of the matter. While cheating your competitors, and your customers, and your government, may not only be good form but even admirable in a predatory dog-eat-dog society, should such habits enjoy the same moral sanction in a socialist society?

"Absolutely not," said Phoenix indignantly. "The situation is fundamentally different. In a feudal or capitalist society, a minority rules the majority. It's a jungle type of existence, where ruthlessness and cunning are indispensable, where only the most ruthless and most cunning make any headway. But socialism isn't like that. Here the majority rules, and every new development is designed to better their well-being. People don't have to worry so much about food or clothing or shelter any more, and taking advantage of others is discouraged. If a person is dishonest, we only shake our heads and say: "How crude. Just a pig!"

This moral regeneration to me was one of the most stimulating aspects of new China. People were changing. As the tension and pressure eased, they became more affable, more kind. Or maybe that's how they were originally before the struggle for survival left them little opportunity for consideration of others.

There still were tensions in China, people had to work hard. Class struggle, the battle of ideas, disagreements on methods, continued. All of the problems and petty annoyances of daily life went on. The Chinese people were not saints. But the degree of selfishness was noticeably diminishing. You didn't feel the need to make pre-emptive strikes. The world, in new China at any rate, was not out to get you.

If I was moved by the new social atmosphere, I was simply staggered by the beauty of Peking. It was a very different China, after pre-Liberation Shanghai.

Shanghai was a mixture of East and West. For a mile along the Whangpoo River ran the Bund with its row of foreign banks and offices, mostly in heavy nineteenth century European style, their majesty somewhat marred by the rickety old trolleys, French owned, rattling before them. The entrance to the Bank of England was flanked by two pedestaled bronze imperial lions. Millions of passing hands, rubbing them for luck, had burnished their front paws a shiny gold.

At one end of the Bund lay the Chinese city — the oldest part of the original Shanghai — a jumble of handicraft shops, restaurants, and crowded dwellings. The other end was graced by the British Consulate and spacious lawns. There the road crossed the steel-girdered Garden Bridge where, during the occupation, Japanese soldiers slapped foreigners who failed to come out of their vehicles and bow to sentries.

On the other side of Suchow Creek, which the bridge spanned, was Hongkew, an area of docks, bars and brothels. Its most visible landmark was the tall apartment hotel called, appropriately enough, Broadway Mansions. Before Liberation it housed American and other newspaper correspondents, as well as some of the highly paid personnel of various foreign commercial enterprises, and in its interior life was much closer to Broadway than to the Bund.

The city was populated by a large poverty-stricken class, a fair-sized middle class, and a small but extremely powerful group of the very wealthy. The poor were everywhere — stevedores, rickshaw pullers, shipyard and textile workers, itinerant drifters, famine refugees — their clothes often little more than rags and patches. Weary men, emaciated women, large-eyed spindly children. The lucky ones occupied crowded warrens resembling tenement houses. Many lived in shacks and shanties, made of whatever material came to hand. Thousands slept in doorways and on the streets.

I was shocked and heart-sore at the sight of such misery when I first arrived in Shanghai in 1947. But the sheer numbers of suffering humanity had a numbing effect. Though each sick or dying individual you encountered was a sharp prick to your conscience, your mind boggled at being immersed in hundreds of thousands. In self-defence it reduced them to statistics. I found, to my horror, that I was coming to accept them as part of the local scene.

That was because I myself was living, though modestly by American standards, much closer to the opposite end of the spectrum. I was comfortably married. We had a car, an apartment, a maid. I ran a law office, listened to big talk at the bar of the American club, partook of the French cuisine at the Hotel Metropole for lunch. When the fancy struck me, I could stroll over to Jimmy's on Nanking Road and have the best American apple pie and chocolate ice cream in the Orient. Feelings of guilt could always be put down by the rationalization that depriving myself could in no way help to solve the inequities of Chinese society.

And I was only on the fringes of the real money. Foreign financial giants — the foundations of whose fortunes had been laid on opium running and real estate speculation. Big absentee landlords from the provinces, Chinese merchant kings, gangster chieftains. And bureaucrat capitalists — the top heads of Chiang Kai-shek's Kuomintang and their coterie who simply used government funds and property for their own private purposes. All these gentry lived in sumptuous manors or in smart new high-rise apartments and tooled about in chauffeur-driven limousines.

I met them at parties, luncheons, banquets, receptions. Whether Chinese or foreign, they talked nothing but business or politics. A few of the Chinese had studied abroad — in America, England, Germany, Japan — and had pretensions of Western culture. In general they were a cynical lot. Most of them knew the end of their day was approaching. It was only a question of time. Discussion tended to center around how to squeeze the last possible dollar out of China and get it, and themselves, abroad before the final curtain fell.

The middle class, though smaller proportionately than its counterpart in the West, also hoped to climb to a higher bracket, and also was whipsawed between low incomes and rising prices, but much more severely. They included office employees, store sales personnel, civil servants, students and teachers. Except for the last two, they knew little and cared less about political affairs, their previous experience having taught them that politicians and officials, of whatever stripe, were greedy and corrupt. They longed only for peace and stability, and an opportunity to earn a decent living.

But try as they might to stay away from it, politics influenced every aspect of the people's existence. Suitable bribes to government flunkies kept your son out of the army, or diminished or exempted the tax you had to pay. Racketeers — musclemen of the politicos — also required financial assuaging for the "protection" they afforded. The great value of the "Old China Hands" was that they could advise foreign concerns exactly who, and in what manner, should be paid how much. Many arrangements had to be made with local political figures to ensure the smooth operation of the black money market, where ninety percent of the city's foreign trade was conducted. Politics was as inevitable as death in Shanghai, and much more inevitable than taxes.

It was essentially a foreign city in flavor. The buildings were in the shoddy European style of the century before, except for a few new elegant apartment houses in what had been the French Concession. Street signs were in both English and Chinese — "Bubbling Well Road", "Avenue Joffre", and were known to the local residents by the way their ear heard the foreign pronunciation. (Bus conductors announced "Petain Road" as "Pei Tang Lu".) My office was in the "Development Building". "St. John's University", an American institution, bordered on "Jessfield Park", established by the British. Turbanned Sikh policemen controlled traffic. European food and dress were popular. Movies were mainly Hollywood creations. Western products flooded the markets. There were even dance halls where charming partners were available, for a set fee per dance. On the outskirts of the city riding stables and a large golf course offered healthful relaxation to the tired executive.

But Peking, that was something else. In the early fifties no city could have been more Chinese. It breathed antiquity, power and refinement. It first became the capital when the Mongol emperor Kublai Khan took the throne in 1280, and was built into its present magnificence in the 15th century by the emperors of Ming.

Situated in the exact center of Peking is the Palace, also known as the Forbidden City, a huge complex of courts, compounds, terraces and tiers, all paved with stone and surrounded by ornately carved marble balustrades. A series of great halls rise gradually to a height overlooking the entire city, each with massive pillars supporting gleaming tile roofs of imperial yellow.

From here the city extends in the four directions of the compass with geometric precision. Ancient places of worship — Buddhist, Taoist, Confucian, Tibetan, Muslim and Catholic, temples, cathedrals, nunneries and monasteries — attest to Peking's diversified religious and cultural influences. The whole city is neatly laid out in regular lines of streets and lanes. And in these lanes, mostly earthen and unpaved when we first arrived, the bulk of the population lived in traditional hollow square compounds of tiled-roof one-storey structures, enclosed by high plastered brick walls.

There was a serenity, a solidness, about Peking. Northern Chinese tend to be tall, big-boned, their movements and speech more deliberate than those of the volatile southerners, their courtesy unfailing. They are a people who have beaten back endless incursions of foreign hordes. Even when over-run, as by the Mongols in the 13th century and the Manchus in the 17th, they absorbed them into their rich civilization and vast multitudes until the invaders were completely assimilated.

Though Shanghai had been interesting in appearance, its European architecture and office buildings, its cars and business suits provided familiar footholds to a person climbing slowly into a new and alien culture. But practically everything about Peking was different. It was a story-book world, filled with colors and shapes the like of which I'd never seen. Princely residences guarded by stone lions, arches of stone and wood painted in beautiful and intricate designs at street intersections, the whole city encased in a thick crenellated wall punctuated at regular intervals by gates — massive brass-studded doors topped by tiled-roof forts.

Now, in ancient medieval cities like Peking, throughout the land new concepts were taking hold, the new regime was strengthening.

III

PEOPLE CHANGE

1953-1955

Though plenty of problems remained by 1953, conditions were fairly stable. Peasants were forming producers co-ops; business too was moving toward socialism. In July, the Korean armistice was signed, and the Chinese Volunteers started for home. China's first Five-Year Plan commenced in 1953.

It also was the year when I joined the Foreign Languages Press. In 1951, when I was still with the Bureau of Cultural Relations with Foreign Countries, we had begun, experimentally, a magazine called *Chinese Literature.* With our main stress on current creations, we chose the best of the latest fiction and literary articles we could find, as well as classics and early 20th century writings, and translated them into English. But it was felt that a broader organization was needed to introduce new China to the world through the medium of books, magazines and pamphlets, and in 1953 the Foreign Languages Press was formed. Our magazine, along with others, was amalgamated under its aegis.

Our office was a delight, housed in the usual one-storey tiled-roof buildings in a large hollow square around a lovely garden, formerly the home of a Manchu aristocrat. Two of our staff, an English woman and her Chinese husband, also lived there, and they usually served tea or coffee during the breaks. She was the daughter of a British business-man and had been raised in China. Her command of the language was very good. She had met her future husband while they were both studying at Oxford. They married and came back to China after the Japanese surrender. His English was fluent, and his knowledge of literary, including classical, Chinese was excellent. They made an ideal team of translators.

All told, we had only about a dozen people, but we managed to put out quite a decent quarterly. In succeeding years this became a bi-monthly, then a monthly.

My job tended mainly toward the translation of contemporary works, especially those with war themes, fighting, and rough and tumble. Having been raised on the diet of violent fiction, which is the privilege of every red-blooded American boy, I seemed to have the vocabulary and imagery required.

Actually, I enjoyed doing them, and felt a rapport with many of the characters. Whether fighting an enemy on the battlefield or a natural calamity in a commune field, Chinese heroes and heroines have a courage and dash strongly reminiscent of the American pioneer spirit. They do what has to be done, come hell or high water, or as the Chinese would say, "fearing neither heaven nor earth". I've often wondered whether the instinctive friendliness between the Chinese and the American people might not be due in part to this common trait they sense in each other.

I liked the work, too, because it gave me an opportunity to read a great deal more in Chinese than I ordinarily would have had occasion to. China is a huge country with a long and involved history. No one, certainly not a foreigner, can thoroughly cover all that time and space. A lot can be learned from a country's stories and poems and plays. They give more of the "feel" of the thoughts and emotions, the people are more vivid, more real, than in purely factual accounts.

As the society changed, we would see the style of writing also changing before our eyes. A few hundred years before, form was all. It didn't matter what you said, but you had to say it elegantly, and within the framework of a rigid formula. Vagueness and circumlocution was the order of the day. Less than half a dozen noteworthy novels were produced in half a dozen centuries. These were mainly in the vernacular, and for this innovation their authors were heaped with the same abuse their European counterparts had met when they tried to break the grip of Latin on the written language in the Middle Ages.

After World War I there arose general revolt against the old ways. Writing in the vernacular became more popular. From the early twenties, the Communists gave the movement considerable encouragement. But it wasn't until the Party came to power that it could push for writing "in the language of the people" on a nationwide scale.

The writers had to feel their way. Many classical phrases had long been current in common speech, even among the illiterate, and they enriched and beautified the language. The idea was to retain these while fostering a gradual colloquializing of the written word. When you added to this new terms and expressions reflecting changing ethical concepts and a developing technology, you got a prose that was very different from what you would find, say, in a Taiwan or Hongkong newspaper.

As a result of the written coming closer to the spoken language, literacy increased, but not spectacularly. You need a knowledge of at least two thousand characters to read in Chinese, and you can learn them only by rote. Some are slightly pictographic, a relic of ancient times when people made drawings to represent what they wished to describe. Many are ideographic, that is, they are a combination of several drawings to express an abstract idea. Still others have become arbitrary, their origins lost in antiquity. A few are independent words. Most are now syllables in longer words.

Not only must you memorize them, but you have to keep reading and writing or you forget what you've learned. This proved to be the case for peasants who took crash literacy courses. By really cramming, they learned fifteen hundred characters in about three months. But reading was a tiring chore, and they had little occasion to write. In another three months they had lost their mastery of a great deal of what they had previously acquired.

A special national commission was formed, which simplified the complex characters. This helped, but still left the fundamental problem unsolved. Ideographic writing is unscientific and cumbersome.

Another commission, headed by a friend of ours, was established for experiments in the use of an alphabet. They worked marvelously, he said, but diehards fought the idea tooth and nail. They insisted that there is a vast body of literature in Chinese — original writings and translations from other languages — which would be abandoned if people stopped learning characters.

Not at all, said the modernists. Students can specialize in Chinese hieroglyphics, just as they specialize in ancient Latin and Greek. And the best of the heritage can gradually be rendered into alphabetized Chinese.

The regional differences in pronunciation are too great, cried the diehards. You can't use the same alphabet when people can hardly understand one another.

That's not true, the modernists replied. Many countries have more than one dialect, but they all use the alphabet. Besides, having an alphabet helps to bring about a standard pronunciation.

To prove their point, the commission sent a team to a primary school in Fukien. The dialects spoken in that province have been compared by folks in other parts of the country to "the twittering of birds". First, the team taught the kids the alphabet and how to use it phonetically. Then, spelling out the words, they corrected their pronunciation. In a few weeks time the youngsters were talking with flawless Peking accents.

The commission published a little newspaper and a number of story books in romanized script. They also explained what a nuisance characters were for typing, printing and telegraph and cable communication, and how much easier it would be to use an alphabet. Chairman Mao himself came out strongly in favor of having an alphabet ultimately supplant the present form of writing. There was also considerable public support.

Nevertheless, the movement seems to have bogged down. Perhaps, for the moment, the diehards and traditionalists have proved too strong. Or maybe it is because the leadership has become involved in other and more momentous struggles. In any event, it is only a question of time before the drive gets rolling again. It will be a major aid in bringing universal literacy to China, and will facilitate the study of Chinese by people in other lands. A modest start was made at the end of 1978 with the decision to use a new romanization of the spelling of all person and place names in translation of Chinese materials for circulation abroad. A small step but nevertheless a beginning.

The reluctance to give up traditional cultural forms is understandable. Brush writing of Chinese characters is an important and beautiful art, though not many people indulge in it nowadays. The brush discipline which Chinese of well-to-do families learned from an early age was markedly reflected in their paintings.

There is much that is of value in Chinese traditions. I was introduced to *tai chi chuan*, an ancient form of body conditioning, while our office was still in the big compound. My English colleague and her husband began taking lessons from an old gentleman who came after hours at the end of the day. I watched them learning the elementary movements in the garden and became so intrigued I joined the class. Our teacher was a man in his sixties. He had spent his life giving instruction in what the Chinese call "the military arts", as had his father and grandfather before him. These included exercises with lance (single) and sword (single or double) and his own particular version of *tai chi chuan*.

Quite a bit has been written about *tai chi,* and its popularity is spreading well beyond the confines of China. My own understanding is that it started in Han times, about two thousand years ago, as a karate for soldiers in the imperial army. It remained a combat drill until Ming (14th to 17th century), when an offshoot developed as a solo exercise. This was increasingly refined until it reached its present form as a kind of therapeutic dance. Often prescribed by doctors and taught in sanatoriums, it is effective in helping sufferers from ailments connected with disturbances of the nervous system — ulcers, high blood pressure, insomnia, and the like.

I certainly have found it an excellent dispeller of tension. The movements are slow, almost dreamy, with a coordination of long deep breathing — not deliberate but in harmony — yet sufficiently complex to keep you concentrating on them, and them alone. There is a procession of rise and fall, advance and retreat, rhythmically flowing. You go along with it, yet you exert your will at the same time, in a floating dialectic. As you expel your breath and sink downward or draw back, you can actually feel the pressure going out. Over a period of months you build up a habit pattern until, even when you are sitting at your desk or walking along the street, you can consciously relax. The whole routine takes about half an hour. You end up perspiring freely, but your breathing is even, your heartbeat normal.

In China in the old days *tai chi chuan* used to be larded over with mysticism. Today, that's out. What used to be "lightness and dark", "male and female", are now simply positive and negative, stress and relaxation. Very straightforward. Amusingly enough, it was in the scientific West, though perhaps that's not exactly the term for Hollywood, that I recently found people learning *tai chi* with a good dose of abracadabra thrown in, linking it up with *Yi Ching* — Confucius' *Book of Change* to which they managed to give an astrological interpretation.

Tai chi is not a panacea. It does not work for everyone and does not succeed every time. For me, most of the time, it does.

Phoenix had been transferred to the Peking Art Players, a legitimate drama company. Her job was to find plays for them to stage, and to help the writers lick their opuses into shape. I saw dozens of performances, usually of dress rehearsals. Directors and actors were always dropping in at the house. They were a lively, interesting bunch, reminding me of left-wing theater people I had known on Broadway in the forties. We had long, animated discussions on the relationship between form and content, what should and should not be learned from foreign theater experience. . . .

Our daughter Ya-mei had started going to a kindergarten run by the wife of Shao Li-tse, a high Kuomintang official who had come over to the side of the Communists. It was several blocks from where we lived, and every morning a pedicab with a little enclosed van in the back with seats for eight kids rolled up to the door to call for the eager pupil. The first two mornings Ya-mei howled as if she was being sent to the North Pole. But when the tiny bus brought her home at the end of the third day, she was completely adjusted and already boasting about her new accomplishments.

"Teacher said I was the best today," she announced with quiet pride.

"The best what?"

"The best eater. I finished first at lunch."

It just shows what good home training will do for a child.

The kids learn that it is bad form to grab things from or slug your little playmates, that people have to be reasoned with. They get into the habit of discussing things in groups, with every tyke encouraged to speak out freely. Bad conduct is criticized, lightly, usually in a private chat with teacher, who does more explaining than scolding. But the main stress is placed on praising the good. They have the usual kindergarten fun and games and, when they become five or six, begin learning to read and write.

Chinese children don't start primary school until the age of seven, though they are obviously capable of doing so at six or even younger. I have never been able to discover whether this late commencement is due to some backward pedagogical concept about children's learning ability, or shortage of teachers and classrooms. Anyhow, the kids are raring to go by the time they hit senior kindergarten, and you simply have to give them a crack at the books.

Ya-mei knew that I was a "foreigner", but she was rather vague about what that implied, and it certainly didn't bother her. Among the children it was not a disparaging term, in fact it gave a certain amount of prestige, for it meant that your parents were invited to the reviewing stands to see the parade on National Day, and that you were taken to watch the fireworks from Tien An Men Gate in the evening.

When I first came to China, the small tots tended to hail all foreigners as "American". It was a good word, then, but it grew tarnished with US involvement in Korea, military bases on Taiwan, and persistent US government hostility. The new operative term was "Soviet", which became the new equivalent for "foreigner" among the half-pints. This too gradually lost its gloss. Now foreigners are "foreigners" or, among the more ceremonious kids, "international friends".

In the early fifties there were not many foreigners in Peking, other than Soviet "experts" and the diplomatic corps. The business people, the missionaries, the idle lovers of the "exotic" had almost all gone home. They didn't fit into the new society. Foreign trade, shipping, manufacturing, were now under government control. Religion was dying in China. There was no market for Chinese monks and priests. What interest was there in foreign preachers?

Even before Liberation, religion had always been a pragmatic affair. The main organized faith was Buddhism, with Taoism second, and various forms of Christianity running a poor third. But it was not unusual for a man to pay lip service to two, or all three, parleying his bets not so much to gain an ultimate paradise as to make sure he would get whatever good fortune was being divinely dispensed in his lifetime.

In a land of strong family ties, China's peasants had an intimate, and quite democratic relationship to their gods. In some villages it was the practice at spring planting time to parade their idol through the streets with exhortations that he provide them with plenty of rain. If in the months that followed he failed to oblige they took him out again — and beat the living daylights out of him with sticks and clubs.

As for foreign religions there were certainly some true and sincere believers. But many more were what were known as "rice Christians". It was the practice of certain foreign pastors to reward their flock with handouts of free rice after services on Sunday morning. As long as the rice kept flowing, the turnouts were good. But if ever it stopped, the congregation mysteriously vanished.

After the People's Republic was formed in 1949 religion began fading away. Not that it was restricted. On the contrary, freedom of religion was guaranteed in the Constitution. The government exempted houses of worship from taxation, and provided funds for the restoration of run-down temples and the maintenance of clergy.

But most folks couldn't see the point any longer. The little niches in walls of village homes where idols had stood or squatted were now empty. I asked an old peasant the reason. He shook his head.

"Those gods never brought us any luck. We had drought and floods and famine. The landlords and usurers squeezed us. The Kuomintang taxed us and dragged our sons off for their armies. We had nothing but misery. Chairman Mao and the Communist Party have put an end to that. Things are getting better all the time. Who needs religion?"

The young people wouldn't be caught dead in a church or temple. Old stuff, "square", was their reaction. They were learning Marxism, the teachings of Mao. Religion was "metaphysical idealism". What they wanted was "dialectical materialism".

So the foreign missionaries went home, except for a few who remained to grace Chinese prisons for activities of a definitely non-ecclesiastical nature.

The last to go were the exoticists, the orientalists, the lads who had found in Peking a home away from home. They usually, but not always, had money of their own, and collected jade, or paintings, or delved into ancient poets, and lived in "quaint" little homes, wore old-fashioned Chinese clothes, and had servants to shield them from the crass intrusions of an everyday world. Generally harmless, woolly, a few good in their particular field, they were a living anachronism of a bygone day, and they gradually drifted off to find another quiet backwater in another old impoverished land.

That left among the foreigners a handful of left-wing journalists and people working in government organizations or teaching school. Social life was pleasant, relaxed. Everyone knew everyone else.

I was a member of a small amorphous group which met every week or two at a bar and grill we had rudely christened "The Dump". It was rickety, the walls tilting slightly beneath the weight of years, and had sawdust on the floor But it had beer on tap and served steak and French fried potatoes which could have held their own in any high-class Flatbush emporium.

Most of the time the quorum consisted of George, Rewi, "Yao" and me, a select, if varied, gathering.

George was Dr. George Hatem, of Lebanese extraction, American born, raised in upstate New York and courtly North Carolina, who had studied medicine in America, Beirut and Geneva.

Not long after his arrival in the early thirties in Shanghai, where he tried to set up a practice, he met Rewi Alley, a New Zealand engineer, who was a factory inspector for the Shanghai Municipal Council. This body, composed mainly of foreigners representing the big imperialist interests in China and a few wealthy Chinese, had meant Rewi's job to be a sinecure, eyewash for the public, part of the humanitarian facade. Rewi, however, took it seriously, and asked George to check the health and sanitary conditions in the chromium plating factories. George was shaken by what he found — children working long hours in filthy, appalling, dangerous surroundings, often beaten, some chained to their machines. He began getting "political". Rewi and Agnes Smedley, one of the best American writers on the early stages of the Chinese revolution, then also in Shanghai, contributed to his education. He did a lot of reading on his own.

When, in 1937, word came down from the Red Areas that more foreign doctors would be welcome, George was ready. He arrived in the revolutionary base, in the company of Edgar Snow, young American journalist, after a series of wild adventures and immediately went to work in the local hospital. He was given the Chinese name "Ma Hai-teh". He married a lovely Chinese girl, Su Fei, who later bore him a sturdy son.

Still the American prankster, George appeared in Yenan in a Chinese opera performance in full costume regalia and elaborate painted facial mask. At the same time, he was a hard-working conscientious doctor in a region where medical men were scarce. He treated literally thousands of patients, from impoverished peasants to some of the highest ranking men in the Communist Party. When Norman Bethune, the famous Canadian surgeon, arrived, George was there to greet him. It was during the Yenan period that George and Edgar Snow grew especially close, in a friendship that was to last until Ed's death in Geneva in February 1972, with George at his bedside.

After the People's Republic was formed, George, who had become an internist, switched to venereology and dermatology because, he said, "that was what was needed". He went tramping all over China with teams which eliminated venereal diseases that had been endemic for years among national minority people in China's border regions, thanks to foreign incursions. Similar Chinese medical teams halted schisto-somiasis, scourge of the Nile and the large watery region of south China where the tiny snail host breeds.

In Peking George worked in the Skin and Venereal Disease Research Institute and seemed to spend the rest of his time solving other people's problems. He was everybody's friend, everybody came to him with their troubles. If there hadn't been the phrase "Let George do it", we would have had to invent it. He would listen carefully, thoughtfully, to what you had to say, then offer some suggestion that suddenly made the whole thing obvious and simple, and usually conclude with a quip that tickled you into a grin. My blood pressure was up a bit, a few years back, but every time George took it I was normal. He's the world's greatest calmer-downer.

Rewi Alley, like George, needs a book to himself. There's one out about him already — *A Learner in China,* and no doubt there will be others, about both of these fabulous guys. Arriving in China in 1927 for "a look around", Rewi remained to devote his life to it. He found-ed China's industrial cooperatives during World War II, when Kuomin-tang corruption and supineness in the face of Japanese invasion had brought a dangerous disruption of manufacture and transport. He set up a school in a remote village in Kansu and taught hundreds of local kids and famine refugee orphans — children of "ignorant" peasants — to become first-rate technicians and designers in preparation for the new day he was sure was coming. He has written over a dozen books on China, and has published collections of verse — his own — about China, as well as translations of Chinese poetry, both ancient and modern. There is hardly a place in China Rewi hasn't been, there is hardly a facet of China's life and culture, past and present, he can't discuss knowledgeably, fascinatingly.

Rewi and George were "old timers", but we kept getting infusions of new blood. Yao, a Chinese friend recently returned from the US, was a wiz at steel making. He left most of us dizzily behind when he soared off into the realms of higher steel theory, but he was a delightful companion (he died early in 1972) and in some ways more American than the Americans. Yao could quote the batting average of every important player in the major leagues, and tell you which shortstop stole the most bases in 1935. He was married to an American girl whom he met in the States and brought back with him. She taught English at Peking University. They had three kids — a boy and two younger girls.

Men like George and Rewi and Yao did much to broaden my cultural and political base in those enlightening evenings at The Dump, while the beer and steak and potatoes did the same for my waistline.

They were more my friends than Phoenix's, for when we were together we talked, naturally, in our native tongue, and Phoenix's English was limited, a sad commentary on my abilities as a teacher. She had a fairly extensive vocabulary, but no noticeable grammar. This was entirely my fault, for I got in the habit of not immediately correcting her when she made a mistake, so as not to break in on her train of thought. Soon I got used to her brand of English. I could understand her perfectly. I rather liked her original reorganization of the old sentence structure. Hers was much more logical, and close to the Chinese. By concentrating hard, her quick intelligence enabled her to follow, and even take part in, our conversation. But anything more than ten or fifteen minutes was too much of a strain.

Then we would switch to Chinese, which we all knew to a greater or lesser extent. But we were by no means fluent in the vocabulary of the artistic fields which were Phoenix's special interest. Over the years we got better at it, and friendship between Chinese and non-Chinese families ripened. Still, it was always easier for her when one, or half of the couple, was Chinese. The ability to communicate in depth was the key.

Another thing that brought foreigners together as foreigners — I'm talking of those working in government organizations — was political study. This was something the Chinese took very seriously. They were always engaged in some course of study, some drive, some movement, which invariably involved them in reading Marxist classics, in reading Mao, in discussing Chinese and world affairs, analysing, arguing, applying theory to practice. It was constantly around us, and very infectious. Those who had the necessary language ability participated in some of the sessions of their Chinese colleagues. But usually the foreigners set up their own groups and conducted their own discussions of whatever was being currently mooted.

To me it opened new vistas. Before I came to China, the Marx with whom I was most familiar was Groucho. Like most Americans I was quick to recognize and resent injustice. I didn't like seeing big guys pushing little guys around. But though I bitched loudly I didn't do much about it. I was cynical, I considered myself a sophisticated New

Yorker. Everyone was out to get his. That's the way the world was and always would be.

Then, in China, I discovered I wasn't quite so clear as I thought. I had been ignorant, naive. People are not born bad, tainted with Original Sin. Nor do they come into the world with a clean copybook which they have to defend frantically from being blotted. It isn't primarily a question of the individual at all, but one of classes, class struggle. A small powerful minority, aided by a culture, a way of life assiduously peddled, keeps the majority toeing the line, brainwashing them into thinking they like it.

This had not only been the Chinese experience, as I learned from reading Mao and talking with my Chinese friends, but the same was happening in every corner of the globe. The foreigners in my study group came from several different lands, and everything they related of the history and struggles in their own countries bore this concept out.

For that matter in America too, as a lawyer, I frequently enough had seen marked class differences in attitude and behavior, and had no illusion, by the time I came to China, that equality or freedom could exist in the abstract, separate from people's class status. The fat purses always prevailed. In America the situation had seemed just bad and hopeless. But my Chinese friends were telling me it wasn't hopeless at all.

What can be done about it? I demanded. The only answer, said the Chinese, is revolution, non-exportable revolution, by each people in their own land. But why revolution? Why couldn't you vote the villains out of office? Why couldn't you vote in a new form of government, an entirely new social system?

They referred me to Mao's *On Contradiction*. I found it easy to understand. Mao says that the physical world is composed of an infinite number of entities within which are two mutually contradictory aspects, and that these entities are at the same time in mutual contradiction with other entities, and so on endlessly up and down the scale through time and space. Unrelenting battle goes on — between positive and negative, between the new and the dying — until one dominates and conquers the other and changes the very quality of the object or state involved. With this, I believe, most scientists agree.

But, says Mao — and here he parts company with the bourgeois philosophers — what is true in the physical sciences is comparably true in the social sciences. Technologies become outmoded, social relationships — master and slave, feudal lord and serf, capitalist boss and worker — are no longer efficient, the concepts which sanctified them — in law, religion, philosophy — are no longer germane. No thing, no condition, is immutable.

"Are you trying to tell me it's impossible to change a social order of minority control by peaceful transition?" I said to an office colleague with whom I was arguing.

"No, not theoretically impossible, under certain conditions," he replied. "Environment — the domestic and international economic and political environment — has a great influence on local change. If all the world were Red, with the exception of the Principality of Monaco, for example, it is quite likely that country could complete its revolution without a shot being fired. But only because the pressure, internal and external, would be so overwhelming that resistance against change would be obviously futile.

"In the world today," he continued, "the ruling cliques, shaky though some may be, still have plenty of power. They don't take their defeat lying down, and they have outside forces helping. Vote them out of office tomorrow and you have a military junta staging a coup within a week, a month, a year. They don't like removing their snouts from the gravy trough, and have no objections to a bloodbath if that will get them back in again. They are the negative aspect of the contradiction, and they keep wiggling and kicking and squirming until, as a class and as an ideology, they are completely supplanted."

Our Chinese friends were many. We knew scores of people in the arts. A few old friends we tended to see a lot of. They were delightful characters, the kind whose counterparts draw listeners in New York or Hollywood with their sharp professional comments. But there was an important difference — these people were socially dedicated, and they cared very little about money.

"Chang" was one of my favorites. A Cantonese, he "joined the revolution" at seventeen. He left Canton rather hurriedly by diving into the Pearl River and swimming underwater, except for intermittent gulps of air, because the Kuomintang police were popping at him with rifles. Later in his career he became a film director, a good one, too, and a film technician. Phoenix played in one of his movies, made in Chungking during the war. In the period of Kuomintang-Communist cooperation, he went to New York in a mixed group, to buy movie equipment. They took rooms in an old brownstone in the east sixties.

Chang formed an instant and hearty loathing for one of the Kuomintang blokes — a fat greasy type who was very superstitious.

One afternoon, while the gentleman was out, Chang ran a wire with a small speaker under his bed. Around midnight, Chang, from his room above, began muttering curses and groans into a microphone, punctuated with eery gibbering. Fatty was pale and haggard at breakfast the next morning. His hand shook as he reached for the butter. After two or three days of ghostly visitations, he moved to other quarters.

Chang was a frequent caller at our stone-flagged home. By then he was working in the film bureau. Like many Chinese men, he's a marvellous cook. He would arrive with a couple of his kids on a Sunday morning, carrying a live chicken or a still faintly moving fish. Commandeering the kitchen, he would line up his condiments and get to work. It's the preparations that take the time in making Chinese dishes. The actual cooking is fast, because they like the fresh, natural flavor.

After a delicious meal, which Chang consumed with more gusto than anyone — it improved your appetite just to see him enjoying his food — we would sit around talking movies, or theater, or world affairs. His job was on the technical end, and he was working on the manufacture and printing of color film, on three-dimensional movies, on a cycloramic theater. . . . We talked and argued, smoked and drank tea, until the children were dozing in their chairs and had to be taken home, grumbling sleepily.

Chinese men not only like to cook, they have no compunctions about holding babies. You often see them outside the front door with infants in their arms, chatting with neighbors. The love of children is universal. It's one of the things by which all visitors are struck. People take their kids everywhere. Babes in arms sleep nestled against one or another parent in movies and through the loudest clamor of Peking opera drums and cymbals. The older tykes dash up and down the aisles, or drag docile mums or dads on urgent trips to the john.

The men also do a lot of the shopping. A large plastic bag — useful for carrying books and papers — often serves as a receptacle for fresh vegetables spotted at the roadside stand on the way home from the office. Male chauvinist pigs are rare indeed. There used to be a bit of wife-beating in the old days, when the miseries of life made tempers short. But it's almost unheard of in the new society. Most women are working — full or part-time. They join in study groups which keep them up on Chinese and world affairs, there are women's associations which specialize in advancing their emancipation. Let any foolhardy male try pushing wifey around and he would be met with such an avalanche of opprobrium and public criticism that he would rue the day he was born.

In fairness to the men it must be said that pressure of this sort is seldom necessary. Though not yet entirely free of the ties of housework and children, women are playing an active role in more and more occupations which formerly were the exclusive province of the men and, by sheer ability, earning their respect. In some fields, like textiles, the women already outnumbered the men. In others, like medicine and dentistry, they are coming up rapidly. Equal pay for equal work is the rule, though still often violated, especially on the farms. Since every boy and girl graduating from school today is given a job, in another generation or so the work participation and responsibility exercised should be about the same.

After only a year in our garden quarters, "Chinese Literature" was again shifted. The new office building for Foreign Languages Press was ready for occupancy in 1954, and we moved in. The various magazines and book departments which had been scattered throughout the city were finally gathered under one roof. I wasn't altogether pleased to be back in an office building. We were on the fourth floor, all concrete and dull colors, with four to six in a room. As a "foreign friend" I shared my room with only one person, our chief editor.

From a law office on the fourteenth floor of the Paramount Building in New York I had moved to the eleventh floor of the Development Building in Shanghai, and now to the fourth floor of the Foreign Languages Press Building in Peking. But there were other differences than a mere change of locale and moving down a few floors.

In New York I had express elevators and steel cabinets and a view of the water cooler of the air conditioning equipment on the roof of the Paramount Theater. The Shanghai elevators were more sedate, the office had wall-to-wall carpeting and large Chinese-made desks of mahogany. Tea and perfumed hot hand towels were constantly available for attorneys and clients.

My Peking office was five storeys high, the ground floor, which had offices as well as a small lobby, counting as the first floor in the British manner. In the middle of the long rectangular building were broad staircases and an elevator reserved for foreigners and invalids.

Hallways with offices on either side stretched in both directions, with more stairs at either end. On each floor the bright sunny rooms on the south side were allocated first to the foreigners, the elderly, and those in poor health. Rooms on the north side went to the younger and sturdier members of our staff. Steam heat in winter was feeble at best, a deliberate economy measure to save coal. You had to wear almost as many clothes indoors as you did out, and the poorly insulated north side required full cold weather garb.

We worked an eight-hour day, six days a week, lunch hours not included. At ten and at three-thirty (4 p.m. in summer) there was a fifteen-minute exercise break. Those who needed it most — the fatties and the bookworms — usually strolled around, chatting and smoking. The young and eager types went through a series of calisthenics, an interesting combination of standard and traditional movements, to broadcast directions in cadence accompanied by music. A few fooled around on the basketball court in the rear compound. Here were three buildings, four storeys high, of apartments with steam heat and hot water, for both foreign and Chinese personnel, and a large garden.

Aficionados of *tai chi chuan,* like myself, worked out on the flat roofs, along with practitioners of other ancient Chinese martial arts, attracting small audiences. There were always some who wanted to learn, and we formed classes. But in a few weeks the novices usually drifted away. It's a tough discipline and requires perseverance.

We had a canteen which served three meals a day. Food was cheap but mostly what my colleagues called "big pot" style, meaning that it ran heavily to dishes which could be cooked, boiled or stewed in large cauldrons for a great number of people. Still, it was reasonably tasty and more convenient than going out to a restaurant. My favorites were the big grilled wheatcakes, which are similar to bread, and dough fritters fried in deep fat. The pickled bits and small side dishes were also delicious.

There were no water coolers, or coke or coffee machines, but everyone had his or her own pottery tea mug and cover. Each room was equipped with one or two thermoses, filled from special boilers on every floor. You kept your favorite tea in your desk drawer, and put leaves in your mug and steeped them when you arrived in the morning, replacing them with fresh leaves when the flavor was gone. People drank tea all day long, taking the mugs with them when they went elsewhere in the building for meetings or discussions.

Tea serves the same function in China as liquor in the West. When you call on anyone, in a home or in an office, a cup of tea is placed immediately before you, and is kept replenished throughout your stay. If workmen are repairing your house, you naturally serve them tea during their rest breaks. There are dozens of varieties and grades of tea, and many Chinese are connoisseurs who can expound on how quality is affected by times of picking and methods of curing.

Our office had no air conditioning, no janitors. We did our own cleaning. On a rotation roster, we swept, mopped and dusted our rooms and the hall outside and filled the thermos bottles. That meant each of us had a turn roughly once a week. It required only about fifteen minutes. Another roster provided for cleaning the toilets. Since every able-bodied person on the floor took part, that job came up approximately once a month. Windows were also cleaned monthly, inside and out, mostly by the young and agile.

For a number of years the first hour was devoted to reading fundamental political theory. You could choose your author — Marx, Engels, Lenin, Stalin or Mao, as you preferred. Two full afternoons a week, and sometimes an evening as well, were devoted to discussion of domestic and international political affairs, usually with people of your own office, in groups of five to ten. Occasionally talks were given on some important topic during office hours by a senior official of the Foreign Languages Press or higher organization. These invariably were followed by discussion in the small groups.

In our frequent *Chinese Literature* work conferences we talked about planning, editing, translations, illustrations. Criticism was offered of methods and attitudes of the leadership and, on rare occasions, of each other. Among the rank and file self-criticism was more common than criticism. The shortcomings of a unit, including those of its members, were deemed to be ultimately the fault of the leadership — for not being more efficient, for not giving better guidance.

To me these meetings and discussions were extremely fruitful. I was kept informed of the country's highest policies and approaches to political, economic and cultural affairs. The agreement or disagreement or suggestions which I voiced were relayed up the chain of command to the top. If a person in my unit was applying for membership in the Communist Party we all discussed his or her qualifications. Applicants would not be considered unless they first won the approval of their peers.

And certainly you had a very direct say in how your own particular outfit was being run. You felt that your opinion counted and that you were, by democratic process, participating in leadership and management. As a foreigner I was technically not entitled to any of this, but I was nearly always asked to attend and my views were courteously solicited.

Frequent confabs improved mutual understanding with my colleagues. They ranged in age from the twenties to the sixties and they came from all over China. They illustrated what they had to say with examples from their own life and experience. This gave me an insight into Chinese ways and mentality, and taught me a great deal about conditions, past and present.

We seemed to spend an awful lot of time in meetings. Often we did more discussion than work. Democracy was a new phenomenon in China, and I wondered whether they weren't overdoing the exchange of ideas aspect. It tended to create what my colleagues called a "relaxed start and rush finish" syndrome. We alternated between intervals of not much to do and intense scramble. Yet once everyone got the idea and swung into action, the teamwork was impressive.

Our chief editor was a tall, handsome Chinese novelist, with a fine command of English and several other languages. He had attended Kings College in Cambridge, and was an active figure in China's literary world. Though not a member of the Communist Party, he enthusiastically supported its principles.

His assistant administratively, an attractive competent woman, was the head of the magazine's Communist Party branch. She had left her well-to-do Honan family as a teenager to join the thousands of young people flocking to the outlawed Communists in the hills of Yenan. There she studied literature and art, which brought her ultimately to her present post of literary editor.

The head of our translators section was a young woman from a wealthy family who had attended Shanghai schools run by American missionaries, and who had served for a few years as a translator in the U.N. She spoke flawlessly colloquial American and was one of those geniuses known as a "simultaneous" interpreter. That meant she could convert your Chinese or English as fast as you spoke it, somehow rattling out your last sentence at the same time she listened to your next.

The other translators were mainly recent college graduates who had majored in English. (Our editorial personnel were usually Chinese lit majors). In the early fifties they came from middle class or rich families, since only these could have afforded to give their children enough education in the old society to qualify them for university entrance. This gradually changed after Liberation as more worker and peasant kids were enabled to attend school.

My relations with my Chinese comrades were pleasant and relaxed. They were curious about America and a bit puzzled by my American ways. I played ball with them during breaks, I wasn't "dignified". We talked freely about my family and theirs. There was a strong family atmosphere in the office. Some of our staff lived nearby and their children also ate at the office canteen. Kids wandered in and out at various hours of the day — to bring something mum or dad had forgotten, or to ask for a missing key, or to have a button sewn on. Preschool-age tots, when whoever was looking after them was ill or away, might stay with us for the day, kept busy at an empty desk with pencils and drawing paper. The Chinese love children, who are usually well-behaved, and someone would always be stopping by to play with or caress them.

My colleagues visited me and I them. Though I lived in a Chinese-style household and Phoenix and the baby were both Chinese, I was still a foreigner, and seeing me in this environment was itself a matter of some fascination.

Their homes varied. Both of the senior editors lived in traditional style compounds like my own, with coal stoves for heat and coalballs for cooking, but with beautiful rosewood furniture, gardens, privacy and quiet. The younger staff preferred the new apartments which had steam heat and hot water, and even gas ranges in some, but which tended to be adorned with a kind of Chinese Grand Rapids furniture and gave me an impression of drabness. Beaming grandmothers and kids dashing about and unstinting hospitality of the inevitable tea, plus peanuts, or candy, or melon seeds, or whatever was the best the family had on hand, brightened the atmosphere considerably.

During the spring and autumn festival days we went on outings to-gether — to the Western Hills, to the Great Wall, to the Summer Palace, to the Ming Tombs, carrying picnic lunches, always with full comple-ments of kids. I often went along when the whole office volunteered to help bring in a harvest on a suburban farm, or dig an irrigation canal, or build a reservoir. The fact that I didn't mind sweating and straining and getting dirty, impressed some of my older colleagues, who came from a more genteel background.

Though on the whole we got along fine, we did have points of friction. I was inclined to be blunt and had a "let the chips fall where they may" attitude. It took me a long while to learn the custom of starting with a little polite palaver, then sidling up to the problem and circumlocuting all around it, before actually identifying it and diffidently suggesting a solution. I still don't do it very well. I considered it pussy-footing, over-emphasizing the saving of face, a fear of coming to grips with conflict.

But gradually I realized it's not a bad approach at all. You get the question solved just the same, with a minimum ruffling of feathers. A strong objection by a translator to one of the editors might go something like this (I'm exaggerating of course): "You've done a marvellous job of editing this short story. I really admire you, I have so little talent in these things myself. The tenant farmer is particularly well done. There's just one small question. It's hardly worth mentioning. But could it be a tiny bit out of character to have him longing for a de luxe fully automated car the day after he's acquired the bicycle he's never been able to afford before? It's simply a thought. I mention it in passing — for your reference."

Although this routine is a bit frustrating to Westerners raised on adages like "Time is money!" and "Do it now!", it is what the Chinese are accustomed to and evokes the best response. They are differently and more delicately attuned. A light touch on an electric organ can give you full volume. You don't have to pound it with two hands like you do a piano.

The attitude which aroused my greatest antipathy was the veneration for authority, rooted in centuries of Confucian unquestioning obedience of superiors and official pronouncements. I remember expressing doubt about some formulation in one of our *Chinese Literature* articles, and being told, "But that's how it appeared in the *People's Daily!*"

With this goes a scrupulous addressing by titles: "Bureau Director X", "Department Leader Y", "Section Chief Z". . . . Interestingly, those who have the best relations with the rank and file and enjoy the solidest repect discourage ceremoniousness and are known simply as "Old Li" or "Old Wang" or whatever their name might be.

Mindless acquiescence to "higher wisdom" inhibits progress. Mao fought it for years. "Ask why more often," he urged. The response was to me most clearly visible in the Cultural Revolution. A widespread and deep-rooted resentment of paternalism, especially among the young who had been raised subsequent to Liberation, burst forth. Although the youth, spurred on to excesses by persons like Lin Piao and Chiang Ching, wrongfully attacked almost everyone in authority, the revolt was a sign that no leader, no matter how exalted his rank, was sacrosanct. Though his office was respected, his performance was open to critical scrutiny by one and all.

This, for China, was a very fundamental change.

IV

ENEMIES WITHOUT GUNS

mid-fifties

All through the years, although dealings between America and China on a government level were virtually nil, I remained in touch by mail with my mother and sister in New York. We corresponded on the average of once a month. Airmail letters arrived in ten days to two weeks. There was never any interruption, even during the Korean War. I followed regularly what was going on in America and the rest of the world. You could subscribe to the various news magazines, or read them in the office library. The Foreign Languages Press reading room also received the London Times and the Paris edition of the Herald Tribune daily by airmail. And you could listen to the Voice of America, Armed Forces Radio, BBC, Radio Australia, and various other English language broadcasts. These were never jammed. (China doesn't even jam the scurrilous Chinese language broadcasts beamed from Moscow.) Once in a while there were visitors from the States.

They had to come quietly because America was at the height of the "Hate China" period. China was anathema. No fabrication could be too fantastic. It used to make the Americans here laugh wryly. China was news, nevertheless, and American periodicals would buy stuff from foreign journalists and then slant it and twist it as best they could.

LIFE, in one issue (in 1959), carried eighteen pages of pictures taken by the French photographer Henri Cartier-Brisson. Certain inescapable facts it reported: China was training 400,000 engineers annually, many of them women. Kids in nursery school were well cared for. Elderly people kept checks on neighborhood cleanliness. China was not over-populated. It had "enormous room to grow".

But this was all too positive. LIFE quickly followed with a bit of pulp fiction in the same issue on the horrors of Chinese communes.

Although Mr. Cartier-Brisson had spent four months and traveled 7,000 miles in China, LIFE was unable to find even one slightly horrible photo among the hundreds he must have taken, and had to rely on the imagination of a hired artist to supply the appropriate illustrations.

The caption for one of the pictures Cartier-Brisson did take says that a hundred million civilians are under arms — in other words the majority of Chinese in their twenties. LIFE's readers must have been puzzled. China was supposed to be a "slave" society. Wasn't it dangerous for the administration to supply most of the able-bodied "slaves" with guns?

Perhaps even then Americans were beginning to suspect they had been sold a bill of goods about China. John Strohm came for READER'S DIGEST. He spent three weeks and traveled 7,500 miles. He didn't like the Chinese hatred of US imperialism and was irritated that "they chatter arrogantly" and call America's military might a "paper tiger".

Still, he couldn't help being impressed. He said the Chinese were creating "a fantastic surge of production". "Nurseries and kindergartens are a fixture in factories and on the farms." "Rent is dirt cheap." "Education is compulsory for seven years." "Most communes and factories hold adult classes." "Various sects are allowed to preach their doctrines, so long as they conform to the aims of the state." "China is a potential industrial giant."

He noted also that petty thievery had ended. ("I left my camera lying around with perfect confidence.") He marveled that "prostitution has been abolished", that "today tips are regarded as an insult."

But honest reports like Mr. Strohm's were rare. Most China coverage in the American press was unadorned fabrication. Reading it here in China, where the facts were staring you in the face, you wondered whether there were not similar distortions in stories about other parts of the world.

And it wasn't that material wasn't available to US editors. Because of the hostility of US China policy the American press was not permitted to maintain permanent correspondents in Peking, but newsmen and press association representatives from dozens of non-communist countries had been covering the China story for years, and their reports were accessible to any American editor who wanted them. There must have been many who knew the truth, but McCarthyism didn't die with the McCarthy period, and it wasn't wise to be considered "soft on Communism".

The Chinese, on the other hand, though far beyond the pale of the Free World, knew a great deal about it. *Hsinhua* coverage was sprinkled liberally with quotations from the Western press services in its foreign news, which was also broadcast several times daily on all national and local stations. Chinese papers carried frequent meaty analyses of international events and conditions. Discussions of those were part of the regular study courses held throughout the year in every form of endeavor from government organizations to neighborhood study groups. I was frequently embarrassed by Chinese friends asking me about some happening in America I had missed.

Admittedly, the Chinese press in dealing with American activities in Asia and the Middle East tended to accentuate the negative. But these were the aspects with which people in these areas were most frequently confronted. In just one week in July 1957, for example, here are some of the items I culled from Peking newspapers:

HANOI, July 24: *There are thousands of US military personnel in South Vietnam. They actually direct South Vietnam's Ministry of National Defence. In some military departments there are more US advisors than South Vietnamese officers.*

TSINAN, CHINA, July 24: *Three agents trained at America's CIA center in Tokyo were sentenced to prison terms at a public trial here. They were arrested when they landed on the Shantung coast in May and June of 1956. Three other spies were killed at the same time resisting arrest.*

BANGKOK, THAILAND, July 25: *The newspaper SANSERI reports that the heads of three ancient Buddhist images in the temples of Phitsnulok were sawed off and stolen recently. Americans here are paying 500 to 600 bahts apiece for such heads. Some have been caught trying to smuggle them out of the country.*

DAMASCUS, SYRIA, July 25: *The US embassy in Jordan is providing $500,000 to King Hussein's uncle, Nasir Jamil, to carry out assassinations in Syria, the paper ALNOUR reports today.*

KAESONG, KOREA, July 29: *Maj.-Gen. Chunk Kool Kok strongly protested US violations of the Armistice Agreement in delivering new weapons to South Korea.*

CAIRO, July 29: *In a 21-page indictment released here tonight, the Egyptian prosecutor charged that, in keeping with an understanding with the US, conspirators planned to assassinate President Nasser and install a pro-US government headed by Mohammed Naguib.*

HIROSHIMA, July 30: *A 54-year-old Japanese woman died this morning from the effects of the 1945 atomic bombing of this city. She developed symptoms of atomic disease only last January. She is the 15th victim of the bombing to succumb this year.*

Is it any wonder that the Chinese tended to take American protestations of friendship for the people of the developing countries with a grain of salt?

China too was subjected to steady and unrelenting American harassment. Besides building a crescent of military bases around China — complete with planes and nuclear-tipped rockets — stationing American troops in the Chinese province of Taiwan, and patrolling the Taiwan Straits with the Seventh Fleet, US forces pushed toward Chinese borders in wars against her Korean and Vietnamese neighbors, and made literally hundreds of intrusions into China's territorial air and waters by plane and by ship. Any trade with China was strictly forbidden.

Yet, amazingly, the Chinese kept their cool. When the attacks came too close — as in Korea — they hit back. A few planes that flew in too deep were shot down. They gave the Vietnamese heavy logistical support. They made no wild moves, but they made it plain they were not to be trifled with. The American top brass learned that in the Korean War. While the US forces in Korea hadn't exactly lost, they hadn't won either, something that had never happened before in American history. In this, the new Chinese soldier had played no small part.

A grudging respect crept into American comments on Chinese fighting abilities. Important generals publicly concluded that a land war against China would be "suicidal". A major clash of arms between the United States and China, while certainly not impossible, was no longer inevitable. Or so it seemed to the armchair generals among my foreign intimates. Many of the Chinese I spoke to had the same feeling.

Where did that leave me, personally? If I were to go back to America, this would be the time. The hostilities had ended. My mother was a widow, earning a slim living at various odd office jobs. The modest sum my father had left her was running out. What I was able to send her occasionally just about covered her rent. Though she never labored the point, she sometimes asked when was I coming home.

I missed her, and my sister and my old friends. I remembered lakes in summer amid green wooded hills, tree-lined residential streets, concerts in Carnegie Hall, comedians with the zany humor on which I had been raised, dancing to soft lights and sweet music, Fifth Avenue on a windy day. The unpleasant edges had been rounded off by time and distance. I was even nostalgic about subway rush hours and the frenetic bustle of Times Square.

I wondered idly about going back, but with no sense of conviction. There was too much against it. I talked it over with Phoenix, and we both agreed. I think she would have gone with me if I really wanted to leave. But she never had to make that decision because I never had any overpowering desire to.

America was in the throes of McCarthyism. Witch-hunters were finding Reds under every bed. The China Lobby, furious over their loss of property and power, were constantly beating the big drum against Peking. Even if I should not be subjected to persecution and harassment I would probably have had to become a lawyer again in the commercial environment I had traveled 12,000 miles to escape.

And where would Phoenix fit in, torn from her familiar roots and plunged into a way of life she disliked? What could she, a professional woman used to decision-making and activity, do in a society like America? Wouldn't she, and later Ya-mei, be discriminated against because of the color of their skin and the shape of their eyes? The disadvantages of returning to America far outweighed the advantages.

But the main reason we never seriously considered leaving was because we were stimulated and pleased by our life in China. We liked our jobs — I translating stories, Phoenix discovering new plays for the burgeoning drama companies. We had plenty of friends, more Chinese than foreign, who dropped in frequently, unannounced, in the Chinese fashion, although we had a phone. Ya-mei was growing prettier daily and more endearing. As to entertainment, we could have gone out every night in the week had we been able to stand the pace.

Financially, we were secure. Our combined salaries, high by Chinese standards, enabled us to eat and dress well, and put money in the bank. Medicare was virtually free, as was education, rent was low. We had no mortgage to amortize, no insurance premiums to meet, retirement pay was guaranteed. Since there were no private cars, we had no installments to keep up, didn't have to queue for gas, or pay for parking, or mess about with repairs (the hours, the days, I spent on details like that in New York!). We got around on busses or trams, or rode bikes.

Most important, I admired the Chinese people and the brave new world they were building. Though naturally there were some exceptions, the Chinese I met were possessed of a gentleness, a courtesy, a reasonableness that to me were a revelation. They suggested rather than demanded, they "offered an idea for your consideration", they were interested in your welfare, your comfort, your opinions.

The Communists, too, were not what I expected. While I didn't believe in the bushy-bearded, wild-eyed "Bolshevik" with a bomb in his hand I used to see as a boy in the Hearst newspaper cartoons, I thought they would surely be dry, austere, sternly puritanical. But, if anything, they were more relaxed, more humorous, than the average Chinese. They drove themselves hard, inspiring by example rather than by words. But their relations with the people they worked with and among were intimate and comfortable as an old shoe.

I had seen something of what China had been like in the old society. Now I was not only witnessing the miracle of people pulling themselves up by their bootstraps out of medieval squalor, but was personally participating. I had a sense of purpose, and accomplishment, and a goal, for the first time in my life. I wanted not merely personal advancement — though there was that too — but to move forward as part of a whole society.

I don't think I said to myself at that stage: "China is my country and my home. I want to spend the rest of my days here." But, though amorphous and unexpressed, that conclusion was beginning to take shape in my mind.

The war was over, Land Reform had been completed, inflation had been checked, industry and commerce were back on their feet. It was time for the next big step. That started in 1953 with China's first Five-Year Plan, with the main stress on economic expansion.

There was a lot to be done. China's per capita income was lower than India's, although distribution was more equitable. As against 190,000 miles of rail lines in the US and 80,000 in the Soviet Union, China had only 16,000. Many plants were backward technically. They weren't suitably located — too concentrated in some places, too sparse in others. Seventy percent of industrial output was being produced by old pre-Liberation factories. Many more new ones had to be built. There was a shortage of trained administrators and technical personnel. Only three percent of China's workers were skilled, as contrasted with thirty percent in the Soviet Union. China's lathe production was a third of what she required. Her railroad equipment was low-speed and light-weight; it all had to be replaced. . . .

But other conditions were favorable. Sixty percent of the peasants were members of mutual-aid teams or farming cooperatives. Their income had risen. And so the taxes they contributed increased by a third, although the tax rate remained low. Fifty-eight percent of all internal trade was in the hands of the state and cooperatives. The state-owned sector of industry and commerce was three and a half times what it had been when the government first took over. Though groping and feeling their way on specific measures, the Party was gaining experience in running the economy, and the broad outlines were taking shape.

Small-scale private trade, still permitted, often clashed with the collective enterprises. One night Phoenix and I were strolling past the neighborhood consumers co-op — which got its supplies and had its prices set by the government. Right in front of the door were private hawkers selling roasted peanuts for forty-eight cents a catty — roughly 1.1 pounds. They were doing a pretty good business until a couple of lads from the co-op came out with a huge sack of roasted peanuts which they began selling at twenty-four cents a catty. A line quickly formed, and we joined it. The pedlars took up the handles of their pushcarts and rolled away.

There had been floods in parts of Hopei province that summer and some of the peanut crop was waterlogged. Smart operators bought peanuts from the peasants at fourteen cents a catty — two cents over the state purchasing price — roasted them and sent them into the city with hawkers to sell at forty-eight. Since this was gouging the consumer, the government stepped in and offered them at half the price.

Daily, the advantages of collective effort were being proven to the general public from the viewpoint of both the producer and the consumer.

On the farms, mutual-aid teams and co-ops were beginning to outproduce the single family units. Foreigners were being shown around the country on conducted tours, and I was able to talk to farmers and ask questions. Many of them had thought when the Land Reform gave each family a plot of land, free and clear, that their troubles were over. But those who had been poor originally — and that was the majority — were still short of draft animals and farm implements, and labor power.

Then, encouraged by the Party, they discovered that if they clubbed together at planting or harvest time and tended each other's land in turn, they did better than singly. The next step, again cheered on and helped by the Party, was to form cooperatives in which the land was pooled and farmed collectively, the proceeds being divided according to the amount of land invested as well as how much work each member did. Those with draft animals or farm implements either sold or rented them to the co-op. The co-op members earned larger incomes than people going it alone. Sceptics who had adopted a wait-and-see attitude began applying to join.

Marketing and supply co-ops were being established all over the country. These were kinds of general stores carrying consumer goods and simple farm tools. They also bought up the things the farmer raised or made in his spare time. Farmers who joined them received dividends from the profits. Since they weren't sufficiently widespread or well-stocked, a lot of barter trade still went on, privately or at village fairs. Still, the marketing and supply co-ops were there and growing, and could and did intervene, buying and selling, to keep prices on private transactions in line.

In the cities too, prices of commodities were stable and quality in general was good. Essentials — like grain, cooking oil, cotton piece goods, coal — were strictly rationed and controlled. This was a tremendous improvement for the average person. People used to spend half their lives trying to ensure that they and their families had enough to eat.

One old lady in a Peking suburb told me how, in the days of the Japanese occupation, she had walked for hours to get to a grain store in the city to buy the "mixed" grain — a weevilly compound of chaff and sorghum and a little wheat — which was all the Japanese allowed to be sold to the public. By the time she arrived, the supply for the day was gone. So she walked back, hungry, exhausted, reaching her village in the hills about three in the morning. The kids were still awake, waiting hopefully. They all wept when she told them what had happened. For three days they had no bread in the house. Finally, her husband begged and borrowed a little flour from a friend. Thousands led that kind of a hand-to-mouth existence under the Japanese.

It was scarcely better under the Kuomintang. After the Japanese surrender, Chiang Kai-shek and his gang of highbinders took over. They were all for the big landlords, the big merchants, the bankers, the foreign "investors", and the public be damned. Unemployment, corruption, scarcity of necessities, was the order of the day. When harvests were poor, the grain merchants hoarded wheat and rice until prices rose sky high. Food was a constant problem. There were always long queues outside grain shops.

But the new administration changed all that. At first, the grain merchants were confident they could lick these tyros. Shortly after Liberation, the big boys in Tientsin went into the same routine, hoarding grain. Prices climbed. There was no response from the government. Encouraged, the grain merchants accumulated big stocks, paying stiff prices in a rising market but sure they could sell at a large mark-up. Still no response from the government. They began offering their stuff for sale, at eighty to ninety cents a catty. Suddenly the government stepped in. Wheat, rice, at roughly twenty cents — for two days, three days, a week. The grain hoarders were wiped out. Nobody tried that trick again.

Due to rigid control on a few basics, and a looser, yet over-all, supervision of commerce in general, prices remained stable and currency fluctuation ceased. It became possible to calculate budgets and pay wages and expenditures in "People's Yuan". The public had confidence in the currency. Instead of changing their money into silver dollars and hiding it in the mattress or burying it in a jug, they put it in the bank. For China, this was unprecedented.

Not all aspects of the economy improved at equal speed. Bureaucracy cropped up from time to time. Well-meaning know-it-alls could create absurd situations. One case caused quite a stir. For a long time the only dress material you could buy in North China had loud glaring designs, running heavily to large flowers. The indignation of China's liberated women piled up like a thunderstorm. They deluged the newspapers with letters of protest to such an extent that three artists of a leading magazine and the head of the Department of Industrial and Applied Arts decided to look into the matter.

They found that the Tientsin printing and dyeing plants which supplied North China had a board of designers, local women and other interested individuals who advised on the selection of new prints and designs. The recommendations were then displayed at a meeting of buyers for different parts of North China. Unless a design received orders for 2,000 bolts, it was not printed. Naturally, the buyer who could place the largest orders had the greatest influence on the choice of designs. In the case of North China, unfortunately, it was a gentleman named Kung, who bought for the whole of Hopei province, and combined with vulgar taste the conviction that he alone knew what the ladies wanted.

The investigators produced proof that the women of North China actually hated his choice and wore them only because nothing else was available. One young wife suspected her husband of cheating on her when he brought back a few yards of a Kung special he had bought in Tientsin.

"You never went to Tientsin at all," she wept. "They wouldn't sell a horror like this in a big city!"

A few weeks after the magazine published the report, it carried a letter from a much deflated Mr. Kung. He confessed he had been all wrong about the ladies' taste and offered evidence of the popularity of a small snowflake design that had recently been printed over his objection. Mr. Kung thanked his critics and promised to mend his ways. The Sunset-over-the-Yangtze-Gorges type of prints rapidly disappeared from Peking counters, and was replaced by a nice variety of designs, with much smaller figures.

Over-all, China was progressing steadily. The main question at issue was how rapidly to let agriculture — in which most of the population was involved — move ahead, as compared with industrial development.

This was a vital problem, and the debate about it waxed hotly for several years. We foreigners also argued the question in our study groups. Here was a country of hundreds of millions, most of them farmers, who had to be clothed, fed, and provided with a higher standard of living. This necessitated an increased output in both industry and agriculture. But what were the priorities? What should be the relationship between the two? What about light industry, which created the consumer goods? Where was the money to come from for all this expansion? Where should the start be made?

Agriculture itself was the obvious answer. China was short of money and machines, but she had plenty of people with centuries of practical experience on the land. Not only had they smashed the grip of the feudal hierarchy and obtained land of their own, they had discovered that combining with their neighbors they could raise their yields. In many places what were called "agricultural producers' cooperatives" were being formed, and farmers were flocking to join them.

This trend, said Chairman Mao, should be encouraged and guided toward still higher forms of cooperation, for it was bringing prosperity to the countryside. Higher yields meant more money in rural taxes, and therefore more state-financed industry, as well as more industrial raw materials. Bigger farm incomes meant bigger rural markets for industrial products. The increased use of these — tractors, trucks, farm machinery, fertilizer, oil, electricity — would bring further rises in agricultural output. Agriculture and industry would interact upon each other in a rising spiral. The key lay in the farming co-ops. They had to be given the full backing of Party and government.

The opposition groaned that this was impetuous and rash. Mao laughed at them. He said they were "tottering along like a woman with bound feet and constantly complaining, 'You're going too fast.' " Mao's estimates of the enthusiasm for collective farming proved to be correct. By 1955 most peasants had joined semi-socialist co-ops (where part of the member's income was determined by the amount of land he invested), and they were in fully socialist co-ops (where income is based entirely on the amount of work done) by 1956.

This pervading interest in things agricultural was something new to me. My grandparents on my mother's side lived on a farm. I had an uncle who ran a feed and grain mill. I traveled a lot in the States, through the dairy and orchard regions of New England, the wheat belt of the midwest. But the farmers did the farming, and the rest of us were interested mainly in its end results — the cost of meat and vegetables in the butcher shop and grocery store.

In China, agriculture is a part of everyone's life. Eighty percent of the population is rural. Farms lap the edges of the town or city wall. Whether there is too much or too little rain or snow, what effect this will have on the corn, or cabbage, are normal topics of conversation in my office and among my city intellectual friends. Though you calculate time by the Western calendar, you regulate your day-to-day life by the divisions of the Farmers Almanac — based on the age-old lunar calendar.

Clear and Bright, usually around Easter, marks the beginning of spring planting on the farms. City and country dwellers alike tidy up their ancestors' graves, shed their winter woolies, and stop the heating stoves. This is followed by such dates as Grain Rains, Small Heat, Big Heat, Autumn Equinox, Descending Frost, Small Snow, Big Snow — at each of which times you wear certain kinds of clothes, eat certain kinds of foods, sun your bedding, pickle this, preserve that. There are many old saws and jingles, known to all grannies and little kids, which tell you exactly what to do.

You get Christmas off if you are a Christian, and everyone is off on New Year's day. But the big holiday is Spring Festival, which starts on the first day of the lunar year. This falls usually at the end of January or the beginning of February. It is still cold, and there may be snow. But homes are warm and noisy with family reunions and almost a whole week of feasting, of admiring new babies and new holiday clothes, of visiting and delivering gifts.

Observance of these farmers' time designations seems entirely natural to a people so widely and deeply rooted in the soil, even those now on an assembly line or in a publishing house.

No wonder, then, that the growth of cooperatives down on the farm aroused such interest. In fact, the idea of socialism was simultaneously catching on in all sectors of society. Private industry and commerce were also fired by it. Cooperation in agriculture had led to a sharp rise in the purchasing power of several hundred million peasants. Supply couldn't keep up with demand. The formation of state-private enterprises — that is, the government buying in as the major partner — had already started, but many small factories were still privately owned, as well as a lot of the retail stores and all of the little service shops.

Not only the workers and employees, but many of the owners were insistent that the socialization process be speeded up. I knew one man who had a small chemical plant which brought him a very good income. He told me originally he wasn't keen on changing. He wanted to leave his business to his sons. The boys were already working in a government organization. When they heard what daddy had in mind, they were horrified. "What do you want to do," they demanded indignantly, "make capitalists out of us?"

With the political and economic changes in Chinese society, moral values were also being transformed. To the younger generation "landlord" and "capitalist" were dirty words. They didn't want any part of it. They had their jobs. Their futures were assured. In a social status sense the rich were all dressed up with no place to go. What was the good of trying to accumulate a lot of money? Their kids wouldn't accept it. Conspicuous comsumption was considered vulgar. The motivation for acquiring a fortune was gone.

Could they ever cleanse themselves of the capitalist stigma? Yes, Chairman Mao told a group of their representatives in November of 1955. If they gave up exploiting their workers and became workers themselves. Their fate was in their own hands. The march toward communism was inevitable. They had to face reality.

They held meetings all over China and discussed this. An honorable and secure future lay ahead. Their wives and children enthusiastically encouraged them. The capitalists organized committees to hasten the conversion of their holdings. Some offered them gratis to the state. These offers were smilingly refused. The change in attitude is what counts, they were told.

Transformation of private enterprise began in Shanghai. At first the changeover was on a business by business basis. Then someone figured out at that rate it would take sixty years. It was decided to do it by entire trades, to be followed by rationalization of production and operation, and ideological reform.

Peking zipped through its capitalist conversion in ten days, from January first to January tenth, 1956. Other big cities followed suit. The original plan, nationwide, was to spend two years, 1956 and 1957. But the whole country's industry and commerce went socialist in two months.

The mechanics of it were simple. Each owner took an inventory and set a value on his own assets, aided by his workers and staff. In most cases it was found he undervalued rather than overvalued. After his figures were approved by the government he received a fixed annual percentage of his capital — varying from trade to trade but usually about five percent — until his investment was paid off. He could not withdraw his capital and could not run the business, but he remained on as a salaried employee or technician.

Businesses were merged, consolidated or expanded, as the situation required. The public interest was borne in mind. Little enterprises — like shoe repair stands or bicycle repair shops — were encouraged to form small co-ops rather than become state-private, and carry on giving service in places convenient to the customer.

There were scenes of great rejoicing. Peking stores and factories were draped with red bunting. Firecrackers popped, drums pounded and cymbals clashed as owners, their faces wreathed in smiles, presented scrolls to government representatives announcing the formal transformation of their business into state-private enterprises. You could see and hear these celebrations all over town, for days.

"Are these fellows really as happy as they look?" I asked a Chinese friend.

He laughed. "Why shouldn't they be."

"After all, they're going to be phased out of business."

"The manufacturers were going broke at the time of Liberation — no orders, no raw materials, labor trouble, galloping inflation. The government put them on their feet again. It gave them everything they needed and bought their entire output. They've had seven very good years, and the value of their equity has greatly increased. It's been the same story in almost every line of business. Now the government comes along again, invests heavily, doubles or triples their capacity, buys them out over a fifteen or twenty year period, and pays them good salaries to boot. Not only that, but they are treated as respectable 'democratic personages'. What more could a capitalist in a socialist country ask?"

State planning could now embrace almost all of China's industry and commerce, and job allocation could be handled more rationally. The capitalists were still capitalists because they continued to draw unearned income in the form of installments paying off their assets, but they could no longer control operations. As salaried members of their old enterprises, they developed a new attitude and their relationship with their former employees improved, as did their status in the community.

By November, 1956, ninety-six percent of China's peasants were members of farming co-ops, eighty-three percent of them in co-ops of a fully socialist type; ninety-nine percent of private industry and seventy-five percent of private commerce had become state-private. Ninety percent of the handicraftsmen and service stores had formed special co-ops of their own.

I had no difficulty in accepting the idea of socialization of agriculture, industry and commerce. It wasn't utopian, it wasn't even new. The Mormons have had a large prosperous cooperative community operating in the state of Utah for well over a hundred years. Nor had the Chinese invented government participation in business. The difference was that in China it was a socialist-oriented government, and all collective endeavor was part of national and local government plans, and was both guided and assisted. I saw no reason why it shouldn't succeed. It certainly seemed to be working well enough.

Just as events in China were proceeding, for the moment, on a fairly even keel, we were fanned by the shockwave of Khrushchov's bombshell at the Twentieth Congress of the Soviet Communist Party in February 1956.

We were all, Chinese and foreign friends alike, startled by the revelations of the excesses Stalin had committed toward the end of his career. The Soviet Union had exercised a profound influence upon Chinese revolutionaries and progressive intellectuals. Its experiences were studied, Stalin's writings and the *History of the Communist Party of the Soviet Union (Bolsheviks)*, edited under Stalin's supervision, were the texts of study courses we all attended. Hundreds of Russian books were translated into Chinese and widely read. Intellectuals discussed Turgenev, Tolstoi and Belinski as well as the moderns. Russian language study was popular. Good inexpensive primers in Russian and Chinese were available at the book stores. Russian plays and operettas were staged. There was a flood of Soviet movies, skillfully dubbed here into Chinese. You heard Russian music on the radio. People sang Russian songs in Chinese. The best of the Soviet artists performed on the stages of many of China's big cities.

Stalin had been the symbol of the Soviet Union, of its Communist Party, of its achievements, besides being respected and admired in his own right. Yet now, three years after his death, Khrushchov, the new Chairman of the Party, depicted him in the darkest of colors. We were disturbed, not knowing about Mr. Khrushchov then what we do now.

My own feelings were mixed. I knew that Stalin had sent help to the Spanish Republicans when Hitler was rehearsing his bombers over Madrid and Barcelona and Guernica for more ambitious future operations. I heard that he had offered to fight for Czechoslovakia after the betrayal at Munich, but that his French and British allies had refused to lend their support. Most observers agreed that life in the Soviet Union had climbed from squalor to, if not plenty, at least to a previously unsavored adequacy.

I hadn't understood the Moscow Purge trials in the late thirties, when important Communist leaders and generals had confessed to being in cahoots with the German Nazis. It just didn't seem possible that so many politically dedicated men should not only suddenly switch to a diametrically opposed ideology, but sell out their compatriots, their flesh and blood, to a foreign enemy as well.

The trials had been conducted under Stalin's leadership and certainly had some queer touches. But in China I had read a number of Stalin's writings. Whether you agreed with them or not, they showed a clear intelligent mind, and didn't at all fit in with Khrushchov's portrait of the man as a paranoic homicidal maniac.

I got hold of my Cantonese friend Chang one night and put the problem to him. "What about it?" I asked. "Has Stalin the hero become Stalin the villain?"

"He's still more hero than villain, I think. But he let them put him on a pedestal and lost touch with what was going on. He made mistakes."

"What kind of mistakes?"

"Serious ones. He suppressed many good people labeled as counterrevolutionaries. He wasn't vigilant enough against Hitler's blitzkrieg. He neglected the welfare of the members of the collective farms. His policy toward Yugoslavia was wrong —"

"Some hero!"

"That's one side of the picture. Don't forget he also continued Lenin's policy of collectivizing agriculture and large-scale industrialization. Without that the Soviets would never have defeated the Nazis. Stalin deserved most of the honor and respect his people gave him. Unfortunately, it went to his head. He exaggerated the importance of his own role and counterposed it to the collective leadership. Ironically, this was at the very time when Stalin was insisting in articles and speeches that the masses are the makers of history, that the Party must never lose touch with them, that it should welcome their criticism."

"If it could happen to a man like Stalin, how can we be sure it won't happen to leaders of other socialist countries?"

"If you mean Chairman Mao, experience has taught us that no leader, no matter how wise and talented, can function effectively without the strength he draws from the grass roots. He must not and cannot feel superior. Chairman Mao says, 'The masses are the real heroes. We ourselves are often naive, absurd.' The Stalin story has only confirmed our conviction that there has to be a continuous interflow between the leaders and the led. The whole thrust of our system and philosophy is against letting any deification take place."

"Won't the difference in appraisal of Stalin put a strain on the relations between the Chinese and Soviet Communist Parties?"

"Not necessarily. We didn't always agree with Stalin. Why should we have to take everything Khrushchov says as gospel?"

"When did you disagree with Stalin?"

"Several times. For instance when Chiang Kai-shek's troops were fleeing south and the PLA was chasing them. Stalin's advice was to stop at the Yangtze and establish our new regime north of the river. We didn't listen to him, and instead drove the Kuomintang clear off the mainland. It didn't seem to hurt our relations with Moscow any."

That may very well have been true. But I don't think Chang or I or most people in China, realized at the time of the Khrushchov "revelations" what a serious rift they presaged. Looking back now with the wisdom of hindsight I would say they marked the beginning of the end of the Big Brother concept. Khrushchov's blast had the effect not of lessening the Chinese appreciation of Stalin's merits, but of causing them to examine more cautiously from then on all proposals and propositions emanating from the Soviet Party.

The Chinese still thought the CPSU was fundamentally sound. The real disillusionment did not set in till some years later. But they had taken off their rose-colored glasses.

In October of that same year, while the Left was still reeling from the impact of the Khrushchov revelations, it was slammed by another blow — the Hungarian crisis. Hungary had been liberated from the fascists by the Soviet Red Army at the end of World War II. With Soviet backing the Hungarians had set up a socialist government, which had economic and political ties with Moscow. Ten years later, a coup is staged, Communists are slaughtered in the streets. The Soviet Union has to send tanks in to quell the uprising. An outcry is raised in the West against the suppression of the poor "freedom fighters". In Poland there is a big workers' strike. What was going on?

The Chinese appraisal was that "the democratic rights of the Hungarian people had been impaired", and counter-revolutionaries, who had never been eliminated, took advantage of the discontent to organize a revolt. Soviet policies were also partly to blame. Poor relations between the Soviet Union and Hungary would have to be "put right by the Soviet Union", said the Chinese editorially. As to Poland, the Soviet Union had been underpaying her for her coal from 1946 to 1953. The Chinese spoke sharply of great-nation chauvinism.

They entirely approved of the maintenance of Soviet troops in Poland and Hungary at that time, for they said the socialist countries were being constantly menaced by outside pressures. The Chinese press ran articles on the activities of American-financed subversive groups against the socialist countries, described the NATO bases ringing them, and discussed the rearming of revanchist forces in West Germany. When the trouble started in Hungary, the Chinese admitted that the situation was "chaotic", but noted the reemergence of the Horthy fascists, the movement of arms across the Austrian border, the American offer of twenty million dollars to Nagy, who held power briefly. This outside intervention only fanned the flames. They scoffed at Western "solicitude" for Hungary, and said it was just a device to divert attention from the imperialist attack on Egypt. Inner and outer forces of reaction were working hand in glove, said the Chinese. The disturbances were proof not of the failure of the socialist system, but of the failure to implement socialist principles.

Not all communists agreed with the Chinese position. Leaders of communist parties in other lands wrote lengthy articles, blaming "Stalinism", and demanding "liberalization". The Chinese press carried their statements in full — the Polish leaders, Togliatti of Italy, Dennis of the USA, Kadar of Hungary, Tito and Kardelj of Yugoslavia. When you consider that the *People's Daily* is only six pages and that Tito's comments, for example, occupied two of them, you can see how far the Chinese went to give complete coverage.

At the end of the year, the Chinese published their reply. It was quiet and scholarly in tone. It affirmed the "tremendous successes" of the Soviet Union in the 39 years since its formation. It said that Stalin's achievements far outshone his failings, although these were serious. And it warned against "revising" the fundamentals of socialism in the name of correcting errors in their implementation.

There is a difference between proletarian and bourgeois rule, between socialist and capitalist systems, said the Chinese. No bourgeois country can become socialist without a revolution led by the proletariat creating a state run by the proletariat. State capitalism isn't socialism. You can't reach socialism by "evolution". Don't forget, the Chinese reminded the revisionists, while you indulge in wishful thinking, the imperialists are mobilizing their military, economic, diplomatic and undercover forces against the socialist countries. Deposed old regime boys, hiding at home or in exile abroad, are working every minute to

make a comeback. We must rally round common principles and close
our ranks. The proletariat, through its party, must lead the country,
with no rights for its enemies and full democrary for the people. (A
story going round at the time said that during the Polish and Hungarian
crises Premier Chou En-lai had flown to both countries. In Poland
he had to persuade the Russians not to fire on the workers, who the
Chinese felt had a right to strike, whereas in Hungary it was only at
his insistence that the Russians used force against armed fascist gangs.)

This was the first public pronouncement of China's stand against
revisionism in the international arena. It marked the beginning of a
long and acrimonious debate which divides leftists all over the world
to this day.

As if in confirmation of the Chinese contention, in 1957 a sharp class
struggle erupted within China's own borders, not an attempt at a
fascist coup as in Hungary perhaps, but a concerted right-wing assault
on everything the young government stood for.

It began with a rectification campaign — one of the periodic house-
cleanings in which the Communist Party invites the general public to
point out and help it correct its shortcomings. The targets set for
this one were bureaucracy, sectarianism and subjectiveness within the
Party.

People with complaints voiced them freely and, on the whole, in
a friendly and helpful spirit. But bourgeois leaders of other political
parties — especially the Democratic League and the Peasants and
Workers Democratic Party — while insisting they wanted nothing
more than to strengthen Communist Party leadership, launched a series of bitter attacks. These were echoed and implemented in speeches
by a few university professors and former capitalists — also prominent
members of these parties — and by articles appearing in one or two
Shanghai newspapers, the *Wen Hui Pao* in particular, which was run
by men active in these same parties.

Lo Lung-chi, Democratic League leader who held the government
post of Minister of Forestry, led off with the claim that the Communist
Party had wronged thousands of innocent people in its drives against
corruption in business and government organizations and in the ideological remoulding of the intellectuals. He offered no substantiation of
his charges.

He proposed the establishment of a "rehabilitation committee" consisting of members of all parties to check on the work of the Com-

munist Party, the implication plainly being that the Communist Party was too inept or corrupt to be trusted to review its own record and needed to share its leadership with other parties.

Chang Po-chun, a leader in both the Democratic League and the Peasants and Workers Democratic Party (composed, incidentally, of former businessmen) had a number of bright ideas. One was to set up a "political planning board" which would be a kind of super-cabinet to draw major policy lines. It would be packed with splinter party leaders like himself, and operate "democratically" on a "one party one vote" basis, replacing Communist Party leadership on the highest level.

Another spokesman for China's capitalists, Chang Nai-chi, was Minister of Transport. He tried to plant a few time bombs under a political theory which was a foundation stone of China's internal policy. He maintained that the annual payments capitalists were receiving for the assets the government had taken over were not a form of exploitation and that, therefore, there was no longer any real difference between China's capitalists and workers. The subtle stinger in the tail of this one was that capitalists and their parties were just as qualified to run the country as the workers and their Communist Party.

Several gentlemen became so carried away by their own rhetoric that they forgot their pose as friends of socialism and the Communist Party, and switched from oblique slashes at socialist theory and forms of government to direct assaults on the Party as such. They said that the workers and farmers were suffering under Communist rule, that bureaucracy in the Party was a "more dangerous enemy than capitalism". They demanded that Communist Party organizations quit functioning in schools and government offices.

Public reaction was angry and swift. People organized meetings in factories, on the farms, in offices, on the campus. Usually there was just a microphone and a makeshift platform. I attended some of those meetings. Audiences were anywhere from a few hundred to several thousand. They listened quietly while some smooth talker went into his spiel. There was rarely any heckling, but you could feel the tension building. When he finished, there would be a dead silence.

Then some man, or woman, would get up on the platform and begin, awkwardly and hesitantly at first but gradually warming into eloquence, and tell the story of their life, or the life of their family, under Chiang Kai-shek's Kuomintang, their poverty, their misery. Then they would detail their life today — the jobs they had, what their income was, the kind of food they ate, the house they lived in, the schools their kids attended. If it weren't for Chairman Mao, if it weren't for the Communist Party, would this have happened? Some members of the Party might have faults, but why should anyone want to remove the Party from leadership?

And then another man would jump up, a student perhaps, and grab the microphone. If the Communist Party is as bad as some people claim, he would shout, how come there's been a steady rise in purchasing power, in real income? How come agricultural production has increased twenty-six percent in the past five years and industrial output a hundred and twenty percent?

But the slanders continued. Day after day articles, cartoons, some snide, some openly vicious, appeared in the press, with never a word from the other side. Indignant people deluged the editors with letters nailing the phony statements of the Rightists, but the letters never saw print. Workers from a Peking radio factory stomped into the office of the *People's Daily* and demanded to know which "people" they thought they represented. Didn't they remember what Mao said in 1949, shortly after Liberation? "After enemies with guns have been wiped out, there will still be enemies without guns." How could they keep publishing reactionary bilge without a word of refutation?

Only later did the reason come out. The Communist Party had instructed all its organizations and periodicals to say little for a whole month, and let the dissidents blow their tops. The people saw them for what they were and defeated them easily in a big national debate.

"What is it all about?" I asked a Chinese colleague.

He laughed shortly. "Some right-wing intellectuals and capitalists hate socialism because it interferes with their private ambitions. They took courage from the Party's silence and the flurry their sniping caused among a few simple-minded individuals. But they exposed themselves completely as irresponsible greedy little men whose only interest was to climb to power."

The Rightists had seriously miscalculated. They had counted on the support of the intellectuals, who exercise an influence disproportionate to their number. But very few joined them. The overwhelming majority of the intellectuals — the "democratic individualists" on whom Dulles and the China Lobby pinned such hopes — rejected the overtures of the Rightists out of hand. Some had run up against Party bureaucracy and sectarianism in the course of their work, and they criticized manifestations of these faults frankly and constructively. But on the whole they felt there had been a great improvement in their lot since Liberation. Their jobs were guaranteed, well paid. Scholarship was encouraged and rewarded. As to the country in general, the enormous advances were obvious to China's humblest citizen, to say nothing of some of her best educated.

During the previous eight years since the establishment of the People's Republic, intellectuals had gone seriously into a study of Mao and the Marxist classics. They had become enthusiastic supporters of the government, and many held official as well as professional posts. Working in close cooperation with the Communists, they were impressed by the Party, and many had themselves become members. This gravitation of China's intellectuals to the Communist Party was one of the things that worried the Rightists most. By way of "reform", they had proposed that intellectuals be encouraged to join other parties instead!

Significantly, it was the intellectuals already in these other parties who hastened the undoing of the Rightist leaders. At a heated meeting of the Shanghai branch of the Democratic League, they persuaded one of the editors of the *Daily News* to spill the beans. He revealed that Lo Lung-chi and Chang Po-chun had built around themselves a small coterie of professors and newsmen who were long-time admirers of "Western democracy". These gentlemen saw the events in Poland and Hungary as evidence of the inherent weakness of socialist government. The few strikes and student demonstrations which had occurred in Chinese cities in the preceding year or two they interpreted as harbingers of similar bloody uprisings in China. Taking advantage of the Party's invitation of criticism, they organized a smear campaign in the hope that this would hurry *der tag* along.

I had never been much of a letters-to-the-editor type, but these birds prating about "freedom" and "democracy" and the beauties of a "bi-cameral legislature" in the West were a bit too much. I sent an article to the *People's Daily*, which they published, telling how these things worked in practice. I explained that two senators in a given state had as much or more power than thirty or forty representatives from that same state, and that if these senators were not free of personal greed they might acquire such appellations as "the oil senator from Oklahoma" or "the silver senator from Nevada" and act against the interests of the people. I told how the term "Cadillac cabinet" originated, and why it was worthwhile for millionaire members to accept salaries which, for them, were trifling. I spoke too of the astronomical legal expenses of those accused of political crimes, of congressional investigative committees, of blacklists against those suspected of excessive liberalism.

These were things most Americans knew, and as a New York lawyer I had seen something of the difference between justice for the rich and justice for the poor. The article was only another drop in the already sweeping flood of evidence against the contentions of the Rightists. But it made me realize that I was becoming more committed to China's cause, that I was less of a spectator and more of a participant, that I was beginning to see better the connection between class struggle in China and class struggle in other parts of the world.

The Rightists' scheme backfired and fizzled out. They had raised a temporary furor but they weren't really very strong. There were indeed some genuine Rightists. Yet in many places thousands who merely voiced mild criticisms were also given the label. This was politically tantamount to a "counter-revolutionary" status and meant loss of jobs, or at least cuts in salary, and social opprobrium. Since most of these persons were intellectuals, who were then relatively few in number, it deprived China of some of the very people she needed most in her drive for modernization.

We knew a few personally — a playwright, an archeologist, a novelist. All were poseurs, big talkers who liked to say "shocking" things. But they were quite brilliant in their own fields and could, if handled correctly, have made real contributions to the new society.

The situation was not fully rectified until 1978 and 1979, when those wrongfully labeled were exonerated, and all regained their civil rights.

V

NORTHWEST TRAVELS

1957

For foreigners working and living in China life was never dull. If you had an interest in the past, well-preserved historical records went back two thousand years. Strata of early dynasties lay only a few yards below the surface of the earth. Art, painting, sculpture, showing vigor and beauty and a great variety of styles, were everywhere in abundance — huge figures hewn out of cliffs, a delicate frieze or drawing tucked away in some grotto, a splendid mural on the wall of a temple. Old operas reproduced the dress, the mannerism, the speech patterns of people in ancient times.

And the present, with its promise of the future, was there under your nose, bustling, free-swinging, groping, but ever cheerfully driving ahead, with all the clamorous good humor of a wide-open frontier town.

It was hard to see it all, to get the whole picture. China was so enormous, so complex. It was particularly difficult for a foreigner. Not only were there language barriers to overcome, but the culture, the customs, the habits, the code of conduct, were very different from those of the West.

The most important difference was the magnificent experiment they were conducting. They were remoulding a whole society — snatching it from a barbaric semi-feudal, semi-colonial state and thrusting it boldly into a new civilization, a highly civilized civilization, reasonable and scientific, yet full of kindness and consideration for the ordinary folk of the world.

You got a good deal of the feeling of this in your daily job, your daily life. But to sense the scope of the thing, you had to get out and travel around. Most government offices and schools arranged periodic tours for the foreigners working there, usually once a year. They lasted from two to three weeks, as a rule, and were well run. You paid only for your meals. The government picked up the tab on the rest.

Each year two or three tours were offered, and you had a choice. You would go out in groups of half a dozen foreigners and an equal number of Chinese from your own office, acting as companions or interpreters. Your husband or wife, regardless of whether they were foreign or Chinese, was also invited, and their expenses were also paid. Before setting out, everyone would sit down together and plan an itinerary, making requests and expressing preferences. This required a bit of discussion, since the foreigners often had different interests and different levels of experience in China. But eventually some compromise would be reached more or less satisfactory to everybody.

I always enjoyed these tours and got a lot out of them. We traveled mostly in cars and special busses in the places we stayed. For the longer distances we generally went by train, and we had hours in which to chat with other passengers, Chinese and foreign, while watching fields and villages and hills roll past our windows.

I'm fond of Chinese trains. They're fast, but not so fast as to make you wonder in a little corner of your mind whether they're going to leave the rails. And their maintenance, inside and out, is excellent. We traveled four in a first class compartment, which meant two uppers and two lowers, with the uppers folding flat against the walls during the day. The single travelers were divided according to sex, but we often had two married couples in a compartment, or one married couple and two singles, either male or female. No one seemed to mind, and all behaved with decorum.

The dining cars served good Chinese and Western food. You had your choice. Since the crews and attendants came from both ends of the line, accent differences sometimes produced amusing results. Once, while traveling to a resort in Shantung province, I told the waiter I'd have *you ping* (oil fritters) for breakfast. He looked at me strangely for a moment, then went off, thinking no doubt that you have to humor these mad foreigners. I must have waited about ten minutes, and I wondered what was taking so long, for oil fritters are only a strip of dough fried in deep fat. The waiter returned with a big juicy hamburger.

"Here's your *you ping*," he said with a smile.

I ate it, and it was very tasty, though I refused his offer of beer. Evidently some other mad foreigner who had eaten in his car had ordered beer for breakfast. I darkly suspected Australian friends of mine, who gargle it in the morning.

I got hamburger instead of oil fritters because Shantung people cannot or will not pronounce the initial letter "r", and they say *you* for both *you* (oil) and *rou* (meat), differentiating them by some filip of inflection that only Shantungers can hear. Still, it was a delicious hamburger. I even wondered later whether beer might not have been such a bad idea.

Most of the Chinese passengers didn't go to the dining car. You could buy a tasty box lunch for only twenty or thirty cents, a packet of tea was five or ten cents, and hot water was free. A lot of people would wait for certain stations, then rush off and line up before the white-jacketed vendors, who arrived with neatly wrapped portions of some famous local delicacy — dumplings or roast chicken, fruits or pastry. I trusted the wisdom of the masses, and did some of the finest eating in my long and varied gastronomical career.

We stayed at the best hotels, which were always comfortable, with piping hot water and boxspring mattress, but often not to my taste where decor was concerned. A few had been built by foreigners in the Victorian period, and were dark and massive and gloomy. Other were designed to satisfy tourist ideas of Chinese architecture, and were more Grauman's Chinese than China's Chinese — Hollywood temples with purple dragons entwined around vermilion pillars. The courteous attendants — mostly bright young boys and girls — seemed as out of place there as I was.

Besides what we saw and learned in factories and on farms, the trips gave us a chance to get to know our foreign and Chinese colleagues better. In a large busy office like the Foreign Languages Press, you seldom had time to exchange more than a greeting and a few words with people in other departments. The foreigners came from various countries. I was intrigued by their accounts of what was happening in their native lands, their views on China and the world.

I talked at length with my Chinese comrades. We exchanged family histories, asked questions, argued, offered opinions. I marveled at their efficiency, always calm, pleasant, keeping to a time schedule yet somehow managing to satisfy most of the requests of a diverse group.

But this type of conducted tour was not very satisfactory to me. I had been living simply but well on a few hundred *yuan* a month, even with sending half my income to help support my mother in New York. My mode of transport was a British bike, a Coventry Eagle which I bought from a departing missionary shortly after Liberation. China was far from affluent, and my Chinese friends, while having all the necessities, lived frugally. I could understand that there was no other practical way to squire around a mixed group of foreigners, but I didn't feel right riding in cars and staying at posh hotels.

And so, in the summer of '57, I decided to do my trip differently.

I would travel as simply and economically as possible. No VIP treatment, no set schedules. Only a general destination of Yenan, visiting Sian on the way up and Loyang on the way back. There would be no formal lectures. We would meet people and just chat.

Working with me in the Foreign Languages Press was "Singh", a young fellow from northern Nepal. Short and stocky with a receding hairline, he came from a poor family in a mountain village. With dogged perseverance he had worked his way through school, not easy for a poor boy in Nepal. But Singh was very bright. His English was as fluent as his Hindi, and he translated from one into the other for a Hindi language magazine we were putting out. He also was picking up Chinese with astonishing rapidity.

We had become quite friendly, and he told me a lot about his life in Nepal. When he heard about the trip I was planning, he offered to come along. He too felt the formal tours didn't go deep enough, and he liked the idea of doing the trip economically, since he was saving to get married. I was delighted to have him. Lin, a young Fukienese from the Hindi section, agreed to accompany us as Singh's interpreter and guide.

At our request, the Press notified the authorities in the places we intended to visit that we wanted only ordinary treatment. Phoenix was too busy to get away. With some misgivings and a long list of do's and don't's, she saw me off.

We took the train to Sian one evening late in August, all three of us in lower berths in a "hard seat" sleeping car. The berths were in tiers of three running athwart the car, with a narrow passage on one side. They were hard only in comparison to the spring upholstery you get in First Class. These were firm, leather-covered, and quite comfortable. The bedding, which you rented, cost only eighty cents from Peking to Sian. It included a thick quilt, which I folded lengthwise and used as a mattress, spotlessly clean sheets, pillow and pillow case, and a fresh blanket.

Above me was a seventy-year-old peasant woman, returning home to Shansi after visiting relatives in Peking. Lin changed berths with her because it was such an effort for her climbing in and out. The berth above Singh was occupied by a young woman with a baby girl, not quite two, cranky with a bad cold, who in her more cheerful moments sang loudly in a strong penetrating voice, regardless of the hour. The mother, around twenty-five, was a native of Szechuan who had served in Korea in the Chinese People's Volunteers. After her discharge she received technical training in a school in the northeast, and was on her way to Sian with her husband, also ex-army, to work in a factory in Sian where there was a big growth of light industry.

Singh was charmed by a girl attendant in our car, one of two who shared shifts. About eighteen, very healthy, very pretty, she worked every minute she was on duty — sweeping, mopping, dusting, bringing bedding, answering questions. She was from Tangshan, a little place a hundred miles north of Peking, and was an elementary school graduate. The run to Sian and back took four days. The crew then got five days off. She used this time to attend a special school the Railway conducted for people with irregular hours, and was taking political and academic courses.

I was restless the first night, but slept like a log on the second, except when awakened from time to time, roughly between two and four in the morning, by arias from the little girl. The mother chose this opportunity to "pee" her from the upper berth, aiming her at the chamber pot on the floor below. Singh later confessed that he feared disastrous results might ensue from bad marksmanship and the lurching of the train. Fortunately we came through dry and unscathed.

We reached Sian at six in the morning and were greeted by a man from the provincial (Shansi) Visitors Bureau with a large car. I said we'd rather go by bus to the hotel. He looked so distressed that I relented. We got there in something under three minutes and were later billed for two *yuan*, not a very auspicious beginning for our "economy tour". (Since this was not one of the Foreign Experts Bureau's regular junkets, we were paying our own expenses.)

Our plea for modest accommodations had been met by delivering us to something called "People's Mansions", a huge new white elephant of a hotel, not bad-looking on the outside, but inside leaning heavily to the Confucian temple decor. The roofs were covered with tons of glazed tile — a type of architectural gambit which had been severely criticized not long before in Peking. Glazed tile roofs are pretty and very "Chinese", but they're frightfully heavy and require extra-strong and expensive beams and foundations to support them. And the dining room was graced with — wouldn't you know — purple dragons on vermilion pillars!

We were ushered to our rooms, large, with boxspring mattress and attached bathrooms complete with baths and showers.

"How much?" we asked.

"Fifteen *yuan* a day."

"Can't afford it," we announced cheerfully. "Where do visiting Chinese cadres stay?"

"Oh, you wouldn't like that."

"Let's have a look, anyhow."

They showed us to a sunny basement room with large windows and a wooden floor. The price? One *yuan* twenty per head for three in a room, bedding and tea included.

We took it. There were showers and toilets at the end of the hall.

We had the same problem with meals. They wanted us to eat in the Confucian temple, where foreign as well as Chinese food was served. We had a hard time convincing them that we didn't want foreign food, and that we could survive without milk. Finally, we managed to arrange to eat in the dining room for hotel personnel and Chinese visitors, a lovely room of white and pale green. The food was delicious and cost a *yuan* a day for three big meals.

Many foreign tourists ran into this problem. Our Chinese hosts were not trying to run up a bill on us. Their prices actually were reasonable, considering the quality of the food and accommodations. Certainly, they meant well. The Chinese are extremely hospitable, and always want to give their visitors the best. But there was a contradiction, for living in that style necessarily cut you off from the local cadres and people who give you the deepest understanding of the places you visit. Fortunately, we were able to convince our hosts that we were quite content with the arrangements, that young Lin could adequately look after us and we wouldn't need any chauffeured vehicles or special escorts.

We set out after lunch and a short nap. I had to learn to take naps all over again after coming to China. I had given them up about the age of five, and thought of them as something only for babies and invalids. But in China it's an old and prevalent custom. Everybody lies down after lunch, under a tree in the country, or on your office desk, if there isn't a bed handy. I tried it once, on my office desk, and became permanently sold on the idea. Even a half hour's snooze sets you up nicely for the rest of the afternoon. Could this ability to relax in the middle of the day have something to do with the low incidence of hypertension among Chinese?

We went to a local museum known as "Pei Lin" — the "forest of tablets" — because it contains hundreds of stone tablets which they started collecting back in 108 AD, inscribed with notes and impressions of various prominent scholars and officials who visited there. It had begun as a Confucian temple in Han, became a "Tai Miao" or emperor's ancestral temple in Tang, had its buildings completely restored in Ming.

They had some Han tomb paintings, fairly well preserved. Early and Late Han together ran from approximately 200 BC to AD 200 and was a period of imperial expansion. The elaborate tombs the wealthy built for themselves were well preserved in the dry friable yellow soil of the region.

The museum is proud of its Confucian analects. Confucious lived five hundred years before Christ, when the Chou dynasty, a slave empire, was disintegrating into brawling petty dukedoms which were developing feudalism, a more vigorous and relatively enlightened form of society. But Confucius longed for the "law and order" of the old days, and scurried about from duchy to duchy preaching against progress. His arrogant presumption that it was "Heaven ordained" for "talented aristocrats" to rule over the masses of "ignorant rabble", his insistence on blind obedience within a rigid system of social relationships, proved very useful to succeeding generations of repressive autocrats, up to and including Chiang Kai-shek, and were piously perpetuated by them. (Lin Piao was also an adorer of "the sage".)

However misbegotten Confucius' nostalgia, he did amass quantities of valuable material about ancient ways, and these were categorized and compiled in volumes. Copies of some of these writings on stone tablets during the Han dynasty are preserved in "Pei Lin".

China is perhaps the one country in the world with an uninterrupted development of thousands of years of civilization. Her sculpture, her painting, have an astonishing variety of styles. Consciously or otherwise, she absorbed a great deal culturally from people of other lands, and gave them much in return. Like any other country, whenever China was under foreign domination — the Western imperialists during the past hundred years — her cultural creativity dwindled, was quiescent. But when she drove out her oppressors and stood again, her culture flourished. Wherever you go in China, this is made plain.

For the past fifty years China has been absorbed not only in fighting off foreign domination but in changing her social structure as well. Only now has the dust of these battles begun to settle. It will be interesting to see what the next Chinese cultural upsurge will bring.

Perhaps because of its ideal location on a fertile plain beside a broad river, Sian is one of the oldest sites of human habitation in China. Both paleolithic and neolithic remains have been found, including a 6,000-year-old neolithic village. It was the site of Western Chou (1100 BC), the earliest Chinese kingdom of which there are written records. For centuries Sian, then called Changan, was China's capital. It reached its heyday in the tenth century, when it was the capital of the Tang dynasty. Changan was three times Sian's present area and had a population of two million. No city in the world approached it for size and splendor. More than 40,000 foreigners lived and worked in Changan. Most of them had immigrated over the Old Silk Road, through Sinkiang from present-day Afghanistan.

By the time Sian was liberated in 1949, the population had dwindled to less than half a million. It was dusty, dreary and decayed. Sian had no running water, no paved roads, little electricity. When we visited there in 1957, Sian was again thriving, and its population had jumped to a million and a half. They said they'd soon be back to Tang dynasty size in area as well.

Our visit to a government textile mill east of the city — Number Three of six built so far in the Sian area — inclined us to believe them. Every piece of machinery used was made in China. Of the mill's six thousand workers, two thousand were youngsters from Shanghai. Sixty percent were girls, primary or middle school graduates. China was very parochial in the old days. Now kids are often assigned to jobs hundreds of miles from home. They like the adventure of going to distant places, and it does the local people good to get infusions of new blood and new ideas. By government regulation, the kids get a paid trip home every year to see their parents.

After wandering through the fresh-as-paint workshops, we dropped in on the bachelor girls' dormitory. The effervescent southern kids made a great fuss over us. They ushered us in to one of the rooms and served us hot drinking water. The room contained six beds and was very neat and clean. Colored posters of fat babies and scenes from romantic operas covered the walls. It was obvious what the girls thought about in at least some of their spare time.

They weren't a bit shy. Two of them sang arias from a Shaohsing opera — greatly favored in the Shanghai-Nanking-Hangchow area. Singh then sang a Nepal poem and I did "Tavern in the Town". Both numbers were acclaimed by fervent applause. Singh took a group picture of the dozens of girls who had somehow managed to squeeze into the small room.

Next we had a look at the nursery. Apparently textiles weren't all they were turning out at great rate in Number Three. They had a thousand kids under the age of seven, with six hundred women in varying stages of pregnancy. The six textile mills in the complex had a combined population of nearly 50,000, including the workers' families. They said they were starting a birth control education campaign.

A printing and dyeing plant was due to be completed that year. The textile mill area was becoming a city in itself. Nicely laid out and landscaped with trees and flowers, it had its own shopping centers, movies, clubs, restaurants, bath houses and post offices.

In the afternoon, we took a bus to the famous Big Goose Pagoda. It had been within the sprawling confines of Changan in Tang times, but now the land around it had become farms again, interspersed with many new schools and institutes. A Chinese Buddhist monk named Hsuan Tsang had the pagoda built in AD 650 on his return from a pilgrimage to India. It was a round stone tower seven storeys tall and covered with carvings of religious scenes. The wooden stairs inside were somewhat rickety, but they seemed strong enough. You got a magnificent view of the city from the top.

The pagoda stood in a compound with a few old temple buildings and was tended by seven monks who lived on the premises. These brethren belonged to a farming co-op composed of about forty monks from various neighboring temples. They were tilling temple land, which they had pooled, and were doing so well that several had bought wristwatches and bikes.

We were told that Sian's Taoist priests also had their own agricultural producers' cooperative, and the Buddhist nuns had organized a sewing co-op. Singh said the clergy in Nepal were very numerous and led a parasitical existence. They were a big problem. He thought the Chinese method very sensible.

In the evening we went to see a "Chin Chiang" opera, a specialty of the region. China has at least a dozen major different types of local opera. Some of these, like Szechuan opera, are still further subdivided into another four or five types. They are not nearly so stylized as Peking opera and have a lot more jokes and local color. There is more dialogue and less singing, and the music is mainly derived from folk songs. For that reason, every word of the arias is understood by the audiences. This is not true of Peking opera, whose unnatural style of singing requires that the lyrics be flashed on screens on the sides of the stage, which is tough on people who read slowly or not at all. Nevertheless, Peking opera draws the largest audiences of all the opera forms, thanks to its superb artistry and improved content, and is nationwide in its appeal.

The "Chin Chiang" we saw in Sian was called "Tale of Pu Mu". Pu Mu was a girl who caught the eye of the County Boss of Hangchow several centuries back — a lecherous dog who tried to steal her from her sweetheart, who was also his friend. It was too long, but we stayed almost to the end. Not that we had any doubts about virtue triumphing, but because the leading lady was so beautiful.

For some reason the hero was played by a woman, though the other characters were cast according to their rightful sex. In old China all parts, male and female, were played by men, like in Elizabethan England, and probably for the same reason. No decent woman would be seen in the company of actors and mountebanks. Mei Lan-fang, perhaps the most famous of China's Peking opera actors until his death some years ago, was a female impersonator.

There were exceptions, however. In Yueh opera, all roles were played by women. Taken over by idle wives and concubines of wealthy Shanghai merchants at the turn of the century, it was mostly historical soap opera, very weepy, about unrequited passion and dying for love. The music mas melodious, though a bit monotonous. Its male impersonator approach may have seeped over into Chin Chiang.

In recent years, this kinky stuff has been phased out. None of the opera companies are training up anything except boy actors and girl actresses.

We spent all of the next day at Lintung, a resort amid wooded hills east of Sian. In the warm mineral springs here, the famous Tang imperial concubine Yang Kuei-fei took her baths. Her personal pool has been rebuilt many times, but it was in the same location and tapped the same spring. You could still bathe in it for one *yuan* twenty, four times the cost of the ordinary pool. We examined it, a sunken pool of dark rose tile, then bathed in some of the cheaper ones.

Chiang Kai-shek stayed in Lintung in December of 1936, while conferring with Chang Hsueh-liang, the "Young Marshal" of the Northeast Provinces, then called "Manchuria" by the Japanese. The Young Marshal wanted to cooperate with the Workers and Peasants Red Army and fight the Japanese who had occupied the northeast. Chiang was more interested in battling the Communists than the foreign aggressors. Chang Hsueh-liang sent men to arrest him in his house at the Lintung springs to force a showdown. Firing broke out. Someone put a couple of bullets through Chiang's front window. We saw the holes. They were still there.

Panic-stricken, Chiang hopped out of the back window, in his nightshirt, and scampered up the mountain. He hid himself in the small dead-end of a steep fissure in the rocky slope, above a pavilion done in the classic Greek style. We climbed up, with considerable difficulty, and peered into the crack. Chiang must have been terrified to make such a stiff climb. There he was caught, minus his false teeth.

Only the intervention of Chou En-lai, sent by the Communist Party, saved him from being shot. The Communists wanted unity in the face of a common foe. The Kuomintang agreed to stop internecine strife and cooperate in driving out the Japanese.

That was the famous "Sian Incident". Chiang Kai-shek soon went back on his word. His armies seldom ventured against the enemy. They spent most of their time harassing the Communist forces and gouging the people.

Local folk at Lintung, to commemorate Chiang Kai-shek's little escapade, have installed a large stone plaque in the Grecian pavilion which reads: "Where Chiang Was Caught." But the popular name for the cul-de-sac in which generalissimo cowered is, contemptuously, "Dog's Hole".

We had lunch in the walled town of Lintung, the county seat. The restaurant was crowded with prosperous-looking peasants who had been compelled to quit work by the rain. After lunch we wandered around and stopped in at their cooperative general store. It stocked everything you could buy in Sian, plus a few new items I hadn't seen in the city.

The rain stopped. On the hard-packed earth of an empty threshing ground a juggler and a trick bicycle rider began putting on a show. We joined the audience of peasants and kids who gathered round. The performers weren't bad. Then they began their spiel. They were peddling "fountain pens" at forty cents apiece, gadgets with glass points which held a bit more than ordinary nibs when you dipped them in the ink. They sold about twenty. Sheer robbery.

Carnival and "snake oil" types had a long history in China. In ancient times before there were doctors, the "medicine men" were itinerant bravos who sold their services to any lord who could pay. When unattached, they put on exhibitions of skill with weapons in the streets and sold nostrums for wounds and injuries. They were enveloped in a romantic aura which persisted through the ages.

There was no need for pitchmen in the new society. Theirs was a dying trade. But I was glad to have seen them before it was too late.

The next day, September 1, we started for Yenan. We took a train at seven in the morning for Tung Chuan, to the north, which was as far as the railway extended. The rest of the way we would have to go by bus. Our fellow passengers were young people from all over China who got off at various stops along the road. Loud, cheerful youngsters from Kiangsu, south of the Yangtze, were working in a local railway administration office. A moon-faced young man with round glasses, from Hainan Island, had become a forestry instructor at a university in Chengchow, in Honan, and was conducting his students on a field trip.

You saw these shifts of young population wherever you went, breaking down the old provincial narrowness, enriching the national culture, broadening people's outlooks. The bobbed hair and smart attire of the pert girl textile workers from Shanghai were being emulated by their sisters in Sian, the langorous southern Yueh music shared popularity with more decisive northern opera arias on the Shensi radio. There were jokes and laughter over the misunderstandings caused by regional differences in pronunciation, but the laughter was good-natured and friendly. The youngsters were enjoying the exciting adventure they were sharing in building a new China.

Our train was a local, with hard wooden seats. The weather was hot and we were climbing continually. By the time we got to Tung Chuan, we were pretty weary.

But we perked up when we saw what lay before us. Tung Chuan, meaning "Copper Valley", is a pass in the mountains guarding the northern flank of the Wei River plain and Sian. It was well-garrisoned in ancient times, for it was through here that Tartar and Turkic nomadic tribesmen poured in raids on their more affluent Han neighbors to the south. The name indicated that there had been copper mines at one time, but these must have been worked out, for coal mining was now the

major industry. Tung Chuan had the biggest coal mine in the Northwest.
It's beautiful country, this land of the yellow soil, known as "loess"
in the West. Sticky and adhesive when wet, it's fine for making bricks
or building dams. When dry it is porous and light. Local people carved
their homes out of yellow soil bluffs, merely boring a hole in the top for
a chimney and adding a front wall of wood, with paper panes for the
windows.

There are few real mountains, but you see great heights and depths,
because centuries of erosion have incised the yellow soil plateaus with
huge canyons, some hundreds of yards deep and stretching miles across.
With a little water, the soil is fairly fertile. The problem is it's dry most
of the year, and then in late summer, usually August, heavy rains form
torrents which race through the gullies and canyons, smashing everything
in their path. The locals had started a drive to build check-dams and
reservoirs, and to plant trees and bushes and grass. But it was difficult,
for the population was small and the area vast.

After a late lunch heavily flavored with garlic in an earthen-floored
restaurant carved out of a bluff, we walked into the old walled city. It
had only one real street, lined with a few stores and government offices.
We were followed by a large gang of kids, very friendly, in high spirits,
average age about nine. They were neatly dressed, many in new cotton
prints. We were struck by the beauty of the children, especially some of
the girls. Tall, well-proportioned, they had large eyes, fresh complexions.
A few were quite Western in their facial configuration. Raiding Central
Asian tribesmen in ancient days were often exiled on capture to Yenan
prefecture, then a garrisoned border region, where they intermarried with
the local girls.

The city had a Tang dynasty pagoda — a nine-storey tower. It was
shabby and neglected. People are not impressed with antiquity *per se*.
A mere thousand years is nothing in a land where recorded history
runs back three thousand and detailed legends commenced four millennia
ago.

Our bus would leave the next day. We were put up in a government
office compound, in rooms of cadres out on field trips. Tung Chuan
had no hotel, only inns "not suitable for foreign guests". We were given
bedding, hot water for washing, good tea. There was no charge. We
went to bed at seven-thirty, worn out. They told us that the Yenan bus,
due to leave at five in the morning, might not. There had been rain up

north, and water makes the yellow soil slick and dangerous on mountain roads.

Most freight was hauled on two-wheeled carts, pulled by horses and mules in mixed teams of four, with one animal in shafts and three in forward traces. The squeal of their brakes — a wooden block pressing on a round metal drum on the axle — never stopped. It was the last thing we heard as we fell asleep and the first thing we heard on awakening in the morning.

By seven a.m. there was still no bus. They said at the station they wouldn't know about the condition of the roads until ten. We had breakfast in our cave restaurant, crisp oil fritters and soybean milk. Singh, ever appreciative of beauty, was favorably impressed by our waitress, a handsome girl of eighteen. At his urging, I asked her about herself. She said she was a primary school graduate and liked working in a restaurant. She was charming and self-possessed.

As we sat dawdling over our soybean milk, we felt strangely at peace. We had already become accustomed to the screech of brakes as the carts, laden with coal, checked their speed down the slopes, and listened with half an ear to the Peking opera and Shensi folk songs winging from loudspeakers across the valley through the clear mountain air.

We finally left on the bus at eleven, due to reach Yenan by eight that night. Our vehicle, an ancient light Dodge pick-up, had been converted by means of building a large wooden box on the chassis. It was intended to hold twenty, but was actually crammed with about thirty, plus their hand luggage and two live chickens in cages. You were distracted from the pain in your butt, thumping on the hard wooden bench, by the agony in your knees, crammed rigid and motionless against the backrest of the seat in front. What saved us was the frequent breakdowns of the bus, which gave us a chance to get out and stretch our legs while it was being repaired. The winding mountain road was still wet and slippery from last night's rain wherever it was in shadow, and we had to go slowly.

At three in the afternoon, we had only reached Huang Ling, the half-way point. The bus couldn't get to Yenan that night. The driver was planning to go as far as the next county town and stay over, continuing on to Yenan in the morning. Singh, Lin and I decided to remain in Huang Ling, which we had heard a lot about, and catch another bus in the afternoon of the following day.

We were cordially received by Comrade Liang, vice chief of the county. A softspoken, enthusiastic man of about fifty, he was as easy and friendly as the old cloth shoes he wore with his faded cloth uniform. He had been a primary school teacher in a neighboring village and "joined the revolution" in 1937, operating as an underground agent until Liberation. He became a county leader in 1950. Liang put us up in the rooms of county cadres who were out on inspection tours of village administrations and farming co-ops. The county government office was housed in an old temple compound worn smooth with age, its tile roofs mellow in the shade of large trees. Temples and landlords' mansions were often used for government offices. They were generally the best constructed buildings and taking them symbolized the ascendancy of the people over their former corporal and spiritual rulers.

The furnishings were simple. Our borrowed beds consisted of boards laid across a couple of saw horses. There was no electricity. Water came from a well. But the place was spotlessly clean.

Our warm-hearted host insisted on immediately going out and showing us around personally. He knew the county like the palm of his hand, and his relations with the villagers were more neighborly than official. As we strolled along, farmers, mule train drivers, boys and girls, hailed him affectionately as "Old Liang". People stopped him and asked him questions, told him their problems. Smiling and patient, Liang had a few words for everyone.

He wanted us to see the Tomb of the Yellow Emperor which is what Huang Ling means, while it was still daylight. We climbed a long tree-shaded hill. It was crowned by a large mound twenty feet high. This was the last resting place of China's first ruler, Huang Ti, the legendary Yellow Emperor, who reigned four thousand years ago. With him began sericulture and weaving; people wore clothing instead of animal skins, built houses; wheeled vehicles and boats were invented; a written language appeared.

We asked Liang whether anything remained in the tomb. He said most ancient tombs had been plundered again and again over the centuries. Archeologists had made no recent check. He grinned and told us local lore had it that it is not the emperor but only his boots which are buried here. The First Emperor was such a beneficent ruler that people were loath to part with him even after his death. As he began his ascent to Heaven, they seized his feet. But the pull of the heavenly hosts was too strong, and the people were left holding his boots, which they entombed with due ceremony.

From the burial mound Liang led us to Huang Ling's other famous attractions. At the foot of the hill were the temple and memorial tablet erected by the Han emperor Wu Ti 2,000 years ago and dedicated to his illustrious forebear. Wu Ti and his armies had been driving the Hsiung Nu (Huns) out of China. When pausing here they discovered the tomb of the Yellow Emperor.

In the temple courtyard are two huge ancient cypresses, both alive and green. One is alleged to have been planted by the First Emperor. Wu Ti left a plaque before it, marveling that a tree should have lasted twenty-five centuries. That would have made the cypress, when we viewed it, about 4,600 years old.

The trunk of the other tree, a mere infant of some twenty centuries, was pitted with small holes. These were caused, the temple custodian solemnly informed us, by nail-studded armor, which Wu Ti and his officers hung on the branches, striking against the tree in the wind while they rested beneath it.

Even allowing for a certain amount of imaginative invention, Huang Ling's antiquities are remarkable. They were beginning to attract visitors, and the government had done quite a bit of repair and renovation. Huang Ling was building some unusual tourist bungalows, made entirely of the famous yellow soil. Domed like caves, the dwellings were faced with brick and whitewashed inside, and grouped in hollow squares around gardens. The use of local materials enabled Huang Ling to cut construction costs to the bone, while providing attractive accommodations.

There was no bus the next day. It was still raining further north. In the morning we were taken on a tour of some of the farms. Huang Ling is in the bowl of a large valley. Although a small river winds through it, bringing some moisture to the land along its banks, most of the fields were on terraced slopes, and irrigation was a problem in spite of the wells and rainwater catch basins that had been dug.

But a lot had been accomplished since the "socialist upsurge" in 1956. The people did so much better in only one year of cooperative farming that in 1957 they switched over to fully socialist co-ops, dividing income solely on the basis of work done, with no return for land invested.

In the village of Chengkuang, they had combined four small semi-socialist co-ops into one large socialist farm of 106 families. Most of them had been poor peasants before Liberation, nineteen had been middle peasants, three had been rich peasants and five had been landlords. They farmed a total of 215 acres and owned twenty donkeys, three mules and sixty-four draft oxen. By pooling their resources they were able to dig ten deep wells. This was something which, operating separately, they would never have been able to afford. With more water for irrigation, their grain yield tripled the pre-Liberation figure, which had been only about 600 pounds per acre. They said Huang Ling would have electricity the following year from a dam being built. Then they would be able to pump water to their terraced fields instead of carrying it up in buckets. Irrigation, plus the fertilizer and modern farm implements they were now in a position to buy, would boost their output.

They were already fairly well off. In families where both the husband and wife worked in the fields, the average annual income was about 300 *yuan*. The man usually earned an extra hundred in his spare time on government road and dam building. Since they paid no rent or taxes and the cost of food was negligible, and education for the children was virtually free, they could buy all the consumer goods they needed and still bank a lot of the money. A far cry from the Kuomintang days when in winter there was only one quilt for the entire family.

Ever since the new regime was established, the people found that when they followed Communist Party policies ("listened to Chairman Mao", was the way they put it), they benefited. They became increasingly receptive to changes the Party proposed. You could see the process at work in what had been a backward mountain region like Huang Ling. Along with the economic structure, traditional social values and attitudes were also being transformed.

We saw an example of this when we visited a primary school and the county middle school that afternoon. The total number of Huang Ling schoolchildren was 4,000 — ten percent of the population. Eighty percent came from families which were poor in the old society. The kids were bright, healthy, well-dressed. The primary school had its own experimental farm, run by the kids, who worked in groups according to age level. They also went to local farming co-ops to pick up pointers from the veterans. During vacations, they worked in the co-op fields of their own village.

Before Liberation the middle school served five counties and had sixty students, all from wealthy families. By 1957 its 700 students were Huang Ling county kids only, 550 boys, 150 girls. The other counties had their own schools. All the buildings were new. Tuition cost two *yuan* per term, and even this could be waived in the event of financial hardship. The school had a chemistry and physics lab and an athletics field. Their day started at seven in the morning and lasted till four in the afternoon. Six classes per day, forty-five minutes each with fifteen-minute breaks in between, plus time out for breakfast and a long break at noon. The second and final meal of the day was served at four. Bedtime was eight p.m. There was no electricity.

The main orientation of all the schools was agriculture. Middle school students had covered a whole barren mountain with saplings the year before — part of a long-range afforestation program. Most of the kids when they graduated were sent back to their village farms, where they filled an urgent need. As agriculture developed from mutual-aid teams to semi-socialist and then fully socialist co-ops, organized farming became more sophisticated. It was hard for the mainly illiterate older folks to keep books and records, to read scientific manuals. But the kids could do it, and they could take special short-term courses in agricultural technique. They were a useful addition to the co-ops.

Some of the parents were hesitant at first about the kids studying agriculture. In the old society children of poor families couldn't go to school at all. It was the dream of every parent to get his son (girls weren't even considered) an education so that he could become an "official" and raise the family out of its grinding poverty. Now the children were able to go to school at last, only to end up as farmers. It took a bit of explanation and persuasion to bring papa and mama round.

But they had learned to trust the judgment of the Party, and they saw how welcome the "educated farmers" were in the co-ops. Besides, the youngsters were able to continue their formal schooling in spare-time study, for which special arrangements were made. Many of the kids were becoming experts in scientific agriculture and farm administration.

The students themselves didn't need much convincing. They had been educated in socialist ideas and felt it only right to place the common good above personal inclination. Of the 150 graduating from Huang Ling's lower middle school the term before, ninety were assigned to their home cooperatives. I asked some of them how they felt about not going on to higher education. They said it didn't make any difference. Whatever served the people best, that they would do.

This wasn't a case of kids being noble and self-sacrificing, of the educated moving down into the ranks of uneducated. Rather it was part of the long-range goal of pulling the uneducated up into the ranks of the educated, of wiping out the gap between brain and brawn occupations, between town and country.

The so-called intellectual had a special place in China's old society. In a country of illiterates, any man who could read and write was an "intellectual". He was rare and respected. Generally, only the wealthy could afford to give their children an education, and so the literate tended to perpetuate the rule of the landlords and the bourgeoisie. The few among the poor who managed to acquire a little book learning adopted the social attitudes of the rulers. People who worked with their hands were considered inferior. The educated man made a point of not exerting himself physically. He didn't have to. His servants took care of the tiresome details. I was astonished when I first came to China and visited the family of a schoolteacher, living in quite squalid surroundings, to find that they had a servant. Human labor was cheap.

The result was that after a working class regime was established and social attitudes changed, intellectuals who began to appreciate the dignity of working with their hands discovered that they didn't know how. I was something of a hero to my wife and her friends because I could fix an electric plug and handle a screw-driver and pliers. The educated were practically all theory and no practice. They had little understanding of the abilities and qualities of the ordinary man. There were agronomists who never guided a plow, mechanical engineers who never turned a lathe, writers and artists in a People's Republic who knew next to nothing about the people. Obviously the educated had to be educated. Programs were instituted enabling them to spend periods of time at practical work in factories and on the farms, to good effect with many.

But this was not enough. China, with her nearly 800 million, needed many more than the mere five million who had then received some formal education. Schooling was provided for hundreds of millions more; but not the old kind. The kids had to be taught, while they were acquiring literacy and technical skills, to be civic minded, to be socially dedicated, not to use their education as a stepping stone to cushy office jobs, but to take what they had learned back to their factory or farm and apply it to increasing production and raising living standards.

By 1957, when the bulk of China's rural population had combined into large socialist farming co-ops, it was vital to get the educated boys and girls back to their villages to assist with the increased bookkeeping, administrative work and scientific development. Most of them went, and gladly, and helped the co-ops dig their toes in firmly for the Big Leap Forward which came the following year.

Raising the educational level of those who once worked only with their hands, and teaching the use of their hands to those who once worked only with their minds — this was the method. It had to be predicated in both instances on the goal of serving the people, otherwise it was no different from the method of capitalist countries. In the main the ethical motivation was there, as China's rapid strides in succeeding years bore witness. But the narrow self-interest of the old peasant mentality, the bourgeois intellectual's desire for fame and fortune, were there too. These were played upon and utilized by the revisionists — bourgeois-minded ambitious men who were already mustering their forces.

Liang told us that Comrade Wang, head of the Yenan Special Region, which embraced fourteen counties, was driving down that evening. Around seven p.m. a long black sedan rolled up to county headquarters. I'm not sure what I expected, but I was certainly surprised when the door opened and out stepped an old peasant. At least that's what he looked like in his loose-fitting tunic and trousers and patched cloth shoes. A man about sixty, he grinned engagingly when we were introduced, apologized for the "poor" accommodations, asked whether our beds were comfortable, whether we could take the food. We assured him the food was delicious, which it was.

We went into one of the large rooms, where a couple of lamps had been lit, and sat down on the big wooden chairs. Wang promptly slipped his shoes off and tucked his legs up under him. He passed cigarettes around as tea was served.

In response to our questions, Wang told us about himself. Sure enough, he had been a peasant, and had fought in the guerrillas, first against the Japanese, then against the Kuomintang. He gave a fascinating account of how the guerrillas and the PLA, closely coordinating, had smashed the army of Hu Tsung-nan — the Kuomintang general who, for a time, had taken Yenan. A self-educated man of keen intelligence, Wang spoke humorously and with gusto, leaping from his chair and gesticulating as he warmed to his story.

His complete naturalness, his absolute contempt for the enemy, his supreme confidence in the way China was going, was typical of the old Party cadres we met. The Northwest was then one of the more backward regions of China, yet the atmosphere was almost gay. Sitting in that dim-lit room of an ancient temple high on a yellow soil plateau, we felt warm and excited, listening to Wang's witty, incisive tale. We knew why the revolutionaries had won, and would go on winning.

Coming down to the present, Wang said they were emphasizing three things in the Yenan Special Region — roads, scientific farming, and water and soil conservation. Formerly, three counties had no auto roads at all. Now all fourteen had good hard-surface highways. Each county was responsible for its own. They were maintained by the farming co-ops, whose members earned extra money keeping them in good condition.

The region had introduced a new strain of wheat the previous year which had raised local output. A sorghum from the northeast provinces was also growing well. Every district in every county had its own agricultural experimental station. The older peasants were slow to accept new ideas, but when they could see results with their own eyes, they were willing to give them a try.

The necessity for water and soil conservation was something the farmers understood, and they cooperated to push it. They were digging catch pools for rainwater, building check dams in gullies, planting trees and digging wells all over the place. The really big projects — like dams — the government built and financed. There was still a lot more to be done.

We had a good weather forecast for the next day and should have gone to bed at a reasonable hour to prepare for the rest of our trip. But Wang wanted to know all about America and Nepal and Peking, and we had dozens of questions to ask him. It was quite late by the time we finally turned in. We slept beautifully.

The sun came out in the morning. It was a fine clear day. The bus wasn't due until noon, so we went to call on the head of the county women's federation. A bright young woman of about thirty, she came from Hopei, the province Peking is in. It was a relief to hear the familiar accent again. The local pronunciation was understandable, but I had to strain to get everything.

She told us Huang Ling had been very feudal in the old days. Women had been restricted to "circling around the cooking stove". Only after Liberation did they begin working in the fields, the real break coming with the formation of the cooperatives the year before, 1956, when larger-scale farming had created the need for more labor. Since the women added substantially to the family income, the men's opposition petered out. Wives generally managed to do 140 days in the fields per year to the men's 200.

Nevertheless, the position of the women was still inferior. They had neither the experience nor the technique of the men and, consequently, were paid less. This was being remedied through on-the-job training. Also they were too tied down by kids and housework to put in as much time as the men. The grandmas looked after the children during the harvests, when ninety percent of the women took part, but you couldn't do this all year round. Regular nurseries and kindergartens were being set up, birth control education had begun. The women were all for it. Some had four or five kids before they were thirty. The men were not opposed to the idea either, particularly those with large families.

Male chauvinism hadn't been eliminated, but it was fighting a last ditch battle. As the women acquired more skills and spent less time around the house, their earnings increased. At the same time, the Party was encouraging them to assume positions of leadership. Some were group or brigade leaders. A few were assistant heads of co-ops. Of the sixteen townships in Huang Ling county, fourteen had women deputy leaders. Coupled with this was the constant nationwide education campaign on the proper role of women in society. A major change was in the making.

Back at the County Government, in the room next to mine, I discovered the county nurse, a young woman from Sian. One of her main jobs was to train midwives. A few were the old-fashioned kind, whom she instructed in modern methods, but most were ordinary farm wives. Already every co-op had two or three trained women who could help with deliveries. The county nurse was called in for the difficult cases.

There was no charge for maternity services, only for the medicines, which ranged in price from fifty cents to a *yuan*. In the event of economic hardship, even this was paid by the county. The nurse said it had been hard to convince the farmers at first that the services were free. Women would be in labor for two or three days before calling for help. Now everyone understood.

Medical and surgical treatment for China's hundreds of millions of farm people was still a problem. How could it be financed? Where were the doctors, the nurses, the medicines, the equipment to come from? Not until the seventies was a start made to solving this question. Today, paramedics called "barefoot doctors" do the preventive medicine, deliver the babies, and treat all of the simpler common ailments — guided and aided by professional government medical personnel. Extensive use is made of acupuncture and local home remedies, with the people themselves gathering the various herbs and roots. They can also join medicare arrangements.

But in the intervening years many steps were taken which greatly improved the backward medical picture. The county nurses led the fight against contagious disease — by inoculation and vaccination, and by teaching hygiene. They did a good job. The kids were clean in Huang Ling. It didn't have any flies.

We left on the bus at one p.m., after warmly thanking Old Liang. Comrade Wang had left that morning. We wouldn't forget Huang Ling, toughly persisting through the ages and now, with youthful spriteliness, moving on with the socialist wave.

Our bus ride was breath-taking. The road climbed and twisted to dizzy heights, and clung by its teeth to the edge of precipices. We traveled for miles along high plateaus so wide and flat we thought we were on the plains again, until suddenly yawning canyons, ten miles across, would open up to remind us where we were. Crops grew at 5,000 feet, a little sparse because of the water shortage. At least they had plenty of sun. Then we started down, staring at the terraced fields mounting like stairs to the very tops of lofty hills. It must have taken people hours just getting to and from those fields, to say nothing of working them. What courage and persistence, wresting a yield from nature under such conditions.

Near the bottom, the road met a winding stream, yellow with eroded soil. We followed it to Fuhsien, another county town. It was five-thirty in the afternoon by then, and we had to stay over. The busses didn't travel at night. The mountain roads were too dangerous.

We took a walk before dinner down the main, and only, street. Our eye was caught by a riot of flowers in a garden seen through a courtyard gate. The owner, a retired peasant whose kids were grown up and working away from home, invited us in. The interior decorations were interesting. Carved wooden partitions screened the *kang* bed, which was covered with small rugs and had a chest, painted with flowers by a local artist, at its head. There were excellent likenesses of the old man and his wife, in oils, on the wall. These had been done by the son in Hupeh. Scrolls of Chinese calligraphy were also hung, paper-cuts decorated the window. A delightful place.

The Chinese are very artistic. Everything is a creation, from a store window display of nuts and bolts that have somehow become a locomotive and cars chugging across a railway trestle, to the homely radish which has been carved into a blushing rose to garnish your plate in a neighborhood restaurant.

We strolled back and had dinner at the local inn, with an audience of about fifty kids watching us through the plate glass window. The proprietor kept shooing them away, but they kept coming back. There were plenty of Young Pioneer red ties among them. The little girls were darling. While we and the kids were smilingly examining each other, big dogs nonchalantly wandered among the tables, looking for scraps. Not one of our most relaxed meals.

Singh and I were quartered that night in a splendid room belonging to the manager of the consumers' co-op, each on a separate *kang* bed. *Kangs* are a feature of north China. They are brick platforms, usually occupying the entire side of a room, heated by flues from beneath. In most homes, they are connected with the kitchen stove, utilizing its heat. The vent between the two rooms can be cut off during the warmer weather. Depending on their size, they can sleep one or two or the entire family, each wrapped in separate bedding. During the day, the quilts are folded out of the way and the *kang* becomes the social center of the house. Meals are eaten there on special short-legged tables, there the women sew and mend while toddlers romp around them and older children do their homework.

The ones Singh and I had were smaller types, meant only for sleeping. We were given brand new colored quilts. The walls had been freshly whitewashed, the glass windows shone behind blue flowered curtains, designs of faint red spots embellished the papered ceiling. A pleasant room, and restful in the soft glow of the oil lamp.

At five in the morning we were on the road. By eight-thirty, our bus was rolling into Yenan. Before the Long March culminated here, it had been an ancient walled town on the banks of the Yen River with a population of 3,400. The wide river valley was surrounded by hills of yellow soil, cut by gullies and gorges. People grazed sheep and goats, gathered meagre crops from the arid earth, and paid exorbitant rents to tyrannical landlords.

Everything was taxed by the Kuomintang government — one *yuan* for getting married, one *yuan* for each son born, fifty cents for a daughter. There was one tax for having an ox, and another for not having an ox. There was even a tax on chimneys from the cooking stoves. Magistrates collected two years' taxes in advance, and they did it every year. Some were decades ahead of the game. When in desperation a poor man sold his land, official "fees" ate up forty percent of the price.

Oppression breeds resistance. By 1926 the province had a Communist Party, by 1935 a people's army controlled the entire region except for cities like Yenan, Suiteh and Michih. They instituted their own land reform, and drubbed the landlord home guards sent to crush them. Regular Nationalist troops had to be called in. The people's army made monkeys out of them, though they had virtually no weapons. Peasants would rush into Nationalist Army strongholds with terrifying invented reports that huge well-armed forces were approaching, and the garrisons would flee.

The people knew every move the enemy made. Whenever a Nationalist Army expedition set forth, a peasant spotter on a mountaintop would fling up handfuls of yellow earth which would blossom out in a fine dust and rise like smoke. The signal would be passed in the same fashion from mountain to mountain. The Nationalists never could be sure who was people's army, for they wore no uniforms. They were peasants working in their fields, until the call came. In 1937, when the Red Army, which had come to Yenan at the conclusion of the Long March, went off to fight the Japanese, the people's militia forces became primarily responsible for the defence of the Yenan Region.

As the headquarters for the Chinese Communist Party, Yenan grew rapidly. Intellectuals flocked to it from all over the country. The population of the region soared to 100,000 by 1939. Then the Nationalists, more afraid of the people than of the foreign invader, avoided clashes with the Japanese and imposed a blockade against the region. Yenan met the challenge by setting up home industries which turned out most of their daily necessities. On the food front, every student, cadre and Party leader guaranteed to produce ninety catties of millet per year. Eighth Route Army troops in the Nanniwan sector, mostly southerners, hacked paddy fields out of the wilderness and planted rice, a crop the region had never known. They performed prodigious feats of production. Some of the men were jokingly known as "ox infuriators", because they could pull a plow through more acreage in a day than the average draft animal, which naturally aroused the jealousy and rage of the ox. The need for and feasibility of self-reliance became permanently impressed on Communist thinking.

Yenan was the center of political and military leadership, the school in which cadres for these fields were trained. Tens of thousands passed through Yenan's short-term courses. In Yenan Mao wrote many of the profound articles which are shaping the destiny of China and influencing the course of world history. Arts of and for the people got their start in Yenan. It became the beacon, the inspiration, for millions of Chinese. Despite the Kuomintang blockade, its fame continued to spread, across China, around the world. Canadian surgeon Norman Bethune, who had served in Spain, came to serve and die in the Chinese revolution. Young American journalist Edgar Snow came to observe and talk with Mao, and ended by writing the classic *Red Star Over China*. Yenan also drew American government and military observers, for it symbolized Chinese resistance against the common enemy.

After the Japanese surrender in 1945, the Kuomintang, with heavy American backing, launched its final attempt to crush the Communist-led revolution. Kuomintang general Hu Tsung-nan attacked the Yenan region with 230,000 troops. The defenders numbered less than 30,000. They had, on the average, only 500 bullets per machinegun, thirty bullets per rifle. The enemy boasted they would take Yenan in three days and capture the Central Committee in three months.

Mao's strategy was to let the foe take the cities but to annihilate their troops. In March 1947 the Communists relinquished Yenan. Chiang Kai-shek was delirious with joy. He held victory celebrations in the large Chinese cities, decorated Hu Tsung-nan and sent reporters to cover the "triumph". Hu enclosed 1,500 of his own troops in ten different camps and had them pose as POWs. He piled up a lot of old weapons and exhibited them as "battle trophies".

But it wasn't quite over. The whole population rose in support of the Communists. In the year that followed, the two million population of the Northwest area contributed 50 million workdays to the support of the People's Liberation Army, delivering grain and serving as stretcher bearers. The women hand-stitched 580,000 pairs of cloth shoes. Guerrillas made life hell for the enemy. Hu Tsung-nan never dared spend a single night in Yenan for fear of being assassinated. Mines and booby traps were planted everywhere. Enemy soldiers were still being blown up months after the occupation.

The PLA wasn't idle either. With Mao personally planning and directing all the battles, it destroyed 15,000 Kuomintang effectives in the first forty days of the campaign, and eliminated another 61,000 by the end of the year. Then it switched over to the offensive. Early in '48 it knocked out another 20,000 of the enemy. In April 1948, exactly one year and one month after their departure, the Communists recaptured Yenan. The enemy got out in such a hurry that actors, performing for them in the city, fled with their costumes and make-up on.

Hu Tsung-nan had worked cruel havoc in the border region. He commandeered most of the people's grain, and an estimated 400,000 died of starvation. During their rout the enemy vengefully committed widespread destruction. Restoration took a long time.

When we arrived, the city was still in the early stages of its growth, but the old Yenan spirit was going full blast. They had great plans. In the next five years the population would expand from thirty thousand to a hundred thousand. They would need that many for all their new projects. On the list were a motor vehicle parts factory, a power plant (they had plenty of coal), and a bone meal fertilizer factory (there already were one million sheep in the Yenan Special Region to provide the bones and they were aiming to double that number). Irrigated land would grow from 10,000 to 50,000 acres. They would raise a lot more grain and expand their orchards. While implementing water and soil conservation measures, they would move farming down from the hillsides to the valley floors and devote the slopes to grazing and orchards.

We got this story after we settled in at our temporary quarters. There was a bit of a hassle first. The hostel was half-way up a high bluff on what used to be the Yenan University grounds. On the lower level they had a fancy new building for foreign dignitaries, with steam heat, hot and cold running water and no view at all, except of the tall chimney of the heating plant. Fortunately, it was not yet completed, and the old hostel was still being used. We were shown nice rooms at eighty cents a head. No thank you, we said. What we were looking for were cave dwellings. Friends who had lived here in the old days had recommended them highly.

Our hosts laughed and showed us a row of caves near the top of the bluff. Hollowed out of the yellow earth in a vaulted arch and fronted with a wooden frame which held a door and paper-paned windows, they were clean and surprisingly bright. The whitewashing probably helped. Furnishings were simple. An electric light bulb, a few wooden beds, a couple of tables and some wooden chairs.

When we said these would be fine, our hosts looked startled. I'm sure they thought we would consider the accommodations too crude. Only our earnest assurances stopped them from carrying up spring mattresses and a few sofas. We liked the caves very much, and the location was ideal. There was a broad terrace before the caves shaded by several large trees. You could see for miles — the Yen River, the Tang pagoda on the hill opposite, the large valley and the mountains beyond.

After supper that night, Comrade Huang gave us the background talk on Yenan as I mentioned above. He had been one of the local guerrillas and walked with a limp from arthritis contracted hiding in damp gullies. Like all the old cadres we met in this region he spoke with infectious enthusiasm. He said in the days when Yenan was the heart of the revolution, life was hard but everyone was cheerful. Wherever you went you heard singing. That buoyancy still pervaded. The mountains were vast, the air was clear. The people were big, rugged, outspoken, and confident in their future.

In Sian we had been joined by "Wu", a young Chinese professor and his American wife "Terry", a corn-fed gal from Iowa. Wu, brought up in Indonesia and educated in the USA, had only been in China for two years. He was teaching science at a Peking university. When we started the uncomfortable trip north, he was annoyed by the delays and inconveniences. But the more he talked with the old cadres, the more evidences he saw of the sweep of Chinese history, the more he learned of the courage of the Party and the people in their long and bitter struggle, the more he saw of the dogged fight to pull this region — with its dry soil and difficult mountains — up by its bootstraps, the more stimulated he became. Finally, he was so thrilled, so proud to be a Chinese, that he confided to me: "I wish I had come back ten years sooner."

The next day we visited the cave dwellings where Chairman Mao lived and worked during his stay in Yenan. They were simple and austere. We spoke with old peasants who knew him. They said Mao was always friendly and relaxed — just one of the people. He refused to accept any special treatment. While directing the course of the revolution and writing his famous articles, Mao tended his own vegetable patch and wore old clothes. Hearing that we were from Peking, the peasants asked us to send him their regards. We could only smile and nod.

Yenan natives were a colorful lot. The men turbaned their heads in small towels, knotted in front. (Towel turbans were worn in many parts of northern China, but in most places they knotted them in back.) The towels were a protection against the dust and handy for wiping sweat. Tunics, padded or lined with sheepskin, were held in place by a sash, often with a brass-bowled long-stemmed pipe tucked beneath it like a dagger. Baggy trousers were lined or unlined according to season. Feet were shod with the ubiquitous cloth shoes, by far the most comfortable of footwear. The soles were layers of cloth pasted and stitched together. Sturdy black cloth made the uppers. The shoes were light, they could "breathe". "Athlete's foot" among Chinese was virtually unknown.

Everybody sang — men and women, young and old. The northern part of Shensi province was famous for it. There were plaintive shepherd songs, sometimes to the accompaniment of a flute. And there were the duets — between boy and girl, between husband and wife — tender, funny, broad, as the case might be. China's first revolutionary opera, later a ballet, the *White-Haired Girl,* composed in Yenan, was based on north Shensi folk songs. Singing seems to come naturally to hill dwellers.

We visited the Yenan Opera Company, which was developing the local music. It had taken over the old Yenan University site — mostly cave buildings not far from where we were staying. Organized in 1950, it had given 160 performances in 1956, about a third of them in Yenan, the rest in other parts of north Shensi. They did mostly folk operas and dances. They had sixteen singers, twenty dancers and fourteen musicians. Nearly all could double — the musicians could sing, the singers could dance. They had their own composer, who was writing modern operettas. These were liked by the younger audiences, but the older people preferred the folk forms.

The singers themselves thought the folk songs were better music, but the modern creations had better content. They were attempting to combine the best of both. Most of them were primary and middle school graduates. One or two had been to college. The kids worked hard and put a lot of time in on political study — especially of Mao's ideas on literature and art. Every few months two or three of them were sent to Peking or Sian for musical training. When they came back they taught the others. The majority were keen on learning local folk forms and building on this basis. Although they sang mainly in local dialect, they were also experimenting with standard pronunciation.

They went on tour several times a year, each time for two or three months, doing one to three shows a day. Tickets were twenty and thirty cents. They painted their own scenery, made their own props. These were carried on donkeys when they toured the remoter mountain regions. The performers walked, toting their luggage.

They lived two to a cave-dwelling room. We looked in on one of them. It was clean and artistically decorated. A well-stocked bookcase included — in Chinese translation — Marxist literature, Ibsen and Stanislavsky. The kids rehearsed in a small auditorium, formerly the meeting hall of Yenan University. On either side of the stage vertical plaques read:

> Everyone both student and teacher,
> All the world a school,
> Everything in life a text,
> At all times serve the people.

The opera company had adopted the motto as its own.

This being Saturday, the hostel threw a dance for us. Friends who had been there in the early forties told me the Saturday night dance was a regular feature of life in Yenan, a scratchy phonograph or a small pick-up band providing the music. Our dance was a bit more elegant — we had the opera company orchestra. The singers and dancers also came, as well as doctors and nurses from the hospital and cadres from half a dozen local organizations.

It was a lively affair. The singers did some delightful numbers, then there were demands for us to perform. Singh responded with two songs in Hindi that sounded quite jolly. I sang "Tavern in the Town" and Terry gave out with "Swing Low Sweet Chariot". For an encore we did "Clementine" as a duet. The applause was deafening, more for our willing spirit, no doubt, than for our musical abilities.

There was lots of dancing, with the girls inviting us in relays. Only when we pleaded the need to catch our breath were we allowed to sit a number out. We slept well that night.

In the morning we were taken to where *Liberation Daily* had been printed when Yenan was the revolutionary center. As a precaution against Japanese and, subsequently, Kuomintang bombings, the newspaper had been housed in the "Cave of the Ten Thousand Buddhas" — a cavern of about sixty feet square which had been hewn out of solid rock over a thousand years ago. Two huge pillars supported the ceiling. Every inch of the walls and pillars was lined with rows of carved Buddhas and female figures in the lush natural style of the Tang dynasty. They had originally been colored, but Hu Tsung-nan had set fire to the printing equipment when he retreated, blackening the paint. The figures were still beautiful. Each one was different, in posture and expression, and had been done in sets by different sculptors over several decades. Beside each set was a plaque inscribed with the names of the artists and the devout Buddhists who had sponsored them.

We looked through the old files of the *Liberation Daily*. The headline of the first issue, October 6, 1941 read: "Soviet Union determined to continue aid to China. England and America watch morosely." Things have changed a bit since then. The final issue was dated March 27, 1947, just before Yenan was temporarily abandoned.

The printing press, no longer in the cave, was now turning out *Yenan News*, a lively little four-page paper, published three times a week and servicing the fourteen counties of the Yenan Special Region.

Next we visited an earthen dam, one of twenty the regional government had recently built with spare-time labor. Between five and six hundred men from the co-ops had finished it in four months at a cost of 110,000 *yuan*. With a base 208 yards long and 20 yards thick, the dam would last from five to ten years. They could construct two such dams a year. At that rate, combined with the small-scale water and soil conservation projects the farmers were building on their co-ops, they estimated they could lick washouts and erosion in the Region in about ten years.

China was a poor country and didn't have much in the way of machinery and modern technology. But she had enormous labor power and the social organization to utilize it. Applying these to local problems and making full use of local materials and methods, she was able to advance. The major capitalist countries all refused to trade with China, and so she was compelled to rely on her own resources. She did, of course, obtain some assistance from Moscow until the Soviet Union began behaving like any other imperialist power. From then on, China was completely on her own.

At the same time, China pushed ahead in scientific research and development. We saw something of that, and its application to a backward rural area, in the large experimental farm we visited outside

Yenan. They had found a good wheat variety for cold climates and were trying to improve it. Their wheat expert turned out to be a man who had been studying agriculture at Cornell while I was there taking the Army course in Chinese. Small world department. His English was very good. He had returned to China in 1945.

My old alumnus said they were also experimenting with local buckwheat and various kinds of millet. These coarse grains were hard to digest if you ate any one kind exclusively. But if alternated with rice or wheat they were good for the health and provided the stamina needed for a hard day in the fields. The local people were very fond of them. Buckwheat was particularly popular. Besides being tasty, it could be planted after the wheat was in and harvested before the cold weather. Getting two crops out of that dry soil was a real accomplishment.

For fertilizer, they used mostly sheep manure which was plentiful and cheap. They were introducing the raising of rabbits, both for meat and fur. The co-ops were interested. It was an easy way to earn extra income.

The farm was also pushing apples. For one thing they had discovered that the slopes held water better when strips of fields were alternated with strips of orchards. For another, apples grew well here. They had several varieties. My favorite, and the one which seemed to thrive the best, was a type called the "banana apple". Crisp and juicy, it did actually have something of the flavor of bananas. The farm had given 10,000 grafts the previous year to the co-ops, free of charge, to improve the local stock. They would bear fruit within three years.

As any farmer will tell you, fruit is a risky crop. If you don't dispose of it all in season, it starts to go bad. You have to preserve it or refrigerate it, and that requires capital and equipment poor hillslope regions usually don't have. Here, again, the experimental farm people distinguished themselves. They discovered that the yellow soil caves were natural refrigerators, cool and dry. Apples stored in October kept most of their natural juice and flavor until the following May or June. Big cities like Sian could be supplied all during the usually apple-less first half of the year. Another source of income for the farming co-ops.

According to the lunar calendar, it was Moon Festival Day, the time of the year when the moon is supposed to be at its roundest and the people celebrate the harvests. In the afternoon we bought moon cakes and lots of fruit and invited the kids from the opera company over. The boys had a basketball match, but half a dozen of the girls came.

A pretty Mohammedan girl from Kaifeng sang Honan opera tunes. (She was the only member of the troupe who had dietary scruples, but they had a special kitchen for her. It's Party policy to respect the customs of national minority people.) Others did some north Shensi songs. We were amused by a cute number called *Husband and Wife Have a Tiff*. They promised to teach it to us. The girls were mostly from Shensi. Their average age was about eighteen. They were direct, frank, but modest, and very interested in their work.

They stayed for dinner, then all left except Kao Min, a mezzo-soprano, one of their leading ladies. From Kiangsu province in south China, she was charming and full of fun. She, the hostel manager and one of the attendants played "five hundred" — a kind of rummy — in our cave with us until nearly eleven. They attacked with all the abandon, passion and wisecracks of pinochle players I have known. Then Kao Min wrote out the words of *Husband and Wife* and drilled us on it for another hour. We did pretty well. She was surprised that I didn't have any of the pear-shaped tones some foreigners use for rendering Chinese folk songs. Obviously she had never heard of unpretentious Brooklyn speech.

The next day was our last in Yenan. We visited the famed Precious Pagoda. Built in Tang times, it stood atop a high hill from which there was a wonderful view in all directions. A big old bell of cast bronze hung from a wooden frame not far from the tower. It had been used as an alarm in the liberated area days. Also made in Tang, it was inscribed with the names of people who claimed they had been cured of ailments, and of women who believed their prayers for sons were answered at a local temple, long since gone. They had all chipped in to pay for the bell and present it to the temple. An expensive gift.

To my amazement, along with various holy figures on the bell, there was Pigsy. Old Pigsy was a folklore figure who was supposed to have accompanied Hsuan Tsang, a devout Buddhist monk, to India a thousand years ago to bring back holy scriptures. Their other companion was Monkey, whose x-ray eyes could penetrate the disguise of the many demons and sprites who beset them on their way. The adventures of these three were an important part of Chinese children's fairy tales and puppet shows. They appeared, too, in Peking opera.

Monkey was a typical children's hero. He could work powerful magic, was fearless, humorless and treated women with disdain. Pigsy appealed more to the grown-ups, though the kids liked him too, as a comedian. Brave enough when he had to fight, he was a good-natured slob the rest of the time, a glutton and a lecher whenever the opportunity presented. Due to certain minor deficiencies in my own character, I have always found Pigsy entirely lovable. But I never expected to see him commemorated on an ancient bronze temple bell. That must have been quite a congregation. No wonder Tang was a Golden Age.

We loafed around all afternoon. In the evening, Kao Min dropped in for a final rehearsal of our *Husband and Wife* song. We asked if there was anything we could send from Peking. A couple of arias from *Carmen*, she said. She had been told that her lower registers were good and wanted to try some foreign contralto pieces. We promised to see to it.

We took off the following morning at five-thirty by bus, arrived in Tung Chuan by three-thirty in the afternoon, got on a train at four-thirty, reached Sian at eleven, returned to the hotel by pedicab, had a wash and fell into bed, bone weary, around midnight.

After a day or two of rest and a bit more sight-seeing, Terry and Wu went back to Peking. It was the middle of September and school was starting. Singh, Lin and I decided to climb Huashan, one of China's five famous mountains, then go on to Loyang. Why I got involved in this madness, I'm not quite sure. Singh came from the mountains of northern Nepal and had done a lot of climbing. Lin, as his interpreter and escort, had to go with him. But the highest I had ever got on my own two feet was the top of the hill in Brooklyn's Prospect Park. Perhaps I didn't want my Nepalese comrade to think the men of Flatbush craven. I was only forty-two, and in reasonably good shape. But more likely it was because I wanted to examine Huashan closely, first-hand. It wasn't simply a high and beautiful mountain. Priests had begun building Taoist retreats on Huashan two thousand years ago, during the Western Chou dynasty. It reached its zenith as a Taoist center in Tang, when hundreds of monks inhabited caves cut into the living rock. Devoted followers clambered up the steep cliffs daily to keep them supplied with food and other necessities. Temples were built. The caves, some of them only niches, and the temples were still there.

At eight in the morning we got on a train and arrived in Huayueh at ten-thirty. We left our luggage in the County Office and set out. We walked for an hour along a peaceful country road. Mountains reared abruptly out of the plain. We started up through a deep ravine, the path crossing back and forth over an icy stream filled with rocks and boulders. We had to step and leap from one to another, constantly climbing. Though it was a cloudy day, we sweated copiously.

Then the ravine widened out into gentler slopes, with groves and mountain flowers. About every mile and a half was a small Taoist temple where you could buy tea or boiled drinking water. Every two miles was a large temple which served food and had sleeping accommodations. The temples were old and dark and cool, set among shady ancient trees. Perfect resting places on a hot climb.

The caves were in the most inaccessible places all the way up the mountain, many perched on ledges above sheer rock. Taoism was a religion of withdrawal, of private contemplation. Among the ancient priests were alchemists and men with knowledge of herbal medicine. But particularly in later centuries "Tao" — the "Way" — led to an escape from society and personal problems.

From the hundreds who had inhabited Huashan in the Tang dynasty the number dwindled to only about seventy at the time of our visit, including eight women. They had all been organized into a service co-op which sold food, drink and lodging to travelers. This covered their expenses.

We talked with them wherever we stopped. They dressed in gowns similar to those of the Buddhists, but neither the priests nor the nuns shaved their heads as the Buddhists did. They wore their hair long, gathered into a bouffant which protruded through a special opening in the top of their hats. They were quiet-spoken, relaxed. In that cool stillness, amid vast distances between towering peaks, we all instinctively lowered our voices.

"What brought you here? Why did you become a Taoist?" we asked.

One man said he had fled from being conscripted into the Kuomintang army. Another had dreams of becoming a second Sun Pin — a doctor who had earned fame centuries ago with cures he had learned as a Taoist. But most had run away from personal danger or tragedy they hadn't had the strength to face.

We asked one priest how he reconciled the Taoist retreat from the world with the socialist concept of serving the people. He couldn't of course, and he admitted it. The government was paying for the repair and upkeep of their temples, but they had to work. Now they were providing food for the people instead of the people bringing food to them. He said there were still believers among the old folks, but they weren't getting any new converts. Although people came long distances to Huashan during religious festivals, most came as tourists, not as pilgrims. He thought Taoism as a religion would be gone from China in another generation.

Wearily we began the last leg of our climb. We were determined to reach the northern peak before nightfall. We had to mount banks of steps cut into the rock at an angle of about 80 degrees, aided by swaying chains hung on both or only one side of the steps. In one or two stretches they were absolutely vertical.

I was pouring sweat. My heart pounded, I gasped for breath. It was a grueling, exhausting experience. At first I could do twenty steps at a time. Then ten. Finally, I had to rest after every five. In a few places, one misstep would have sent us hurtling down into the abyss. I remembered the priests' instructions — you can look up, but don't look down. Surely, I thought, one little peek can't hurt. I tried it. Immediately, the gorge below and mountains behind and the sky above began to rotate. I clung desperately to the chains and faced inwards till my dizziness passed.

At last, more dead than alive, we reached the temple on the north peak. The interior was gloomy and full of ancient trappings — all worn stone, faded tapestries and weathered bronzes. But the half dozen priests had the healthy ruddy complexions of mountain men. They provided us with a hot meal of rice and vegetables. I was so tired I could hardly eat.

But I couldn't help feeling a little proud of myself. It was seven p.m. The climb had taken eight hours. It had been pretty strenuous in spots, but we made it.

"I don't suppose you get many visitors up here," I said to one of the priests.

"Not this time of the year," he said. "But in April during the Incense Burning Festival we sometimes have as many as a hundred a day. They're all kinds — even little old women with bound feet."

That properly deflated me. I felt even smaller when, asked about how they got their supplies they explained that a couple of men brought them up every day on shoulder poles, returning the same day. Since shoulder poles, being weighted with loads at either end, have to be supported with one hand, that meant the men had only one hand free to get them up the vertical cliffs. And they traveled so quickly they could breeze up to the summit and back to the valley in the time it had taken us to crawl to the top.

We fell into bed at eight that night, all three of us sleeping on a wide platform in a room perched on the edge of a cliff. I was over-tired, and in that ethereal mountain stillness the squirrels scurrying around on the paper ceiling seemed to be making an awful racket. Just as I was dozing off, I thought I felt one of them run across my face, and woke with a start. Maybe I only imagined it. Anyhow, I slept badly.

The next morning I didn't have much energy. I let Lin and Singh go off to climb the other peaks. I stayed and chatted with the Taoist priests. They told me that when the Kuomintang armies fled, a gang of officers and men had climbed up to the temple and hid themselves, intending to hold out until Chiang Kai-shek made his "comeback". It was an ideal location. The only path was steep and narrow. A single man with a machinegun could hold it indefinitely. All the other sides of the peak were sheer rock.

But a daring team of seven PLA men and a peasant guide scaled one of those "inaccessible" cliffs in the dead of night and took the enemy by surprise, killing some and capturing the rest. Looking at the precipitous rock face, I was amazed. They must have had incredible courage.

After Singh and Lin returned we had lunch and started back. Going down was relatively easy, but we were stiff and awkward, and Singh sprained his knee. The sun was out. It was hotter than the day before. We stopped at every temple for tea to replenish our streaming perspiration. The Taoist priests were friendly and talked with us freely. The vitality of the new society seemed to have broken centuries of silence imposed upon them by religious mysticism. One of them presented us with some home-grown walnuts. They knew a bit about Nepal and America, and quite a lot about what was happening in China. Newspapers were delivered almost every day. From time to time they went down to the county town for meetings. There was no longer any necessity for them to "get away from it all". But they were doing a useful job, running way-stations for tourists, and would remain in the quiet mountains they loved.

We were fairly fresh when we reached the foothills, but fatigue caught up with us during the last hour's walk on the flat. We arrived at the County Office at seven in the evening. After supper we washed our sweaty clothes and ourselves, read the newspapers, and were in bed by ten.

We rose early the next morning and shaved, for the first time in three days.   In the rural areas the movement against the Rightists was just starting.   The office walls were plastered with cartoons and posters. After breakfast we chatted with the county cadres and thanked them for the excellent treatment they had given us.   It was the same in every local government office we stayed at during the course of our trip — good food, clean bedding, and a friendly concern that was almost embarrassing in its solicitude.   The men and women we met were modest, hard-working, competent, and full of optimistic plans for the development of their particular region or district.   They gave you the feeling that China's rural foundations were solid, secure.

At ten-thirty we boarded a train to Loyang, arriving at six p.m. Although the hotel had been notified, no one was at the station to meet us. We telephoned them.   A quarter of an hour later, a young man showed up. He said the section chief (who, as it later turned out, had received our message) had "gone to the theater" without saying a word about us to anyone.   When we got to the hotel we had a long argument over quarters — they trying to give us something lavish and expensive, we insisting on something simple and cheap.   After the question was finally settled, to our satisfaction, we went to bed — only to be awakened an hour later by the shriek of a train whistle which sounded as if it were right outside our window.   The hotel was built much too close to the station.   It had good, expensive equipment, but it was dirty and poorly run.   Our first and only encounter with bureaucracy throughout our journey, it was all the more shocking because it was so unusual.

I think Lin, our Chinese comrade, rather worried the section chief — a languid fellow — with his critical comments when we met the next day. From then on, he left us strictly alone, except for a few cautious suggestions about points of interest we might visit.

We took pedicabs to the city's outskirts, and then a bus for Lungmen — the "Dragon's Gate" — site of huge idols carved out of the cliffs. Loyang had been China's capital during most of the first six centuries AD.   When we saw it in 1957, what remained of the original city was very run-down.   But the outskirts were a different story.   Schools and machine tool factories had risen.   China's first tractor plant was in the process of construction.

The famous Lungmen grottoes lined both sides of the Yi River, a wide shallow body of water.   Remnants of two bridges blown up by

Kuomintang armies when retreating from the Japanese stood forlornly in mid-stream. There was a heavy traffic of trucks and ox carts fording the shallows. The creaking carts, hauling coal from a mine across the river, over the years had spread a layer of coal dust inches thick on the cobbles of the ancient road. The tomb of Pai Chu-yi, great poet of the Tang dynasty, as well as one of Chiang Kai-shek's villas, was visible on the opposite shore. Glory and disgrace, cheek by jowl.

Carving of the Lungmen figures began in the fourth century with the growth of Buddhism. In that period China had as many as thirty thousand temples and two million monks and nuns. The Lungmen carvings ranged in size from rows of figures only a few inches high decorating the grottoes to towering Buddhas of thirty and forty feet cut out of the cliffsides. In the more waterproof caves many of the images, their niches and ceilings, retained their original colors — soft and of beautiful artistry. The paints are believed to have had a mineral base, but the secret of making them is lost.

Considerable damage had been done by rascals who worked for foreign collectors. Hands and heads, artistically expressive and easy to ship, had been ruthlessly chopped off. Even larger operations had been undertaken for customers in a position to pay. The New York Metropolitan Museum had acquired two wonderful Northern Wei (4th to 6th century) frescoes of a devout king and queen. The Kansas City Museum got another. Lions and flying fairies ended up in the Boston Museum. Ugly scars of chipped stone were infuriating reminders to the Chinese of what imperialist countries meant by "cultural exchange".

A fresh layer of dust was churned up and spread on the classic sculptures with every passing ox cart. We were told the Ministry of Culture had allocated funds for paving the cobblestone road and repairing the grottoes. The whole area would be turned into a large public park.

The following day was our last in Loyang. We spent it in the White Horse Monastery, a twenty-minute train ride away. It was established in AD 38 for two Indian monks brought from India by an expedition of nineteen Chinese sent to investigate Buddhism. Han Ming, the emperor, had heard of the influence of Buddhism in neighboring countries and was curious.

China has not merely tolerated varying religious beliefs over the centuries, she actively encouraged the establishment of their orders within her empire. Nearly every civilized religion has at one time or another been freely preached and practiced. This seems to have been inspired less by a desire for spiritual salvation than a search for new ideas. In ancient days it was generally only the clergy of the world who had any education. China gained quite a bit of her scientific information from resident foreign priests and monks and Chinese religious pilgrimages abroad.

We were shown around the White Horse Monastery by a humorous old monk who spoke with the colloquial quips of the professional storyteller. He said that the place originally had been the "Foreign Relations Bureau" of the Han court, where visiting dignitaries were entertained. When the Indian monks came, the officials moved out and handed it over to them. As a mark of respect, the emperor had a temple and pavilion built for their use. The stone floor of the temple was all that remained of the Han period. The present structures were erected later. Buddhist scriptures were translated by means of the Indian monks reading them aloud and the Chinese writing down the sounds phonetically. The Chinese didn't know Sanskrit, and tried to figure out the language on the basis of sound patterns. They didn't do too well, according to Singh, who could read Sanskrit and was familiar with Indian religions. He said much of the translation was incorrect.

The government had started to repair the temple idols, some of them of high artistry. We asked our guide who the little green-faced demon was, being crushed in the hand of a huge Heavenly spirit. He grinned and said: "The Imp of Rightist Reaction."

After a lunch of fried noodles in the village, we walked back along the railway. There wasn't any train due till nine p.m. We did it in three hours and reached the hotel at six. We had dinner with a recent arrival, a young woman doctor from Chengchow, accompanying a couple of epidemic experts from Peking who were on their way to the Sanmen Gorge dam to inspect health conditions. Slim, soft-spoken, graceful, with large expressive eyes, she simply floored friend Singh. He raved she was the best yet. He confided that only the fact that he was engaged to a fine Nepalese girl kept him from going overboard on several occasions during our trip.

Singh and Lin decided to spend a few more days, taking in Kaifeng, Chengchow and possibly Anyang. I had already seen more than I could fully digest. I left Loyang at eight a.m. on the eighteenth of September, reaching Peking at six the following morning. I traveled "hard seat sleeper" and dined on snacks of noodles and meat pies at various station stops. I was home before seven, in time for breakfast with Phoenix and Ya-mei.

VI

BIG LEAP FORWARD

1957-1958

The Chinese are as "racially pure" as the people of any other large society, mixtures in ancient times of many different local tribes, each with their own physical characteristics, then infused by Mongol invaders, Central Asian raiders, Arab traders and — with the advent of European imperialist expansion — Western paraders.

On first arriving I had some difficulty in remembering faces. (Chinese friends have confessed that, to them, "all foreigners look alike".) But it didn't take more than two or three weeks and I was easily recognizing varied, and quite distinctive, features. By the end of the month the Chinese no longer appeared "foreign". Another month after that and I was marveling to myself on how many of them resembled people I knew back home. One day I prevented myself just in time from calling out to a man who, at a quick glance, was the image of my brother-in-law.

I developed a real interest in the movement and blending of people throughout history. At one point I harbored a strong suspicion that Phoenix had gypsy blood, though I could find no basis in my anthropological studies for the presence of Romany caravans in China. I never met a girl with such a passion for moving. She had only to see an attractive vacancy and she was ready to go.

This is a family joke. Actually, we've had only five different homes in the past twenty-five years, which isn't much when you consider the hectic clip at which the new society is developing. I certainly enthusiastically concurred in each of our moves, being a bit of a traveling man myself, in fact in a couple of cases I was responsible for them.

A young woman we knew, who had learned American brashness by spending her teenage years in New York, called to see me. The first time I met her, in 1949, she got us both into hot water, herself literally and me figuratively. I had been home alone one afternoon when a stunning Chinese girl came breezing in, introduced herself as a friend of a friend, and said she heard we had a bathtub — then a relative rarity in Peking. This was true enough, since we were still living in a foreign-style house in the old College of Chinese Studies compound. If I didn't mind, she added pleasantly, she would take a bath, and strolled off before I could close my gaping mouth.

Ten minutes later, Phoenix came home and headed straight for the bathroom. Twenty seconds later, she marched up and confronted me.

"Who is that woman?"

"I never saw her before in my life —"

"Hah!"

I was pure as the driven snow, but it wasn't until the lady herself emerged, pink and fragrant from her bath, and explained who she was, that the suspicious look in Phoenix's eye faded somewhat.

Now, in 1957, this high-voltage beauty was astonishing us again. She was planning to move, she said. Good housing was still pretty scarce, but somehow she had got on to not one house, but two. She asked whether we would be willing to take one of them off her hands. Since the place she offered was more conveniently located to both Phoenix's office and mine, besides being larger, brighter, and with more rooms, we quickly agreed. Rent was not much. All premises where fifteen rooms or more were let for profit had been taken over by the city. You paid your rent directly to the municipal authorities, who gave a fixed share to the former owner over a period of years till the value of his equity was paid off.

Moving was no problem. We had beds, a sofa, two wicker chairs, woven mat rugs, pots and pans, iron heating stoves — very modest. At the same time we had a good foreign-made radio, bought from a departing Westerner, bureaus and clothes hampers (traditional Chinese homes have no closets), and several antique tables and mahogany bookcases. These last I had bought for a pittance in secondhand shops when the wealthy of the old regime were retrenching and flooding the market with beautiful hardwood pieces.

Our main item of kitchen equipment was the stove — a vertical cylinder of sheet iron about three feet high, lined with thin firebrick and cooking with coalballs. We were not encumbered by a refrigerator, since Chinese families buy only whatever perishables they eat that day. China is now manufacturing refrigerators — good but costly — as well as radios, which are good and inexpensive, and you can buy nearly anything you need with "Made in China" labels, most of it of excellent quality. But in the fifties home furnishings of foreigners were a mixture of local and imported products.

It didn't take long to move us. My office sent a small truck and a couple of strong young men, and we finished the job in two trips.

Our new quarters were in another hollow square compound. It must have been very old. On either side of the front gate was a square stone about two feet high. These were mounting blocks, for getting on your horse, or into a sedan chair. The compound was a yard lower than the lane outside, always a sign of age in Peking, for the dust of centuries, while swept out of the courtyards daily, piled up and raised the level of the earthen streets.

Full of large trees and flowering shrubs, it was very pleasant. We were in the outermost courtyard, in a single row of one-story buildings which used to be the servants quarters. The only trouble with the place was that our rooms were paved with large stone flaggings laid directly on the earth. In the damp of spring and early summer, our floors and walls sopped up moisture like a sponge, and we all developed aches in our joints. But houses were hard to come by then, and we stuck it out for several years until we found our present place, which has wooden floors a good three feet off the ground.

Our neighbors — three families living in the handsome inner courtyard — were all connected with civil aviation. The main and best building, facing south, housed our landlord. He had been a manager in the Kuomintang's China National Aviation Company. When the old regime collapsed he had been pressured onto a ship, with various other officials, heading for Taiwan. As the ship was leaving the harbor, he jumped overboard and swam ashore. The People's Republic gave him a position in the new airline at a high salary. He owned quite a bit of real estate in Peking, of which the compound we lived in was part. With him was his wife, a sharp efficient woman thoroughly disliked by the poorer people in our lane for her arrogant manner, an unmarried son who had recently started working in a government office, and a little grandson — the child of a married daughter.

The family in the east wing consisted of a young aeronautical engineer, kept on when the CNAC was taken over, his wife and two kids. Except for a tiny fraction of fervid counter-revolutionaries and crooks, everyone working in the numerous Kuomintang government offices and agencies had been retained when the Communists came to power. The wife was a typical middle-class housewife, rather beefy, and always expensively dressed.

In the west wing lived a bachelor — at least for the moment. A lean good-looking fellow who had been married and divorced, he lived alone, when not being solaced by a young woman who wore high heels and form-fitting gowns. He had a good radio-phonograph combination, a stack of American dance records, and a well-equipped bar. I dropped in for a drink occasionally, and he told me his story.

He had been an airline pilot under the Kuomintang, and had just finished a flight to Hongkong when Chiang Kai-shek fled the mainland. The Communists broadcast a statement that they would welcome all returning airline personnel and would pay bonuses for planes brought back, the price ranging with the size of the plane. He had no illusions about the Kuomintang — "a pack of turds", he called them — and had no desire to spend his days in Taiwan. Besides, the bonus offered was substantial. He drove down to the airport, said he had to test his plane, took off and flew to Shanghai. Not only was he paid for the plane — in gold — but was given a job as a flight instructor with a very good salary in Peking.

He should have been happy, but he wasn't. He had nothing against the new administration — he could see how much better off the people were. But it wasn't the kind of life he was used to. He had no interest in the political study going on. His smartly cut clothes were conspicuous among his casually dressed colleagues. It was hard to rustle up a card game or throw a big party. People were busy. They didn't care much about such things any more. He had his girl friend, of course. No one seemed to mind that they were living together. People only smiled and asked when was he planning to get married. Even his money didn't give him any special status. He could buy expensive canned goods with it, but who wanted food in cans when fresh meat and vegetables were plentiful and cheap?

He was pretty frustrated, but there wasn't anything I could do to help him. It was just part of a process all bourgeois-minded people, including myself, were going through. You had to decide. No one was opposed to fun and games, as such. The Chinese enjoyed their amusements as much as anybody. But it was a question of values, of emphasis. To what did you devote your main energies? What was your primary interest in life? Your personal comforts? Your immediate family? Or did you raise your sights higher and work for your local community, your national community, the world community? True, you could keep your nose clean, go through the motions on your job, say what you felt was expected of you and, on your own time, indulge in all the material pleasures and comforts you wished. You could live that way, no one would stop you, as long as it didn't infringe on the rights of others. Yet, unless you had the hide of a rhinoceros, you couldn't help feeling that most people — your colleagues, your friends, your children — watched you with a pitying scorn.

That was what was disturbing our pilot. What was the good of a little ostentation if no one envied you, or — even worse — thought you vulgar? The braggart, the show-off was like a fish out of water in the new society. The vast majority were moving toward a more civilized and humane way of life. Our pilot was a dying breed. Yet even he might change. I'd seen it happen in worse cases. They suddenly realized that "Serve the People" was the only creed that brought any lasting satisfaction.

Ya-mei started primary school that year. It was two long blocks from the house, about a twenty-minute walk, the way the kids dawdled along. We let her go and come back by herself. She was taller and leggier, and self-sufficient for a girl of seven. She was proud of her textbooks and covered them with fancy paper, keeping them scrupulously clean for two whole weeks. Then artistic doodles and decorations began appearing in the margins and inside the covers. Ya-mei was not the most conscientious pupil in her class.

It worried us a little because she was an only child and our standard of living was higher than that of her average classmate. To prevent her from becoming spoiled we taught her to keep her room clean, to help around the house and, when she was older, to wash her own clothes. She got, if anything, less candy and trinkets than her little pals. We often fed her coarse grains, like sorghum and millet, instead of only highly polished flour and rice. We probably over-did it, but while her grades didn't noticeably improve, she was a normal enough child, and very healthy.

Phoenix was then editing a monthly magazine for the Dramatists Association called *Playscripts*. She did a lot of theater-going in Peking, and I almost always went along. I had been interested in the theater since my days as a lawyer on Broadway, and I liked the friendly, informal atmosphere. We went usually to dress rehearsals or opening nights.

Sometimes a meeting and general discussion would be held backstage after the performance. I would be invited to listen in and once in a while was asked for my opinion. They talked mainly of staging, direction and performance. How to bring out the positive qualities of the hero without making him stuffy; how to show him as human without reducing him to a jelly of indecision and self-doubt. How to point up the villainy of the villain without making him a caricature; how to portray him in depth without turning him into an odd type who was good to his mother. They were aware of the one-dimensional quality of some of their characters but, in trying to round them out with a little flesh and blood, it was all too easy to go to extremes.

I had by then translated half a dozen novels for the Foreign Languages Press and scores of short stories. These on the whole, perhaps because we were able to cull through and pick the best, were of good literary quality. Most dealt with war situations — against the Japanese, against the Kuomintang — and were dramatic and fairly straightforward. The difficulty arose in material concerned with the ideological struggles of the post-Liberation period. To present these well required a thorough rapport with the thoughts and feelings of the workers and peasants constituting eighty to ninety percent of the population. Many of the authors were petty-bourgeois in their background or upbringing and tended to superimpose their own attitudes upon their characters. Or for the sake of suspense they would invent a mental conflict where none existed, at least not typically or to any appreciable extent.

Like everyone else, we were busy. Working in a Chinese office is a pretty demanding affair, with plenty of meetings, some after hours, in addition to regular business. Phoenix nevertheless found time to join an election committee formed by our block association. There was an election of district councilmen all over China that year, the district being a subdivision of the county, as in the USA. The district councilmen, besides running the district, also elected the congresses of the larger cities and the provinces, whose members in turn elected the representatives of the national congress. Members of the district councils held office for two years, provincial, big city and national congressmen four.

The mechanics of it was simple and democratic. In each district, spokesmen for the Communist and other political parties, plus representatives of various people's organizations, got together and worked out a list of nominees, in excess of the number of councilmen to be elected in that particular district. Detailed reports of their qualifications were sent to the block associations within the district. The block associations held a series of meetings — usually in the neighborhood school in the evening after work — where the candidates were discussed. Then the block associations organized election committees — like the one Phoenix belonged to, and sent them to question the candidates and form personal impressions. Sometimes the candidates came and spoke at block association meetings. After the election committee reported back, the voters recommended that certain candidates be dropped and others added. This was passed on to the district nominating commission.

On the basis of these recommendations, the district nominating commission revised the list and returned it to the block associations. More discussions, more recommendations, more revisions. The list kept shuttling back and forth between the nominating commission and the block associations until the majority of the people were satisfied. Although by this time the voters were fairly much in agreement, on election day they could still cross out candidates and write in new ones. All voting was by secret ballot.

Five million deputies were elected to district councils that year, twenty-two percent of them women. Roughly half the original incumbents were returned to office, the rest were new. They included workers, farmers, teachers, doctors, nurses, scientists, technicians, businessmen, religious leaders, members of various political parties and national minority people. Ninety-two percent of all eligible voters took part. In a country of more than 800 million in which every citizen over eighteen — regardless of race, sex, occupation, social origin, religion, education, property status or length of residence — is entitled to vote, that's quite a number.

Although none of the parties proposed their own slate of candidates, a large proportion of those elected to office were members of non-Communist parties. In Shanghai these constituted sixty percent of the municipal congress. They held twenty-three percent of the top posts in the city's bureaus and commissions.

Pre-Liberation China had only two real political parties — the Communist Party and the Kuomintang, the first representing the people, the second representing the landlords and the big bourgeoisie. The rest were not true political parties and had no mass following. They were spokesmen for certain groups and interests — smaller businessmen, intellectuals, civil servants, overseas Chinese. During the Second World War, sickened by Chiang Kai-shek's persistent capitulation to the Japanese and the fascist methods of his Kuomintang government, they tended to unite with the Communist Party in its fight for independence and democracy. Chiang Kai-shek never held any genuine elections, and he kept all important posts in the hands of his own party.

With the advent of the People's Republic, the non-Communist parties were imbued with new life. A Consultative Council was formed in which these parties took part. Its job was to propose and discuss legislation, and to offer comment and criticism of methods of the Communist Party. Members of the non-Communist parties were also elected to the National People's Congress — China's legislative body. Several were appointed to high government posts. The parties had their own clubhouses, held regular discussion and study meetings, and recruited new members.

For a time, they had a considerable growth, membership increasing by eighty percent in 1956. Those who couldn't meet the stringent requirements of the Communist Party but wanted a more active political life joined the other parties. Not all motives were pure and disinterested. A young actor we knew who was dying to become a film director enrolled in one party because some of the members were influential in the movie industry.

Just about that time, however, a few prominent leaders of these parties made scurrilous attacks on the Communist Party and socialism, and were exposed and ridiculed in the mass anti-Rightist campaign. The prestige of the non-Communist parties suffered as a result. Their membership dwindled but they still exist today.

The main current was overwhelmingly toward socialism. An interesting development appeared at the end of 1957 — the movement of intellectuals toward the rural areas. I became aware of it when a pretty girl I was dancing with at a party one Saturday night said with a smile: "Next week at this time I'll probably be sleeping on a *kang*." She explained that she and others from her office — one of the ministries — were leaving on Monday to work on a farm.

All government offices were sending a third of their people to the country for a period of from one to three years. When they returned, the next batch would go. This was a forerunner of a permanent policy of teaching class concepts to intellectuals through periodic stints in factories or on farms. There were several advantages.

In the first place, it brought the white collar lads closer to the people and enhanced their appreciation of the dignity of labor. Most of the middle-aged and older intellectuals — who held the more responsible positions — came from relatively well-to-do families, since these were the only ones who could afford to give their children an education in the old society. They knew little about people who worked with their hands — the very people they were supposed to be serving.

A second advantage was that it brought badly needed trained personnel to the rural areas. With the formation of the big cooperative farms, life was improved, but operations became more involved. A single co-op might contain hundreds of families and control miles of land. There were problems of planning, record keeping, improvement of agricultural technique, the use and maintenance of better and more complex farm implements and machinery. Since the average farmer was only at the stage of learning to read and write, the arrival of well-educated people from the city was welcome. When not working in the fields, they helped with technical problems. In addition they gave part-time courses in a variety of cultural and scientific subjects.

Thirdly, government offices generally were over-staffed. Departments worked just as well, or better, with less people. The Personnel Bureau of the Peking Municipal Government reported that it was doing nicely after having cut down from thirty-eight to eight.

Many of the intellectuals formed a real liking for country life, and asked that their transfer be made permanent. They enjoyed the scenery, the fresh air, they became stronger and healthier. They found that the farmers were fine hospitable people who were happy with the contribution the intellectuals were making. They felt closer to the masses and the revolution.

But at the end of their stint most of them would be coming back, either to their original jobs or to other administrative work. By November 810,000 had gone. The figure reached a million by the end of the year.

It wasn't only government staffers — across the country all sorts of people were turning out and getting things done, without waiting for money, special machinery or trained personnel. Between October 1957 and January 1958, for example, one hundred million co-op farmers pitched in and dug irrigation ditches and built check dams, converting nearly 26 million acres into irrigated land. In four months they brought water to more land than their ancestors had been able to irrigate in the previous 2,500 years.

I managed to get in on one of those projects when they built the Ming Tombs Reservoir. About twenty miles northwest of Peking was a wide bowl of arid mountains. When the rains came in July and August water rolled down the bare slopes in torrents, swamping some 50,000 acres in the lowland. It happened almost every year. Only the tombs of the Ming emperors, high and dry on the mountainsides, escaped damage. Thirteen monarchs who reigned between the fourteenth and seventeenth centuries are buried here in magnificent structures that cost fortunes in terms of money and human labor. That was China's old society — lavish extravagance for dead rulers and dire poverty for live subjects.

When the people themselves came to power they decided to put an end to the annual scourge by building a dam across the mouth of the Tungshan Gorge. But this was a big project. Where was the labor to come from? And the steam shovels and bulldozers and dump trucks? Thousands of projects were in the course of construction in China, and all needed machinery. The dam was tentatively scheduled for the Third Five-Year-Plan, that is, between 1963 and 1967.

Why wait? said the farmers in the neighborhood of the Ming Tombs. Since the job was too big for them to handle alone, they asked the various organizations in and around Peking whether they could help. The response was tremendous. Soon there were 120,000 people working right around the clock in three eight-hour shifts of 40,000 each. All the labor was voluntary, at no charge to the project. Each office or enterprise sent, in relays, groups of volunteers — not exceeding ten percent of their personnel — for periods of ten days. During this time the volunteers continued to draw their regular salaries, while their jobs were taken over by the remaining ninety percent of their colleagues. Farmers got the same work points for laboring at the dam as they would have received if working in their agricultural co-ops — these determined the share they received in their farm's annual income. Army men participated as part of their duty, at no extra compensation.

Ordinary tools — mostly picks and shovels and carrying poles with baskets suspended at either end — were either loaned or contributed. Electrical equipment had to be paid for, but its installation, including all the wiring, was done free by technicians in their spare time.

Of all the factors going into making the project a success, unquestionably the most vital was the enthusiasm of the volunteers. I did a stint with some people from my office, and it was an astonishing experience. Men and women who ordinarily did nothing more vigorous than tickling a typewriter or taking half a turn in a swivel chair were suddenly shoveling earth and toting gravel in baskets slung from shoulder poles, day and night, rain or shine. It was tough heavy work, but what with the singing and wisecracks and high spirits all around, you thought you were at some sort of jamboree rather than at the site of one of the largest earthen dams in the world.

Our cuisine consisted of gruel, bits of pickled vegetable, and coarse corn muffins, but we wolfed them down as if they were epicurean delights. We slept eight in a tent, with only pallets of pine branches between us and the ground, but our slumber was deep and dreamless. I heard many a white collar worker say he never realized manual labor was so difficult — and so satisfactory. The camaraderie and drive knocked some of the stuffiness out of the stuffed shirts, and made everyone better at his job when he got back to his desk.

In less than five months the dam was finished. Fifty thousand acres of land which before were constantly hit by floods now came under controlled irrigation. Local grain output was raised by 27,000 tons a year. The value of the increase in the first year alone covered the entire cost of construction. The reservoir was also used for fish breeding and generating electricity.

Ecological and medical problems are also tackled on a mass public participation basis. An intensive two-year campaign (1957-58) was waged against the "Four Pests" — flies, mosquitoes, rats and sparrows. I was one of the warriors in the Peking battle against the birds, which demonstrated the ingenuity and organizational skill of the Chinese.

Sparrows were listed for extermination because every year at harvest they descended on the fields in droves and consumed large quantities of grain. A spring day in 1958 was set as the time for the final crushing assault. On every building, in every street, in front yards, in back yards, people stood or sat and waved white cloths and shouted, whistled, or beat on pans, whenever sparrows appeared.   I was perched on a high garden wall with a pillowcase, and I flapped and whooshed for hours.

Confused and hungry, the birds plunged into net snares, alighted on limed branches, ate poisoned food laid out in areas purposely left open. Thousands upon thousands were eliminated that day.

Later it was found that our enthusiasm had been misdirected, and that sparrows destroy certain insects which do much more harm to crops than the birds themselves. The authorities, with characteristic candor, admitted that they were in error, and the birds were given a reprieve, though measures are still taken to keep them out of fields when the grain is gathered. Bedbugs were substituted for sparrows as the fourth pest. The experience reminded the Chinese of the need to maintain an ecological balance.

They do this pretty well. Although wide use is being made of chemicals, the main fertilizer is organic waste — human and animal manures, sewage and garbage. Human waste is carefully hoarded and collected. In the cities and towns big tank trucks syphon it out of public toilets. If you have a cesspool, as we do, you can expect a visit every spring from an organization which cleans it out, free of charge. In Peking, the stuff is carted to special areas in the outskirts where it, together with the city's garbage, is processed into fertilizer. Some cities, like Shanghai, have huge mains piping the waste directly to communes miles away.

With the rats (and mice), flies and mosquitoes we had an even harder job, but we did very well. The favorite stamping grounds for city rodents are the sewers. First we drove them out of homes and buildings by plugging their holes, setting traps, spreading poisoned bait. Then, on a given night, powder which emits poisonous smoke when ignited was lit and lowered into the sewers, and every surface opening tightly sealed. The same routine was repeated a few nights later, and then again several nights after that. Everything depends on full intelligent public participation, for the operation must be coordinated to the minute throughout a city of millions. You don't utterly destroy the rodent population. No one has discovered how to do that yet. But you sure as hell discourage them, and if you repeat the process periodically you can keep them down to a minimum.

A slightly different approach is used with flies and mosquitoes. Flies are attacked first in the grub and larvae stages. Kids know where to dig them out — in soft spots along the bottoms of outer walls, and a lot of other places that I would never think of. Swatting is taken seriously, against those flies which manage to get born. People are embarrassed if you see a fly in their home, and the whole family, and the guests, promptly zero in on the offending creature.

With mosquitoes, everyone checks around his own house, and lane or street, to make sure there are no puddles or water-filled cans or jugs in which they can breed. Stagnant pools anywhere are flushed out or filled in. Several nights during the summer at fixed hours you fumigate your house with smoke bombs, keeping the doors and windows closed while you stay out in the garden. Then you air the house and let the surviving mosquitoes, if any, stagger out, and you go inside and shut all the doors and windows again. At this point, planes come skimming over, spraying insecticide. About half an hour later there is an all-clear signal and you emerge into a virtually bugless evening.

The glue that sticks all this together is the neighborhood committees — mostly retired oldsters and housewife volunteers. They are part of a city-wide organization, and notify you of the time schedules, issue the smoke bombs (at a few cents a pack), supervise the operations, and check the results. Quite efficient. The kids help a lot, as messengers doing most of the legwork. They get a big charge out of it, and so do the adults. It is very satisfying being part of a positive community action, particularly when you feel you are helping get rid of dirt and disease, quickly and cheaply. Of course the campaign against the Four Pests is never-ending, but it gets easier and more effective with each succeeding year.

This "do-it-yourself-with-what-you've-got" approach was spreading like wildfire all over China, always carefully watched and encouraged by the Communist Party. Someone would have what looked like a good idea. He would need time or money or conditions to try it out. These, the local Party organization would provide. If it worked, it would be tried on a somewhat larger scale. If that also succeeded, a complete report would be sent to the Central Committee of the Party in Peking. After investigation, the CC might decide to introduce it nationally.

One of the most important developments in modern Chinese history — the advent of the communes — occurred in just this manner. It began in Honan Province early in 1958. Honan for centuries had been tormented by floods and droughts. Determined to put an end to these disasters once and for all, the high level cooperative farms to which most of the rural population belonged began to merge. This offered obvious advantages in dealing with the vagaries of a river. The co-ops on the lower reaches couldn't do much without the help of those on the upper. But they discovered other benefits as well. With manpower and capital pooled into large units, they were able to allocate their personnel more rationally and invest in costlier projects. They could make more appropriate use of their fields, according to soil conditions. The coal in the hills of one cooperative farm, for example, could be combined with the iron ore of another to make iron and manufacture farm implements.

Mergers proceeded apace. Under the guidance of the Honan provincial committee of the Communist Party several thousand more communes — as people then began to call them — were formed on an
experimental basis. In addition to agriculture, the communes did
small-scale manufacturing — mainly of things they needed themselves —
set up their own supply and distribution units, ran their own schools and
their own militias. They organized dining rooms, tailoring and mending
groups, laundries, homes for the aged, medical dispensaries, maternity
clinics, nurseries, kindergartens. Women were freed from much of their
household drudgery and could take a fuller part in the work and
administration.

I was eager to see them in action in the province where they were
born, but I had to delay my visit for several weeks because of the arrival
in China of A.L. Wirin, defense counsel in the Powell case. I was in
the legal section of a committee of Chinese and foreigners in Peking
supporting Bill Powell, his wife Sylvia, and Julian Schuman, charged in
a San Francisco federal court with conspiracy to commit sedition. As
spelled out in the indictment this consisted of publishing in *China
Monthly* (formerly *Weekly*) *Review,* the English language magazine
founded in Shanghai by Bill's father, statements regarding the use of
bacteriological weapons by US forces against Korea and China during
the Korean War, of revealing the extent of US casualties, of exposing
American stalling at the armistice negotiations, and of suggesting that
Chiang Kai-shek was corrupt! The charges were brought in 1956 when
the China Lobby — big business and missionaries who had been shown
the door by the new regime — were hysterically fulminating against the
Peking government. By then Julian and the Powells had closed down
the *Review* and returned to the States.

The defense of the accused was truth. They said they could and
would prove everything they had published in the *Review.* But they
needed a fair chance to prepare their case. For a year and a half defense
counsel had been struggling, against strong opposition on the part of the
US government, for an opportunity to interview potential Chinese
witnesses. The State Department had persistently refused to give Wirin
a passport for China. It broke down only when the judge threatened
to throw the case out if the government continued obstructing the
defendants' constitutional right to secure evidence in their own behalf.

Through the efforts of Rewi Alley and Tang Ming-chao, a friend of
Bill and Sylvia who is today an Undersecretary at the United Nations,

Wirin was able to meet over forty people in Peking, Nanking and Shanghai willing to testify in their behalf. Character witnesses included a former president of the World Council of Churches, the Chairman of the National Committee of Protestant Churches, the Secretary General of the Chinese YMCA, and an Episcopal Bishop. There were military men ready to identify the dog tags taken from the bodies of GIs killed in Korea. (Long after the name, rank and serial numbers of these men were published in *China Monthly Review,* the US Defense Department continued to torment their parents and wives with false hope by listing them as "missing in action".) Scientists and civilians by the score were prepared to come forward with eye-witness accounts, special bomb canisters carrying insect hosts, and reports of elaborate tests, to prove the commission by the US of germ warfare.

Wirin was anxious to get these people and their evidence before the court, but the US government refused to conclude a judicial assistance pact with China. These pacts are standard international practice. Without them some countries — Switzerland, for example — won't permit a foreign lawyer even to interview a potential witness. No country will allow its citizens to give depositions or go into a foreign court in the absence of such an agreement. Since the judge of the Federal court trying the case had written to the Chinese Ministry of Justice requesting that judicial assistance be granted, the Chinese delegate raised the question of a proper pact at the ambassadorial talks in Geneva. The US representative refused to consider it. Premier Chou En-lai commented on the inconsistency.

"The proposal that judicial assistance be given came, in the first instance, from American judicial authorities," he said. "The Chinese government is quite willing to see this brought about. But until the US government changes its inflexible and hostile attitude, all efforts by the Chinese government are in vain."

He scoffed at State Department insinuations that China was insisting on a judicial assistance agreement as a means of forcing diplomatic recognition, and indicated that this was the least of China's concerns regarding the US. "The central problem in Sino-American relations today," said Chou, "is not that China wants American recognition, but that America wants China to recognize as legal America's occupation of Chinese territory. China will exist and continue to grow whether America recognizes us or not."

Wirin returned to San Francisco empty-handed. Stalemated, the case hung fire. Eminent scientists from half a dozen European countries who had made on-the-spot investigations of germ warfare in China and Korea offered to testify. Dr. Theodore Rosebury published his book about the extensive bacteriological warfare experiments conducted in Camp Dietrich, Maryland, in which he personally took part. Protestations of innocence from Washington grew weaker. After dragging on for five years, the case was finally dropped by the US government in 1961.

Mr. Wirin came to China in 1958 and I had left Shanghai in 1948. It struck me that I hadn't had any occasion to use my legal knowledge in ten years. Among the Chinese I knew, or even heard about, there had been a strange lack of court proceedings. One member of the Powell defense committee was a Chinese lawyer who was also on the faculty of a university law school. When I mentioned this to him, he laughed.

"We don't have much litigation here."

"But surely there are civil and criminal cases?"

"Ninety percent are considered contradictions among the people and are settled by the people themselves, through their own committees."

"And the other ten percent?"

"These are limited to serious crimes like treason, counter-revolution, murder, rape or arson. They are acts by enemies of society and must be heard in court."

"What if one of the parties in the ninety-percent category doesn't agree with the decision of the local committee?"

"He can insist on taking it to court."

"Are there many such proceedings?"

"Very few, because there aren't many civil disputes in the first place."

"How come?"

"We're oriented toward community ownership and enterprise rather than individual expansion. There are no private businesses or corporations, no way you can personally make a profit on other people's labor. In the cities you can own your own house and the lot on which it stands, but you can't rent them. If you sell, the price must be approved by the municipal housing authority. In the country communes you own the materials that went into the home you erected, but you can't sell or rent the buildings, and you and your descendants have only a use-right to your so-called 'private plot'. So there isn't much to dispute about."

"Are you saying there's no personal property at all?"

"Oh, no. Your clothing, household furnishings, bike, tools, books and the like all belong to you. You can sell them or give them away, or dispose of them in a will."

"I can't believe there are never any squabbles over inheritances." I must have looked sceptical, for my Chinese lawyer friend laughed again.

"Sure there are squabbles now and then, but we try to get equitable rather than strictly legal settlements. If a man dies without a will, his survivors are urged to dispose of his property according to their financial positions, in other words give more to whoever needs it most. Even if he leaves a will, priority is given to surviving spouse, children and parents, in that order. Any testamentary provision which would deprive them of necessary support would be disregarded."

"Don't husbands and wives ever fight, or separate, or want to get divorced?"

"Yes, some do, though the rate is low. Most of the frictions which cause marital dissension — money problems, drink, moral laxness — are relatively rare here."

"But suppose, for whatever reason, a couple are determined to get a divorce?"

"The neighborhood committee and the organizations for which the husband and wife work do everything they can to effect a reconciliation. If that fails, the local council grants the divorce."

"Suppose one party wants the divorce and the other doesn't?"

"Usually grass-roots efforts can persuade them to give the marriage another chance. But if the party demanding the divorce is adamant, the case goes to court."

"What happens to the children when a divorce is approved?"

"In matrimonial matters first consideration is always given to the wife and children. Regardless of blame both parents after divorce must contribute to their support. Custody is also determined on the basis of what is best for the kids."

"Can a wife get alimony?"

"Yes, to the extent that she needs it for her own and the children's support. The alimony can be cut or eliminated if she remarries."

"What about personal injuries? Are there negligence or malpractice cases?"

"Not court cases. Personal injury matters are settled by arbitration. The party at fault has to compensate for any financial loss, but nothing more. An injured office or factory worker has complete medical coverage and his pay never stops. But a member of a rural commune, though his medical bills would be paid under the rural cooperative medical insurance scheme, would have no income without working. The guilty party would have to compensate him for that. There are no punitive damages, however, or special damages for pain and suffering. If there was malice or criminal negligence, the defendant might be subject to criminal prosecution, but that wouldn't affect the remuneration he would have to pay. The local committee, or traffic police, or whatever organizations happen to be involved, are able to settle all questions of fact, and the law itself is plain. There's no need to go to court."

"What is the procedure in those cases actually tried?"

"The judge, aided by two assessors selected from the local community, hears all the evidence in informal proceedings. Anyone can testify. He may go to the scene of the dispute or crime and conduct his own interviews and investigations. Before reaching a decision he consults with everyone concerned — the litigants or accused, their local committees, the places for which they work. The case may also be discussed at a mass meeting if it has some educational value or special interest to the general public. The judge's opinion isn't final. It must be approved by the local government council or congress, and even this can be appealed to a higher court or governmental body."

"Suppose one of the parties wants a lawyer? Can he get one?"

"Yes, free of charge, on request, though a lawyer's really not necessary. Legal procedure is simple. There are no rules of evidence. People can say anything they like. The judge makes his own evaluation of their testimony. Anyone can plead on the parties' behalf, or testify as to their character and past record."

"Not much point in training lawyers, then, is there?"

"We still need people with legal knowledge for judicial, security and administrative work. We have law schools with regular three-year courses. But there are no jobs for lawyers as such, in the Western sense."

I suppose I hadn't thought much about courts and lawyers and litigation because there was so little of that sort of thing. In all my years in China, only two or three people I knew personally ever became involved with the law.

The first was Little Liu, a boy about seventeen in my lane who always was playing hookey. He took up with a few others like himself, and they hung around, smoking and playing cards. Then one day he was caught walking off with a neighbor's radio. His parents, his teacher, and members of the neighborhood committee urged him to reform.

He was sent back to school with a reprimand.

For several weeks Little Liu behaved. Then his parents discovered among his clothes a jacket that didn't belong to him. They took him and the jacket down to the police station. He admitted he "borrowed" it from a schoolmate, but said he had "forgotten" to mention it to him. The police lectured him on good citizenship and let him go.

The next time, a neighbor returning from night shift caught him scaling a courtyard wall. He was escorted to police headquarters. There Little Liu was confronted with several other boys and a man named Hsia, all of whom had also been arrested. Only then did he confess that he was a member of their gang.

Hsia, a former petty official in the old Kuomintang government, had never lost his penchant for parasitic living. He worked during the day in one of the department stores, where he pilfered whenever he got the chance. Hsia made friends with the idle boys, flattered them and loaned them old books about ancient robber gangs bound by pledges of "brotherhood". Hsia fostered in the boys the notion that they too were "heroes" whose thievery was "gallant". He took the bulk of their plunder, giving them only small handouts as "awards".

When Little Liu wavered after his first two adventures and wanted to quit, the benign Hsia suddenly turned nasty. He and the older boys threatened reprisals against Little Liu and his family unless he continued to take orders. Now that the gang was apprehended, the boy told the whole story.

A mass meeting was held on the large playing field of a branch of Peking Teachers College, a few blocks from where we live. I went with Phoenix. Everyone brought his or her own little folding bench or stool. Nearly three thousand people from in and around the neighborhood had congregated. It was a bright sunny afternoon in September. Members of the neighborhood committee, a senior police official, and representatives from the city's eastern district Communist Party committee and government sat at a long table on a raised platform at one end of the field.

The meeting was opened by the chairman of the neighborhood committee. He said the city had been little troubled by crime, but lately there had been an outcropping of thievery. A small gang in our neighborhood had been broken, and the masses were being asked to discuss the case and recommend a disposition.

Hsia was brought onto the platform in handcuffs, guarded by two security men, and was led to one side. He stood with lowered head. "Down with the criminal Hsia!" yelled the crowd. "Down with the corrupters of youth!"

One by one, three of the boys who had been arrested stepped up to the microphone. They told how they had joined the gang, what they had stolen, and how Hsia had masterminded their operations.

Little Liu spoke last. He said school was boring, and his parents never seemed to have much time for him. He was fascinated by the story books Hsia loaned him about brigands. When Hsia told him that stealing required daring and skill, it made him feel important. Yet he knew it was wrong and wanted to quit, particularly after the second time he was caught and the police spoke to him so nicely. But the gang threatened him, and he hadn't had the nerve to expose them.

A lady from the neighborhood committee then addressed the meeting. She said she felt the committee was partly to blame. They knew the boys were behaving badly, and they hadn't talked with them often enough, or reminded the parents to pay more attention. The committee thought Hsia should be given the full penalty of the law as a criminal corrupter of youth. The boys should go for brief periods of labor reform.

"All reactionaries will come to a bad end!" a girl's clear young voice rang out. Three thousand people, shouting in unison, echoed her cry.

A teacher from the boy's school said he and his colleagues should have noticed when the boys' grades remained low. This seldom is due to any inherent stupidity, he said. Usually it means that something is troubling the student.

The father of one of the older boys spoke. He said originally he had been a poor peasant. He joined the people's army and fought the Japanese, then helped drive out Chiang Kai-shek. After the People's Government was formed he and his parents were given land under the Land Reform. Later, he had been sent to school and now was a technician in a Peking factory.

The revolution had changed his whole life. He was very happy. But he had forgotten that while the landlords and bosses and running dogs of the old regime had been defeated as a class, they still existed as individuals and some were very reactionary. Also, new bourgeois-minded people sometimes developed among even workers and former peasants. His own son had fallen victim to one of them. He felt that he had been remiss in the boy's upbringing.

"We fought the revolution so that our kids wouldn't have to endure the miseries we did," he said. "But if we want to retain our freedom we must keep alive the revolutionary traditions of class struggle, hard work, self-reliance, and serving the people."

In conclusion he said he thought it would be good for the boys to work for a time in a village of some commune. They would learn the fine qualities of China's peasants, and see how much sweat went into producing the food they ate and the clothes they wore. They'd see how indispensable community effort was. They'd be ashamed to take anything that didn't belong to them ever again.

As to Hsia, his kind are the scum of the earth. Killing would be too good for him.

Finally, a representative of the east district Communist Party committee got up. He said he agreed with the opinions of the masses with regard to the boys. There was no need for them to go to trial. No criminal charges would be brought against them or placed upon their record. They would go to an outlying commune village to work for three to six months. When the villagers (the production team) felt they had their thinking straightened out, they could come home. If any of them required more than six months, he could stay longer, subject to the approval of the east district government.

Hsia was a different proposition. He had committed a serious breach of the law and public morality. He would be formally tried, and the recommendations of the masses would be relayed to the tribunal. The Party and government representatives did not agree that he should be executed. "The old society turned men into demons, the new society turns demons into men." Hsia should be deprived of his liberty for several years, but he should be educated and given a chance to rehabilitate himself. It would be up to the court to try him and determine his sentence.

On behalf of the east district Party committee and government, the representative said, he wanted to thank the people for their participation. He hoped that, as masters of the new society, they would continue to educate their children and expose criminals in accordance with the principles laid down by Chairman Mao.

Any further questions? No? Then, meeting adjourned!

Hsia was led away, the boys went home to pack, and Phoenix and I filed out with the slowly dispersing crowd. Young people were talking animatedly. The older folks nodded and expressed approval.

"What exactly is going to happen to those boys?" I asked Phoenix.

"When they get to the village they'll be boarded out among different families, ones that have boys the same age. They'll live, eat and work together with their hosts. They'll earn the same work points and take part in the same activities as the village boys — political study, sports, theatricals . . . what have you. The only difference is that they won't be allowed to leave the village."

"Mightn't they run away?"

"They might. But where would they run to? If they came home, their parents would only send them back. Besides, they'll probably enjoy it."

I met Little Liu in our lane four months later. His face was ruddy brown, his body had filled out.

"When did you get back?"

"Two weeks ago. They said my thinking is O.K. now. I put in a good day's work and am considerate of others. They gave me a great send-off. We had peanuts and apples and pears. I helped pick that fruit myself. Say, you should see our pears. They're enormous. This big!"

"So you really liked it?"

"It was super. I'm going out there again during summer vacation. They invited me. I'm making a radio for the boys."

"And you're back at school?"

"Yep."

"How's it going?"

Little Liu grinned cockily. "A snap. Nothing to it."

The second case I had personal knowledge of involved a "niece" of Phoenix. She showed up at the house one day in the early fifties and introduced herself. Questioning showed that she was the daughter of a third cousin and came from the town in Kwangsi where Phoenix's family originated. At sixteen she ran away from her feudal home and joined the people's army then demolishing the forces of Chiang Kai-shek and his warlord allies. She was demobilized in Peking at the time of Liberation and given a job in the municipal government. Learning, a few years later, that her "aunt" was also in Peking, she looked us up.

A pleasant but rather plain girl, she surprised us by marrying a strikingly handsome boy. A young technician, bright, ambitious, he proved to be a good husband and good father to their two children, a boy and a girl. They visited us on the average of once a month.

Then, a few years ago, the boy, now a man in his thirties and still handsome, began to change. He was surly to his wife and rough on the kids. He stayed out late, and some nights didn't come home at all. Though he persistently denied it, there was, of course, another woman. Our niece demanded a divorce. She said he was never home anyway and was a bad influence on the children. He didn't mind letting things go on as they were. Why should he? He had a home, his clothes were washed and mended, his meals were cooked. And he could still stay away when he was "busy".

Neighbors and people from both of their offices urged giving the marriage another chance. An attempt was made, but the man kept sliding back into his old ways. Angrily, the niece said she would take the matter to court if it could not be settled by agreement. The parties and representatives from their places of work got together and evolved the terms of a divorce. He moved out, she kept the children, and he contributed a fixed amount monthly to their support. The kids, both teenagers, could visit him freely.

They don't see him very often, since their sympathies are with their mother. He has since remarried, to the lady he claimed didn't exist. The niece has remained single. She seems reasonably content, busy with her children and her own career.

The third legal proceeding with which I was familiar would have been a negligence case in the United States. The "defendant" was the son of our steel-making friend Yao, who spent so many years in America. He gave the poor boy the unlikely name of "Skippy". It had to be rendered into something more intelligible in Chinese.

They lived out near the Summer Palace in the western suburbs, where there is still a lot of farmland interspersed among the universities and institutes. One day, when Skippy was about twelve, he went tearing hell-for-leather down a lane on his bike. At a turn, he misjudged his distance and side-swiped an old man, knocking him down and twisting his knee.

People hurried around, a contrite Skippy included, and carried him home.

Old Sung lived alone in a small bungalow not far from the Steel Institute, where the Yaos resided. He was a widower, and his children were grown up and working in other parts of the country. He refused all of their invitations to join them, preferring to stay in the Peking where he was born, near the coal mine from which he was retired and his old cronies. A pension, at eighty percent of his last wage, more than covered his needs.

The neighborhood committee, a person from the Steel Institute, someone from Skippy's school, the boy himself, and his parents met to discuss the case. Skippy admitted he was at fault and apologized. The old man suffered no financial loss. His pension payments continued as usual. As a retired worker he was entitled to free medical care. But, laid up with a sprained knee, he couldn't do the household chores or go shopping.

It was decided that Skippy should stop by twice a day, on his way to school and on his return. In the morning he would sweep, clean, boil the water, fill the thermoses, and cook breakfast. In the afternoon he would do the shopping and anything else the old man required. This arrangement would last until Sung recovered.

Skippy started the next day. Before long, he and his patient were quite friendly. Sung told him thrilling stories about his days in the coal mine, the strikes they waged against the foreign owners, how they dealt with the musclemen the bosses employed, how he joined the guerrillas and fought the "locusts", as he called Chiang Kai-shek's ravaging armymen.

The boy told him about school — which subjects he liked and which teachers he didn't like, and who his friends were, and of the disagreements he had with his parents. The old man gave him patient mature advice, teaching him to widen his petty childish viewpoint.

They grew very fond of each other. Sung always kept tidbits for the boy to eat. Skippy got into the habit of doing his homework in the old man's bungalow after he finished his afternoon's errands. The two would sit in quiet contentment as the boy pored over his books and the old man read his newspaper, the smoke from his pipe filtering through the sunbeams shining in the west windows. Skippy called Old Sung "Grandpa", and the old man called him "Child".

By the end of a month or so Old Sung could hobble about on a cane. At the end of two months he was almost as good as new. But Skippy went on visiting several times a week, right up to the time he left for college.

These three are the only instances I recall of people I knew who were involved in anything that might in America be called a legal case. My own personal involvement was with the Powell affair, and that, strictly speaking, was an American, rather than a Chinese, proceeding.

Some weeks after Wirin's departure I was able to arrange my trip to Honan, where the communes were born. In the summer of 1958 I traveled with a young photographer from *China Pictorial* named Hsieh, who was looking for material on the same subject. We went first to Hsuchang, an ancient city in the center of the province, and spent the night in the compound of the special region Party committee. It was situated on a square half-acre of land that rose abruptly some twenty or thirty yards out of the surrounding plain, with four almost vertical sides. Legend had it that this had been the headquarters of Tsao Tsao, a third-century general and statesman, one of those dynamic figures who keep cropping up in Chinese history, and who had become the subject of centuries of debate. Was he a hero or villain? For a long time he had been condemned as a mass murderer, and was always cast in that role in the numerous historical operas in which he appeared. Recently some scholars, notably Kuo Mo-jo, China's famed historian and archeologist, were claiming that Tsao Tsao had been wronged, that he had in fact played a positive part. Either way, he was a familiar figure to all Chinese theater-goers, and Hsuchang was proud to be the site of his old stamping grounds.

The Party committee was generous and helpful. They provided us with a jeep and driver, and one of their cadres to show us around. We set out the next morning for Two Temples, a township in the county of Hsiangcheng. Two Temples had formerly contained several high level farming co-ops. Recently it had become one of thirteen sub-communes in a commune embracing the entire county.

Though not all communes were as large, their general structure was similar. A dozen to several dozen families formed a team. A dozen or so teams constituted a brigade. A dozen or so brigades made up the commune — which could be anywhere from a township to an entire county in size. The brigade leadership also functioned as village government. The commune leadership, depending on the area the commune embraced, governed either the township or the county.

Even before we reached Two Temples we could see the enthusiasm the formation of the communes had generated. As we rolled along in our jeep, I was struck by a series of little signs that lined one side of the road, each carrying a few words of a slogan, like the Burma Shave ads you used to see along US highways.

There were as many women as men in the fields we drove through, all bright with red banners. On arches of boughs built over the road were announcements by brigades challenging each other. The harvest was in and they were turning the soil to make it more fertile for the next planting. The brigades were vying to finish their respective fields first.

At my request we stopped our jeep and walked into one of the fields. It was like stepping onto a stage. The brigade members — mostly young — were working steadily and fast in a long moving row, turning over the soil with spades.

Behind them, actors and actresses, in full make-up and historical costumes, were singing rhythmic arias, to the accompaniment of pounding drums and cymbals, while dancing around on stilts — a peculiarity of the local opera. This gave the shovel-wielders added vigor, though they didn't seem to need any encouragement. They were chatting and laughing as they worked, some of them singing along with the performers.

We were introduced to the brigade's Communist Party secretary. He looked harassed and tired. He said they had estimated the earth-turning job would take two weeks, but the kids had made up their minds to finish in one. It looked like they were going to do it. They had been working in shifts, twenty-four hours a day for three days, and were already more than halfway through. The brigade's Party committee had been begging them to slow down, but in vain. Everyone was determined to make the communes a success.

A joyous frenzy of energy and creativity, soon to become known to the world as the Big Leap Forward, was sweeping China. Much of it was unscientific and unpractical.

In Kwangtung Province, dizzied by the sudden large increase in rice harvests, some communes allowed their members to eat as much as they liked in the public dining rooms, free of charge. They soon consumed not only the expanded yields but much of the reserves. In many places, while harvests were honestly calculated according to the condition of the crops in the fields, they were less than anticipated when actually gathered. Too many commune members were busy digging irrigation ditches, building dams, making iron, and engaged in the many new collective enterprises the communes had made possible. "Over-populated" China was suffering from a labor shortage. Crops went to seed, toppled in the fields, got soaked on the threshing grounds. The difference between estimated and final harvest figures was not always corrected.

Not all the mistakes were innocent. Many were instigated by false leaders. Men who much preferred private enterprise adopted a complete reversal of tactics when their initial obstruction of the communes failed. They deliberately exaggerated the communes' accomplishments and fanned every utopian tendency. They made wild claims about industrial progress as well, hoping to discredit the Big Leap when the truth became known.

In this they failed for, on balance, it was found that the gain exceeded the losses. For the first time in history China was able comprehensively to control her floods, drain her fields, and provide irrigation when needed. Thousands of miles of dams, dykes, canals and roads were built. New agricultural techniques were discovered and spread. Small home-grown mills and workshops sprouted like mushrooms. There were many inventions, some mechanization, even a little automation. In science and the arts there was a lively ferment of new methods, new ideas. China had made another qualitative leap.

At the Two Temples Sub-Commune this leap was unmistakable. Tobacco and wheat output had risen considerably. Everyone was delighted, the women most of all. They were taking part in everything — agriculture, industry, the schools, the militia. At least half the trainees I saw in the Two Temples iron foundry and farm implements factory were girls.

For the first time most families had a little money left over, after buying their necessities. People were beginning to accumulate savings. "In four or five years you'll have quite a pile," I said to one of the women jokingly. "What will you do with it all?"

"Buy more machinery for the commune."

"Don't you want anything for yourself?"

She hesitated. "Maybe I'll buy a car. Walking to and from the fields wastes so much time."

"I'll come and see you and take a ride."

"Don't bother," she laughed. "I'll drive to Peking and pick you up."

New horizons had brought new outlooks. Women, in the old society the oppressed of the oppressed, were blossoming out. They wore gay cotton prints to the fields, they took more pains with their appearance. One of them recited a jingle she had composed. I wrote it down:

Nurseries, kindergartens, tailor shops,
You don't do the cooking or feed pigs the slops.
Machines make the clothing and grind fine the flour,
When you give birth you're cared for every hour.
Freed from household drudgery let's produce more every day,
And drive ahead to communism, it isn't far away.

Over-optimistic, of course. Communism is still a long way off. Some of the measures were impractical, a bit utopian, at that stage. But there was no doubt that the communes had lent wings to the mind and the spirit of China's millions.

We climbed into our jeep again and took off for Yuhsien County, where 9,000 homemade furnaces were going full blast, turning out thousands of tons of iron per day. People had known for a long time that the Yuhsien hills contained coal and iron, but they had no skilled workers, no decent roads, no large investment capital.

The communes had brought a unique strength — huge concentrations of well-organized manpower, people who had learned to think boldly and big. In September, after the harvests were in, 150,000 commune members — half the county's working population — moved into the hills. First they built a highway, 250 miles in eight days. They dug coal and iron ore with pick and shovel. Transport consisted of anything that could carry. Trucks, rubber-tired mule carts, wooden-wheeled ox carts, wheelbarrows, people with shoulder poles and baskets, traveled in endless procession up and down the slopes, bringing iron ore and coke to the flame-belching furnaces, food and supplies to the busy workers.

The furnaces were miracles of ingenuity. Guided by only a few dozen persons with any technical training, the farm folk in two or three weeks learned to improvise furnaces and blowers that were cheap, quickly built — and that made iron. At the time of our visit a large variety of furnaces were in operation, producing from half to three or four tons each, daily. Most of them had thick earthen walls and used little or no firebrick. Some cost only twenty *yuan* apiece to build. The majority of the blowers were hand-operated. Teams of two, in relays, rotated vertical wheels connected to the motors of the blowers by leather belts — the cow hair still on them more often than not.

In all of these operations women played a considerable part. I saw them digging ore, toting it in big baskets slung from poles supported on their shoulders — one woman in front, the other behind. Others sat on the ground pulverising chunks of ore with small hammers. Many tended the furnaces, from the mixing to the tapping, and pouring the iron into moulds.

The policy was to give the men the heavier jobs and the women the lighter. But in one "mill" of 500 people the women outnumbered the men three to two, and they insisted on running the whole show. Ranging in age from thirteen to thirty-five, the women were strong, healthy and mostly single. They had tried to restrict their volunteers to young women with no family ties, but this had proved difficult.

One lady in her sixties had demanded that they teach her to make iron. She said she had learned to do everything there was to do on a farm, she didn't see why she couldn't learn to tend a blast furnace. After much persuasion, they finally induced her to go home. Another woman came — she was only forty-eight — and refused to leave. She just wouldn't take no for an answer. They had to keep her on as a cook.

I asked Wei, an unmarried girl of twenty-one who was leader of the "mill", what brought her into the rugged hills. She said she had learned to read and write. When the co-ops merged into communes and the drive to expand industry started, she was among the first to volunteer to learn to make iron and steel. As a Communist, she felt she should set an example. Before long, she mastered all the processes, from prospecting for ore to casting the pig iron ingots. Recently, the women had elected her leader. She loved her job and hoped she could stay with it permanently.

Another woman, thirty-four, mother of two small boys, knew precisely why she had come. China needed steel, she explained. Steel would make guns and tanks to protect the nation and machines that would raise farm yields. She said she hated to leave her kids, but it was only temporary, and she was working for their sake and the sake of all the children.

I was cheered by what I saw at Yuhsien. Men able to view long-range perspectives, to exercise their inventiveness and organizing skill to widen vastly their fields of operation. Women able to break out of the narrow confines of cooking and babytending to stand beside the men as equals, shaking them up occasionally with demonstrations of superior skill.

About half of China's iron and steel production was coming from crude furnaces in the countryside, close to sources of iron and coal, and tended by people fresh from the farms with no previous experience. Later it was found that too many had left agriculture. The communes were short-handed, and the quality of some of the iron produced was not worth the effort. Most people returned to their farms, and many of the "mills" were abandoned.

But a lot of the iron had been quite good, and was turned into much needed farm tools. Mass prospecting had unearthed a large number of previously undiscovered mines. More important, homemade iron and steel production had given millions a basic familiarity with tools and machinery, sadly lacking in a country which had just emerged from centuries of feudal backwardness. When small and medium iron and steel plants were subsequently set up all over the country these people were the reservoir of technical trainees. Others became the indispensable "handymen" who serviced the machines that growing prosperity brought to the communes.

As we traveled back to Peking, we stared from our train window in awe at the little furnaces spewing flames into the night sky for miles along both sides of the railway. All China was making iron and steel. In the city our taxi had to drive slowly. Some streets were so thick with smoke it was difficult to see. We could have been in Gary, or Pittsburgh. Every school, every government office, had its backyard furnaces. Teachers, pupils, civil servants, took turns tending them.

Inefficient, yes, but exciting, stimulating. I doubt whether the iron turned out behind the Foreign Languages Press served any practical purpose. The cost of transporting coal and iron ore to the center of the nation's capital must have exceeded the value of the steel we produced. But the value to intellectuals, rising from their swivel chairs and sweating beside a blast furnace they had built themselves, carbon smudges on their noses, was incalculable. They were identifying, for the first time, physically and directly, with industrial production. They weren't just talking and writing about things — they were doing them. It was very satisfying.

The atmosphere was positively festive. There was a great feeling of togetherness. "Me" and "mine" tended to give way to "us" and "ours". Doctors of traditional medicine made public formulas which had been jealously guarded in the family for generations. City people also tried to form communes. Although as economic structures they were not yet feasible in the cities, many of the social amenities they evolved were useful and practical. Older women whose children were grown would call at the homes of young mothers, if desired, with thermoses of water already boiled for drinking and washing, dress the children, feed them, and get them off to school, leaving mama free to go to work, easy in her mind. They would also do the housework and deliver the dirty clothes to another, specially organized, laundry group. In the late afternoon they would feed a snack to the kids returning from school, clean them up a bit, and put the kettle on, so that all mama had to do when she got home was cook supper.

There were also tailoring and mending services, and grocery and butcher shops that delivered right to the door. Unfortunately the small home industries organized by the city communes could not earn enough to pay for all these services, especially when the rest of the city was being run on a different financial basis. But they made their mark, and many of their methods, in slightly different form, still prevail.

As always, it was Chairman Mao and the Communist Party who saw beyond the small mistakes and excesses into the essential merits and power of this massive forward surge. They knocked off the rough edges, straightened out a few kinks, and molded it into a General Line, a political and economic blueprint for China's next stage. The General Line reaffirmed that China was a proletarian-ruled country led by the Communist Party. Unity between the Party and the masses, it said, was imperative. It criticized, without mentioning any names, those who were trying to restore capitalist ways to socialist countries. We knew this was referring to revisionists in the Soviet Union, but only high-ranking members of the Party realized that the criticism was also being directed against a few persons in leading positions in the Chinese Communist Party.

The General Line also finalized the question of priorities in China's economy. How do you build up a backward country starting virtually from scratch? Some wanted to mechanically copy the Soviet Union and put the stress on heavy industrial complexes. First steel, machine tools, modern transport, chemicals, power. Then, and only then, an expansion of light industry and agriculture.

This wasn't suited to China's conditions. China lacked heavy industry. That was a weakness. But she had enormous rural manpower, now organized in communes. Their success confirmed Mao's previously stated position. Agriculture should therefore be recognized as the base of the economy, with industry providing the drive, said the General Line. A rising agricultural output would supply the grain and industrial crops and the finances (through taxation) for industry, and provide it with workers. As industry grew it would turn out the farm tools, the chemical fertilizer, the consumer goods needed by the people on the farms. Agriculture and industry would complement each other. "Walking on two legs," the Chinese called it.

The same dialectical approach was taken to all aspects of the economy. Developing in tandem would be light and heavy industry, modern factories and the home-grown kind, small and medium plants as well as large ones. Most factories were then concentrated in the coastal areas. These would continue to be used. But new enterprises would also be developed in the interior. In administration, too, the "two legs" pattern was maintained. The central government held overall control and ran certain enterprises directly. At the same time the initiative of lower levels of government and their management of local plants was encouraged.

Working out a comprehensive viable economic policy in less than ten years after coming to power was no small accomplishment. China's situation was unique among socialist countries. It all had to be done by trial and error.

We and our friends were carried along at the time by the joyous frenzy. Today in retrospect, the Big Leap Forward, commune formation period are seen as flawed by an impetuosity that ran ahead, in some respects, of common sense. Later, adjustments had to be made, China's countryside was not ready for commune operation as economic organizations. The unit of accounting was returned to the production teams (the villages) rather than the brigade or the commune as a whole.

There were also signs of a growing intolerance to criticism within the Party leadership, and harsh measures against those who dared to voice contrary opinions. This had already been manifested in the anti-Rightist campaign. It was to grow and plague China until its ultimate eruption in the form of fascist take-overs during the Cultural Revolution.

VII

THREE BAD YEARS

1959-1961

All in all, 1958 was an exciting, inspiring year. But it was too good to last. While China was leaping forward, various poodles were yapping at her heels. New threats were muttered in America of "unleashing" Chiang Kai-shek. In December 1958, Khrushchov, in a talk with Hubert Humphrey, labeled the Chinese communes "essentially reactionary". At the Twenty-First Congress of the Soviet party early in 1959, he raged that developments in China were "skipping over a stage", that they were a form of "egalitarian communism". In March, the ruling nobles and the big lamas in Tibet began a rebellion. In August and October, Indian troops attacked. The Chinese drove them out.

Tibet had been part of China for centuries. Though it had mineral and metal resources of some potential, it was so high in the Himalayas and so lacking in transport, they never were developed. The Indians, across the border, had a few trading posts in Tibet, where they did a bit of business. The British had sent a military expedition at the turn of the century, occupied Lhasa, and built a strong sphere of influence which they maintained, via India until the Chinese People's Liberation Army marched in, in October 1951. Everything was owned by the nobles and the Buddhist lamas. The people were slaves and serfs living in conditions that would make medieval Europe look like the Age of Enlightenment. For any infraction of the "rules", eyes were gouged out, hands or legs cut off. Floggings were everyday affairs. Human skins were used for drums, skulls mounted in silver were popular as bowls among the high lamas. Thigh bones of virgin girls were said to make the best horns for religious services.

Peking tried to encourage gradual reform, but did not interfere in local government and left the big land holdings intact. The clergy and the nobles were not content. In collusion with British, American, Indian and Kuomintang agents, they staged an uprising in 1959 which was quickly put down. It was only then that Land Reform was commenced, starting later and moving through mutual-aid team and co-op stages more slowly than in the rest of the country. Today Tibet has communes, factories, schools, hospitals and a people's government.

At the time of the '59 rebellion by the reactionaries, crocodile tears gushed copiously in the West over the loss of freedom and democracy by the poor Tibetans.

Imagine the jolly celebrations if restoration of the old order had succeeded, quaffing toasts out of skull bowls, while virgin thigh-bone horns sound sweet songs to the tender beat of drums of human skin. . . . I saw some of those mementoes in an exhibition in Peking, including a neatly flayed skin, complete to the very finger tips, an offering to the gods in a lama temple. It was sickening. Holy lamas, soul brothers to Ilse Koch.

1959 was the first of what was to become known as the Three Bad Years. When it wasn't floods, it was droughts, or insect plagues. Farm output dropped sharply. The supply of food was short, and China was paying for a good part of Soviet "aid" in foodstuffs. Could these payments be delayed a few years? asked China. Nothing doing, replied the Soviet leaders. The contracts had to be observed to the letter.

In July of 1960 Mr. Khrushchov suddenly went a step further. He recalled all the Soviet experts working on important engineering projects, and stopped supplying the machinery, equipment and gasoline the Russians had contracted to deliver. Why were Nicky and his friends stabbing China in the back?

The first signs of malaise between the two parties surfaced in 1956, after Khrushchov made his dramatic "secret" exposure of Stalin at the 20th Congress of the Soviet Party, which somehow immediately found its way to the pages of the *New York Times*. He alleged that Stalin had a "persecution mania", that he indulged in "mass repressions and terror", that he was a "criminal . . . bandit . . . idiot . . . fool. . . ."

The Chinese, in two newspaper editorials, politely but firmly disagreed. They said Stalin had committed some serious errors and it was correct to criticize him. But his accomplishments far outweighed his failings. After all, it was under his leadership that the Soviet Union built up a solid economy, and defeated Hitler's Nazi hordes. Stalin also made important contributions to Marxist theory and stood for working class rule. Why try to negate him completely? In Peking, Stalin's portrait continued to be prominently displayed, and translations of his writings remained on sale throughout China.

In 1957 the next clash occurred when a world conference of Communist parties met in Moscow. China obviously thought the meeting important. Mao Tsetung personally led the Chinese delegation. The Soviet delegation with characteristic modesty touted the "majestic results" of the "splendid" 20th Congress, reiterated their attack on Stalin and tried to steamroller through a Declaration confirming their brand of "peaceful transition", plugged by Nicky at the congress.

According to Khrushchov the world had changed and it was now possible to go from capitalism to socialism by following the "parliamentary road". In other words, vote capitalism out of existence and the rulers, the boys scraping the cream off the top, would meekly give it up if only you mustered enough votes at election time.

Absurd, said the Chinese. Even if, in a particular country, you might get a majority vote for socialism, the power gang would definitely come shooting and blast you out of the chairs of office. That didn't mean the Left shouldn't take part in elections and public debate. These were a means of educating the public. But you were mad if you thought they would create any fundamental changes in the system.

As for the attack on Stalin, one of its "majestic results" was to delight the enemies of communism. The director of the US Information Agency said Khrushchov's speech had "never so suited our purposes". A *New York Times* editorial acclaimed it as a "weapon with which to destroy the prestige and influence of the communist movement". And John Foster Dulles had mused thoughtfully that it might help to bring about a "peaceful transformation" of the Soviet Union.

After much consultation and discussion a compromise was worked out at the conference which straddled the issue by stating the possibility of both positions. The Soviet Union pulled another fast one and had a reference to the glories of their 20th Congress inserted, on the plea to the Chinese that it would help smooth differences within the leadership of the Soviet Party. Mr. K and his lads later used this to claim that the resolutions of the 20th Congress had thereby been incorporated into the Moscow Declaration and were binding on all communist parties. Pretty slick.

Due mainly to Chinese efforts, certain important principles were included in the Declaration, in spite of the wheeling and dealing of the Soviet Party — US imperialism was the center of world reaction and the sworn enemy of the people, it was not the people who would be destroyed by a new world war but imperialism itself, a socialist country had to fight bourgeois influence within and imperialist pressure without or it would go revisionist and the people would lose power.

Mr. Khruschov's love for the Chinese Communists was not enhanced. They were spoiling his pitch. He was trying to tell everyone how sweet and reasonable the American power structure had become, while freezing doubters with the prospects of an atomic war if they didn't knuckle under to imperialist threats. The Chinese were saying that the tiger doesn't change its stripes, but that even with its atomic teeth, in the face of solid resistance by people the world over, it was only a paper tiger, hollow inside.

And what was this about revisionism? fumed Khrushchov. No names had been mentioned, but a shoe, however dramatically pounded on a United Nations desk, had a nasty tendency to fit, and people noticed.

Though irked, Khrushchov doggedly pushed ahead. In September 1959, he had his Talks at Camp David. "A turning point in history," he called them. Gromyko said they marked "a new era in international relations". The Soviet leaders praised the "sensibleness" and "good will" of American presidents. They foresaw "a world without weapons, without armed forces and without wars", and burbled that universal disarmament would "open up literally a new epoch in the economic development of Asia, Africa and Latin America".

To their Chinese allies and friends they were not quite so kind. In 1958 they arrogantly put forward demands "designed to bring China under Soviet military control", as the Chinese cryptically described them. Peking coolly declined.

Khrushchov's rage was mounting. The Chinese would not allow themselves to be browbeaten. They would not join Comecon — an economic grouping of socialist states serving mainly as suppliers to the Soviet Union of raw material and semi-finished products at lower than world market prices, in exchange for Soviet manufactures at higher than world market prices. The Chinese stressed self-reliance. They were following their own interpretation of Marxism in the light of their national conditions. They treated the Soviet Party as an equal but not as a superior.

The Soviet revisionists squeezed harder. In June 1959, they unilaterally abrogated a treaty on technical military assistance concluded less than two years before, and refused to provide China with a sample atom bomb, previously promised, or any data concerning its construction.   On the eve of Khrushchov's departure for America in September 1959, a *Tass* statement blamed China for an Indian incursion across the Chinese border.

Wild Nicky was splitting the communist camp wide open with his pronouncements on imperialism, war and peace, revolution, and how a socialist country should be governed.   The Chinese Party had to speak out. In April 1960 it published an article entitled "Long Live Leninism", restating its view. Yet even at this point the Chinese refrained from criticizing the Soviet Party and its leaders by name.

A week later, as if to underscore the Chinese contention that the lion had no intention of lying down with the lamb, an American U-2 spy plane flew over the Soviet Union, aborting a scheduled four power summit conference.   Moscow, instead of closing its ranks with Peking, only intensified its invective.   At a Romanian Workers Party Congress in Bucharest in June 1960, which other communist parties attended, Khrushchov took the opportunity to sound off in typical style. He said the Chinese Communists were "madmen" who "wanted to unleash war", that they were "picking up the banner of the imperialist monopoly capitalists", that they had behaved in a "purely nationalist" manner in the Sino-India border clash, and that their attitude toward the Soviet Party was "Trotskyite".   Delegates from other revisionist parties chimed in with charges that the Chinese party was "dogmatic", "sectarian," "pseudo-revolutionary", "worse than Yugoslavia".

The Chinese would not be cowed.   They issued a calm, reasoned statement, sticking to their guns.   A number of parties, notably the Albanian, supported them.

Khrushchov simply blew his stack.   In July he abruptly broke all 343 contracts under the "Sino-Soviet Treaty of Friendship, Alliance and Mutual Assistance", canceled 257 projects of scientific and technical cooperation, and called home 1,390 Soviet experts, instructing them to bring the blueprints with them.   (Many were hard workers eager to help China.   Some were outraged by Khrushchov's behavior, and worked day and night to copy the blueprints for the Chinese before leaving.)   Suddenly there were incidents on the Soviet border and unrest fomented in the province of Sinkiang.

A final attempt was made to heal the breach in November 1960, when a meeting of eighty-one communist parties was called in Moscow. The Soviet Party, as its contribution to unity, distributed a 127-page letter to all delegates, attacking the Chinese Party more savagely than ever. It then put forward a draft for a common Statement it wanted all parties to sign. Again China led the opposition.

One of the main points of contention arose over the Soviet insistence that "peaceful coexistence" be stipulated as the supreme foreign policy line of all socialist countries. What the Chinese objected to was not the principle of coexistence, which they themselves had advocated at the Bandung Conference in 1955, but perversion of it into a peace-at-any-price attitude. There is a basic antagonism between the socialist and capitalist systems, class struggle is international as well as internal, said the Chinese. Imperialism is out to destroy the socialist countries, to smash national liberation struggles, to put down any opposition to capitalism in their own countries. Hot wars, cold wars — it never relents. Sometimes, circumstances force it to ease up a little, and give out with a lot of sweet talk, the Chinese noted. We're willing to go along with that. As long as they don't attack us, we won't attack them. But that doesn't mean becoming spineless. If they hit, we'll hit back. The Chinese position was that socialist countries not only have to defend themselves and each other; they must support all peoples fighting to get iron heels off their necks.

The revisionists tried to push through a criticism of socialist countries which "go it alone", a thinly veiled assault on China for rejecting the blessings of Comecon and relying on her own efforts to build her economy. It was rejected.

Khrushchov also tried to wave the big stick against "factional activities" within the international communist movement, and demanded "majority rule". This would have enabled the Soviet revisionists to use their political steamroller to flatten the opposition.

The Chinese managed to win almost every round and obtained the support of most of the delegations. When the Statement was finally adopted, it proclaimed that imperialism never changes, that US imperialism is the enemy of the people of the world, and called for a broad united front against it. The Statement said national liberation struggles and newly emerging nations should be supported. People in capitalist countries dominated by US imperialism politically, economically or militarily should fight it as well as their domestic reactionaries. Communist parties should consult and decide on questions of principle unanimously (no more Big Brother knows best). The danger of "revising" basic Marxism was particularly stressed.

Khrushchov signed the Statement on December first, but it was a hypocritical gesture. The Soviet Party from a Marxist point of view went from bad to worse. Not only big China but even spunky little Albania became an object of its venom. At the same time Mr. K showered sticky kisses on the rump of the US imperialists, scrupling at nothing to fawn and win favor. The Soviet Union supplied transport for UN troops to suppress revolutionaries in the Congo, it agreed — without consulting the Cuban government — to "inspection" in Cuba during the missile crisis, it called the bloody slaughter of the Algerian people an "internal affair" of France, it announced that it would "stand aloof" when the US invented an "incident" in the Gulf of Bac Bo as an excuse for escalation in Vietnam.

Though communists the world over had long proclaimed their goal to be the emancipation of all mankind, the objective of Soviet communists, according to Mr. Khrushchov, was "a good plate of goulash". "Goulash communism" became the new ideal.

Bourgeois ideas, bourgeois methods, bourgeois values revived. Chauvinism in international affairs inevitably followed. And, of course, ruthless attacks on anyone who tried to stop them.

To the West, Khrushchov was a hero. He was definitely on their side. "Nikita Khrushchov has destroyed, irrevocably, the unified bloc of Stalin's day. That is perhaps Khrushchov's greatest service — not to communism, but to the Western World," said *Newsweek*. *US News and World Report* said: "We ought to be grateful for his mishandling of his relationship with the Chinese. . . . We should be grateful for his introducing disarray into international communism by a lot of quite bumptious and sudden initiatives." Again *Newsweek*: "The administration is now convinced that the US should offer Khrushchov maximum support in his dispute with Red China."

By July 1960, the handwriting was already on the wall. The Soviet Union was moving back toward capitalism, it was itself becoming an imperialist power. China would not bow, China made pointed comment, China, therefore, had to be crushed. What better time than now, when her harvests were failing and she was beset by economic difficulties?

But the Chinese proved to be surprisingly uncrushable. In the first place, they understood the situation. Every office, school, farm and factory, every branch of the armed forces, held formal political study sessions several times a week. In these, Mr. K's antics were closely analysed. The nature of revisionism and how it manifested itself in socialist countries was discussed. Though Khrushchov and the Soviet Party were never criticized in public, all China was aware of their growing hostility.

Yet the savagery of the open betrayal, when it came in the summer of 1960, was something of a shock. Reaction among Chinese friends and colleagues went from incredulity to anger to determination. There wasn't enough to eat. Rationing tightened. Protein was in short supply. (This was thought by some doctors to be a factor in the hepatitis epidemic which followed a few years later.) Several young people in my office swelled up with edema. Foreigners, as usual received special treatment. But there wasn't much food to buy, and who had the heart, anyhow, to stuff himself when everyone else was plainly in want.

Incredibly, there was little grumbling. Unruffled, even cheerful, some of them, people went about their regular tasks. Several large vats were set up in the back yard of the Foreign Languages Press. They were raising algae — served in daily soup to fill in the protein deficiency. Calisthenics and sports were out, and we were advised to rest when possible and go to bed early. But we kept the same office hours and did the same amount of work. Matronly ladies laughed and said they were wearing clothes they hadn't been able to get into for years.

Privation and hardship were real enough, however. While Chinese freight cars continued rolling toward the Soviet border with foodstuffs, as per contract, there were cases of starvation in hard-hit parts of the country, and relief supplies had to be rushed. 1959, 1960, 1961 — the Three Bad Years. What saved China were the communes — at which K sneered, and the Big Leap Forward — declared to be a failure by the West. The communes, with their huge, well-organized forces of men and women, could build dams and dig canals to bring water to parched fields. Or drain off floods and replant quickly and extensively. Or turn out by the thousands and flail locusts to death. The Big Leap Forward meant more roads and railways, more machines and fertilizer for the farms, more improvements, inventions, a livelier, more scientific frame of mind for dealing with emergencies and seeing beyond.

The Soviet betrayal left China with newly started or half-finished projects which, in a way, were worse than none at all. For they were being built according to Soviet plans and specifications, were designed to be equipped with Soviet machinery, and the plans had been taken home and delivery of the machinery canceled. I continued my annual tours in those years. Everywhere I saw empty silent plants and factories. Only two and a half of six projected rolling mills in the Wuhan steel complex had been completed. Projects had to be abandoned or completely redesigned and equipped.

No help could be expected from the West. America and countries under her domination were boycotting China. Those willing to trade demanded exorbitant prices. The Chinese had no choice but to make their own plans, design their own projects, supply their own equipment. They had to practice the self-reliance which Mao had always taught, self-reliance rooted in the earliest traditions of the revolution.

It was slow hard work, but China made a virtue of necessity. The Soviet betrayal and the American boycott turned out to be blessings in disguise. Chinese machines, Chinese industrial processes were born. There were new and original approaches in science and scientific method. Most people remained confident in spite of hardships.

But there was strong disagreement over the methods to be used and the pace at which to advance in China's socialist stage. Should markets be permitted, for example, at which commune members could sell produce raised in their own gardens? If so, what items should be excluded? How should the markets be supervised? Were some of the communes too large for efficient operation? Should they be cut down in size? How should the smaller ones be strengthened? What about industry? Was some retrenchment necessary? How should it be effectuated? Was the social system too advanced for the existing technology?

Mao's position was that it was not. He said it was true there were some imbalances between the social system and technology, but the advanced quality of the social system was precisely what was enabling labor organization and technology to develop quickly. What was holding things back was bourgeois ideology, bourgeois methods. This was because class struggle and the battle of ideas still existed in China. It was too early to be complacent and say that socialism had won. Contradictions existed everywhere, they were a law of nature and of human society. In socialist society, too, this law had to be recognized and applied, giving due consideration to the differences between antagonistic contradictions with the enemy and non-antagonistic contradictions among the people. China's socialist system had to be strengthened and problems met as they arose.

The arguments over differences in approach continued among the Communist Party leadership. Phoenix and I, and most of our friends, agreed with Mao's views. Whatever the failings of various particular methods, the overall direction appeared correct, since the people of China were certainly better off than they ever had been in the past.

A junket through the lower Yangtze region in 1961 demonstrated that to me clearly. I went with a few friends in September, when the weather had cooled off. We visited Nanking first which is fiercely hot and humid in summer, being surrounded by hills which keep the moisture in and the breeze out, while the temperature soars to 104. We arrived at six in the morning, after an airless soggy night on the train, stupid from lack of sleep.

An elegant Volga sedan — remnant of the Soviet friendship days — met us at the station and whisked us to a hotel amid beautiful gardens. Nanking's moist heat, which makes northerners so droopy, is marvelous for vegetation. Trees and bushes flourish and the air is fragrant with flowers. The food was superb. It and our handsome surroundings soon revived us and we rolled off to visit the memorial to Sun Yat-sen.

His tomb lies within a temple atop a large hill. We mounted 342 steps in the broiling sun. After paying our respects, we came out and gazed at the surrounding view. Nanking is very old. Its outskirts are dotted with mossy stone edifices, worn and rounded by the years. Hung Wu, the first Ming emperor, is buried not far from the Sun Yat-sen mausoleum. Only the stone bases of pillars remain of the temple dedicated to Hung Wu 600 years before. A soft nap of grass all but obliterates ancient walks and steps. The Manchus burnt the wooden temple a hundred years ago while fighting the Taiping rebels, who had made their capital in Nanking.

We visited another kind of burial ground in the afternoon. Yu Hua Tai — Terraces of Rain and Flowers — is an area of wooded ravines were Chiang Kai-shek and his Kuomintang murdered well over 100,000 revolutionaries between 1931 and 1949. They were mostly young, in their late twenties and early thirties. A few were only sixteen, but the Kuomintang upped their age to eighteen in the records so as to make it "legal" to shoot them. They were fantastically gallant. Even the reactionary press remarked on how bravely they went to their deaths, shouting slogans, singing the "Internationale".

A Martyrs Museum has been set up in buildings where the Kuomintang butchers had their offices. We saw kerchiefs embroidered with

defiant slogans. One or two were in English, for many of the young
people were students. You can see letters from those waiting to die
written to their families. Though containing touching personal admonitions, they were absolutely fearless, calling on children or younger
brothers to carry on the fight, expressing full confidence in the revolution.

Most of the ravines have been filled in and planted with trees, and
the whole area has been turned into a park. On the hill in the center
a memorial obelisk has been erected. Parties of school children come
almost daily from all over. One old comrade who is now a guide at
the Museum said: "We want the younger generation to know what we
had to go through to win the revolution."

Not much market here for the Rightists' contention that the Chinese
people were better off in the old society.

In the next few days we went to factories, housing developments,
communes.

Our first stop was the Nanking Motor Vehicle Plant. Before 1949,
when the People's Republic was established, it was just a repair shop
with thirty workers. In 1952 they began making spare parts. In 1953
they went into trial production of auto engines. Within four years
they could make two kinds — one 50 and one 70 h.p. In 1958 they turned
out their first truck, a two-and-a-half-ton job, known appropriately
enough as the "Leap Forward", going into full scale production the
same year. They did their own planning and designing. Most of
their machinery and all of their materials were Chinese.

From thirty people in 1949 they increased a hundred-fold to 3,100. Of
these twelve percent were engineers and technicians, thirteen percent
office staff, and seventy-five percent workers. Women, 640 of them,
worked in every department. The plant had its own hospital, children's
nurseries and schools. There were three shifts a day. The average
wage was 52 *yuan* a month. The highest paid men in the plant were
some of the engineers. They drew 195 *yuan*. But the highest paid worker
received 104, so the differential was not too great.

From there we went to Shanghai and visited the big Machine Tool
Works. Before the new regime it had been known as the National
Agricultural Engineering Corporation, and was owned by American
businessmen and Kuomintang bureaucrats. In spite of its high sounding
title, it manufactured nothing but hoe blades — in four years 1,000
workers produced only 40,000. Mainly it repaired broken American farm
machinery, which was then resold in China. In 1950, after being taken

over by the government, it began building precision grinders. Personnel increased from 1,200 to 5,000. The area was doubled and three times as much machinery was installed.

1958 was the year of the Big Leap. Between 1958 and 1961, when we visited the Machine Tool Works, the workers had put forward 30,000 ideas for improving production. In that same period output value rose to 2.6 times the pre-Liberation figures and quantity tripled. Besides mirror-smooth grinders, they also made complicated bearings.

Of the 800 women in the factory, half were technicians. When a woman became pregnant she was given light work starting with her sixth month, and had 56 days maternity leave, with pay, after birth. (This is the same in all Chinese factories, schools and government organizations.) On return to work, she had a half-hour off every morning and afternoon to breast-feed her baby, who was cared for in the factory crèche.

Most of the workers were young. The average was twenty-seven. Seventy percent were junior high school graduates. The majority continued their education in part-time schools run by the factory, ranging from primary to college level. The average wage was 72 *yuan*, the average technician got 93, engineers were paid 250. All personnel had free medical care. Members of their families were treated for a small charge. There were also movies twice a week, plus amateur theatricals. They had their own hospital, clinics, shopping center.

We went to a workers' residential area in the outskirts of Shanghai. It had eight sections, the first built in 1951, the last completed in 1958, and housed 12,700 families — 65,000 people — mostly textile workers. Many of them had lived in mat sheds in the old society. I spoke to a carpenter with a family of seven whose monthly wage before Liberation was 60 kilograms of rice. They had subsisted on scraps which the wife and kids collected. They had one bed and a hammock for the whole seven, and only two old quilts among them. The carpenter was often out of work and had to beg for a living. The kids were always sick.

I met a woman textile worker who had given birth to six children in the old society. All had died, three of illness and three of starvation in infancy because mother was so undernourished she had no milk.

Now every family was earning wages. In fifty percent of them both husband and wife worked. Their average pay was 72 *yuan* a month each. Rent cost from 2.30 to 5.00 per month, water and electricity seventy cents per person, food about 10 *yuan* a head. In 1953 total bank deposits for the community were roughly 1,000 *yuan*. When we visited in 1961 they were 760,000. The woman whose six children had died had 1,000 *yuan* in her account. The carpenter had 600.

The area boasted a department store, a movie theater, a hospital, clinics, nurseries, kindergartens, nine primary and two high schools.

In Shanghai there were thirty-four such new residential areas for workers, each housing about 50,000 people.

We visited a commune in the Shanghai suburbs, raised from a high level co-op in September 1958 when the move into communes was swelling across the land. It had 23,000 people in 5,500 families, farming 36,000 *mu* of land — about 6,000 acres. Their main crops were grain and cotton, but they also raised vegetables, pigs and aquatic products. Their rice yield in 1961 was thirty-seven percent higher than in 1957 — before the formation of the commune, and seventy-one percent above the pre-Liberation figure. Wheat increases were fifty and sixty-three percent for the same dates. For unginned cotton, a hundred percent and 535 percent. They also had large increases in pig and vegetable production.

The experiences of these people strikingly illustrated the advantages of the commune organization. For two days in August 1960 they had very heavy rain — 280 millimeters in forty-eight hours. One third of the crops were swamped. Everyone turned out, all the pumps were put to work, and the water was expelled. They still got a pretty good harvest.

When we called on them in September 1961, although they hadn't had a drop of rain for three months, their harvest was excellent. "If this were the Kuomintang days," one old farmer said to me, "the earth would have cracked and the water buffaloes would have collapsed. Even if we raised blisters on our feet carrying water, the crops would still have withered in the fields."

Now, flood or drought, they were able to cope.

The commune had 16 tractors, 14 fixed pumping stations, 13 roving pumps, 33 modern threshing machines, 400 homemade threshers, 6 trucks, 4 motorboats, and did its own maintenance and repairs. They kept up all roads, bridges and high tension lines within their boundaries.

Strolling around, we dropped in on one of the homes. It belonged to a husband and wife in their early thirties. They had three kids. The husband's mother lived with them. They had received the house and part of their furniture during the Land Reform. The house had an earthen floor and a thatched roof. But they were quite well off. With all three adults working, they had a total income in 1961 of 800 *yuan*. Of this they would spend around 650 for necessities and a few luxuries and put 150 *yuan* in the bank. The thatched roof was new and so was some of the furniture. They had electric lights and a little radio. On a bureau was a bottle of toilet water and a framed photo of the family in their holiday best.

Nanking, Shanghai, Hangchow, Shaoshing — we found pretty much the same thing wherever we went. An end to poverty, malnutrition and the horrors and humiliations of the old society, a steady rise in the standard of living, jobs, schools, medical treatment, security, and a feeling of togetherness.

In 1961 I began translating my twelfth novel for Foreign Languages Press, a lively affair called *Tracks in the Snowy Forest*. The author Chu Po comes from a poor peasant family and rose through the ranks of the People's Liberation Army to the post of regimental political commander. The story is based on his own experiences in the 1946 campaign to wipe out Chiang Kai-shek forces in the wooded mountains of what was then "Manchuria", and the local bandits — long a scourge of the impoverished population — with whom the Chiang soldiers had combined. The style is strongly influenced by the blood and thunder tradition of classic folk tales about heroes. The characters, though stereotyped, are stereotyped in the manner of Peking opera, particularly the main protagonists — exaggerated, and strikingly colorful.

Take Butterfly Enticer, who appears in our story as the Third Wife of the nasty Chief of Police of Peony River City. Chu Po offers an earthy sketch of how the lady got her name:

> Her looks were enough to turn your stomach. An incredibly long head perched on her neck like an ear of corn. In an attempt to disguise her fantastic ugliness, she covered her enormous forehead with bangs right down to her eyebrows. But nothing could help her. The combination of dry yellow skin and the black freckles made her face even more revolting. She coated it with powder, so thickly at times that the powder flaked off when she blinked her eyes. Because her teeth had turned black from opium, she had them all crowned with gold. When she smiled, the glare was painful.

Since Fatty Chiang had no son, but only this precious daughter, he announced that he was seeking a son-in-law to enter the Chiang family and inherit his property. Sons of officials and landlords came flocking to his door.

Of course, these young gentlemen weren't interested in his daughter; they wanted his money. The competition put a high price on the prospective bride. Fatty Chiang forgot his unhappiness over not having a son. He carefully picked through the list of suitors.

The lady had her own method of selecting a mate. Bedding down three days with this one and five days with that, she soon became very notorious. In spite of her ugliness, not one of her gallants failed to tell her that she was "as beautiful as the Heavenly Maidens".

Old Fatty and his daughter became prouder than ever. Standing with his big belly poking out before him, holding his cane, Fatty Chiang announced one day with heartfelt satisfaction, pompously enunciating each word:

"A fragrant flower attracts a swarm of butterflies. My daughter is truly a butterfly enticer."

Thus the name originated. The story spread from one person to ten, from ten to a hundred, and soon the name was known far and wide.

Whoever heard it, snorted. Someone composed a line to match Fatty Chiang's: "A pile of shit brings the dung beetles in droves. Miss Chiang is truly food for the dung beetles."

A lot of good writers came out of the army. They fought the Japanese, the regular armies of Chiang Kai-shek, the battalions of local tyrants, and all sorts of armed scum and riffraff. But in addition they were deeply involved with the people of the areas in which they operated — protecting them, enforcing reductions of land rent and interest on loans, organizing the women, the youngsters, bringing medication, sanitation, education. The relationship between the army and the people was, as the popular saying put it, that of "fish and water".

Of course there were problems. The army lads were handsome and brave. The village girls were pretty and impressionable. It was inevitable that some should fall in love and want to marry. But army policy did not permit this during wartime, and emotional conflicts were created. Shih Yen, another army writer, deals with this theme delightfully in *It Happened in Willow Castle*, which I translated fairly early. We hear the political officer talking:

I explained to Li Chin carefully: The peasants were still full of feudal concepts, especially in the newly liberated regions. They weren't educated yet to the idea of freedom of choice in marriage. The girl's father would raise a row if a man whom he didn't select himself married his daughter. Furthermore, if Li Chin were given permission to take a bride, every other soldier should have the same right. What kind of army would we have then?

The boy and his squad are billeted in the girl's home. He answers:

"You know I've always listened to you. As I talk here with you, I think — break it off and be done with it. What's the use of dragging this thing out? But when I get back to the house and see her, my ideas change fast. I can't make up my mind. You don't know what it's like — the way she's been looking at me the past two days. Her eyes shine like she wants to cry. Living with her in the same house — it . . . it upsets me!"

The political officer, who is the narrator of the tale, concludes the chapter with:

No question that she had captured the boy's heart. If this situation continued there was no telling what he'd do. Although it wasn't the best solution by any means, I determined to move him out of that house.
"How would it be if I found another billet for Squad Four?" I asked him.
"Fine," he replied, without an instant's hesitation.
"Ai! He could make quick decisions! The big kid!"

Chen Teng-ke, who as a boy worked as a hired hand, caused a minor sensation with his short novel *Living Hell* by the intensity of its passions. While translating it I was quite moved. It tells of guerrilla operations in south China, in coordination with the New Fourth Army — the southern forerunner of the People's Liberation Army — against local despots and the Chiang Kai-shek troops. Its language is rich. When the village head announces he is going to conscript the young men into Chiang's army, the peasants discuss the problem thus:

Chu frowned. "Their backsides sit firmly on the horse. It can't fly away, it can't crawl away. You can't move your family or your land. If you rip the stitching open wide, it'll be hard to sew it up again. Let's talk about this again some other time. We hear a lot about the Communist counterattacks but who knows when they'll be able to liberate us here?"
Standing beside him was Ta-shun, his face flushing an angry red and the cords in his neck bulging. "You sexless old monk!" he fumed. "Who among us isn't eating from a makeshift stove? We kick it over

and go! What kind of big property ties you down? When they bind you with rope and throw you on the conscripts' cart, you'll never get to any home again! We have to act —"

Tuan-tse jumped forward. "We only have to keep our nerve. Why should we be afraid of them if we've got guns? Sure we have families to think of, but so have they."

"Docile men are cheated, docile horses are ridden," the widow of the murdered Hsueh-shu said to Chu. "When they came to tear down our houses and Hsueh-shu knelt before Chang the ward boss and pleaded with him, Chang shot him dead on the spot. But when we all stuck together and refused to pay the conscription levy they couldn't do anything about it. You *will* die if you're afraid to die! Do you want to live to be a thousand!"

"That's right," Li chimed in. "They want our guts, so we must tear their hearts out! Strike, I say!"

Chao Shu-li, one of China's most gifted writers, dealt mainly with life in the Liberated Areas, where the Kuomintang enemy had been driven out and local people's governments established. He humorously described the battle between the new enlightened ideas and the old backward feudal practices. Chao wrote the way people talked, in lean unpretentious prose that cut right to the core of social problems. I enjoyed particularly translating his *Rhymes of Li Yu-tsai and Other Stories,* a collection of four short pieces. The title story begins like this:

In the village of Yenchiashan there was a man by the name of Li Yu-tsai, sometimes called "Old Unsinkable" because of his irrepressibly cheerful nature. He was more than fifty years old and had no land. He earned his living by herding cattle for other villagers, and in the summer and autumn by keeping an eye on their crops. Alone in the world, he had no wife or children. He used to joke, "When I eat my fill, my whole family is satisfied."

Our hero considerably enlivened life in the village:

He had a way of making people laugh. The most ordinary words coming from his mouth could cause his listeners to practically collapse with laughter. He also had a great talent for composing satirical rhymes about village events and village characters, which were catchy and easy to recite.

Before the war he wrote one about Yen Heng-yuan who, year after year, got himself elected mayor of the village. When election time rolled round again, Li Yu-tsai wrote this:

Mayor Yen Heng-yuan
Is a mighty tower,
Since we've had the job
He's remained in power.
For a "change in office"
Though we vote each year,
When the votes are counted
Yen's still there, no fear.
Why bother writing ballots
When elections come about?
Just use a stamp with Yen's name,
For years it won't wear out.

Yen had a son named Chia-hsiang, who was a teacher in the local elementary school. This son had never been to college but took the post upon graduation from the county teachers' training course in 1930. He was rather ugly with bulging cheeks and a receding chin. When he spoke, he blinked furiously. But you couldn't judge him by his grotesque appearance and write him off as a fool; actually, he was full of shrewd dirty tricks. Whoever had any dealings with him always came out the loser. Li Yu-tsai composed in his honor:

Bulgy-cheeked, flat-nosed
Yen Chia-hsiang flutters
Long-lashed eyelids
With each word he utters.
He's a schemer, a swindler,
A crook, a cheat,
Nothing pleases him better
Than a quick profit neat.
When he can't get enough
His angry mouth opens big,
While his swinish eyes narrow
Like a fat grunting pig.

Li Yu-tsai turned out rhymes like these at a rate of almost one a day.

In *Old Customs* Chao wryly sets forth the problems of the new bride and the traditionally harsh mother-in-law:

Our story is a true one. It takes place in a little village in the mountain fastness of the southwestern corner of Hopei Province, in North China. People used to say of the village: "It's on a high mountain, far beyond the reach of the emperor." Even after it was liberated, they only changed to: "It's on a high mountain, far beyond the reach of the people's government."

Because the village was so remote, its customs were still those of seventy-five years ago. After a girl was married, she was scolded and beaten by her mother-in-law. When she grew older and became a mother-in-law herself, she scolded and beat her daughter-in-law in turn. If she behaved any other way, she wouldn't be considered a proper mother-in-law.

The accepted attitude of a man toward his wife was summed up in the old saying: "A wife should be treated like a horse — driven and beaten regularly." If any husband didn't beat his wife, people thought he was afraid of her.

Meng's *popo* (mother-in-law), besides observing all the customs of conduct toward her daughter-in-law, had another distinguishing feature. She was a strong talker. In her younger days, she had quite a number of male friends, even after marriage. While her husband didn't like it, he couldn't out-talk her, and he certainly couldn't out-scold her. If her husband didn't dare cross her, what chance had her daughter-in-law?

The old customs of the village plus her *popo's* big mouth made things difficult enough for Meng. But there were other factors that sealed her lot as an unhappy daughter-in-law.

In the first place, there was no one in her own family to look after her. When she was nine, both her parents died, leaving her thirteen-year-old sister and her brother — then only a babe in arms — as her sole relatives. Her sister had married into a family which was on bad terms with Meng's in-laws and which had not even permitted her to attend Meng's wedding. And so when Meng was beaten, there was no one to speak for her.

Secondly, Meng came from a poor family and had no dowry.

Thirdly, because her mother died when she was very young, she had not learned to sew well.

Fourthly, she had nearly natural feet. Although they had been bound, she had wrapped the bindings loosely, and the normal growth of her feet had been only slightly impeded. People in the village looked on women with ordinary feet with the same wonder as city people regarded women with bound feet.

Fifthly, since from childhood she always had to run the household herself, she had learned to argue reasonably. She was unwilling to accept arbitrary abuse, and that, in her mother-in-law's eyes, was reason enough to scold and beat her.

Nevertheless, in the new society, the girl is able to emancipate herself finally and become a competent organizer in the district women's association. But the author offers no pat conclusions. He says:

> I have been asked: Why are Meng's mother-in-law and husband so much against her? Are they afraid that her feet are so big she'll trip over them when she walks? Or that if she does too much work there won't be anything left for them to do? Or that she'll pluck the ground bare of wild herbs?
>
> To that I can only say: Meng is a labor heroine and only twenty-three years old. Events and people connected with her will be recorded for a long period to come. Let's wait and see who will march with time and who will lag behind.

Chao Shu-li, in *The Marriage of Young Blacky* relates how, with the support of the government, two young people fight off the attempts of their parents to choose their mates for them and ultimately succeed in marrying each other. The young lovers are in the district government office when Liu the Sage, the boy's father, storms in:

> Pointing at his son, he exclaimed: "Trouble-maker. They've let you off. Why don't you go home? Are you trying to worry me to death? Shameless wretch."
>
> "What's all this?" the district chief interjected. "Is the district government office a place to swear at people?"
>
> Liu the Sage fell silent.
>
> "Are you Liu Hsiu-teh?" the chief asked him.
>
> "Yes," retorted the Sage.
>
> "Are you raising a girl at home to be Young Blacky's wife?"
>
> "Yes."
>
> "How old is she?"
>
> "Twelve."
>
> "She's too young to be engaged. Send her back to her mother. Young Blacky is already engaged to Chin."
>
> "She has only a father, and he's a refugee who's gone heaven knows where. There's no place to send her back to. I know the law says she's too young to be engaged, but lots of girls in our village are at her age. Be merciful and let this engagement stand."
>
> "Any party to an illegal agreement who's not willing can break it."
>
> "Both families agree."

The district chief asked Young Blacky: "Do you agree?"

"No, I don't," replied the boy.

Liu the Sage glared at him. "That's not for you to decide."

"You didn't ask his consent when you made the engagement," said the district chief. "He doesn't need yours to break it. Today people choose their own partners in marriage, old neighbor. You have no say in the matter. If that little girl you're raising has no other home, you can consider her as your daughter."

"I can do that, all right. But I must beg you to be merciful and not let him become engaged to Chin."

"You can't interfere in that."

"Be merciful, I beg you. Their horoscopes don't match. They'd be miserable all their lives," cried Liu. He turned to Young Blacky. "Don't be such a muddle-head. This will affect your whole life."

"Old neighbor," said the district chief, "don't you be such a muddle-head. Your son would really be miserable all his life if you forced him to marry a twelve-year-old girl. I'm telling you this for your own good. If Young Blacky and Chin want to get married, they can whether you agree or not. You can go home now. The little girl can be your daughter if she has no place else to go."

Before Liu the Sage could renew his pleas for the district chief to "be merciful", a messenger escorted him to the door.

Because our historical and cultural backgrounds were so different, I frequently had difficulty in comprehending the thought processes and motivations of my Chinese colleagues and friends. Two of the books I translated, *The Family* by Pa Chin and *Spring Silkworms* by Mao Tun, gave me the beginnings of understanding.

The Family is about the hopeless love of a young son of a wealthy household for a sweet bondmaid in Chengtu, Szechuan, in the twenties, against a background of warlord strife, student unrest, and the ferment of new ideas. The boy writes in his diary:

> She seems to be avoiding me lately, I don't know why. Today, for instance when she saw me coming she turned and walked the other way. I ran after her and asked, "Why are you avoiding me?"
>
> She stopped and looked at me timidly, but the light in her eyes was warm. Then she dropped her head and said in a low voice, "I'm afraid . . . I'm afraid Madam and the others will find out."
>
> Very moved, I raised her face and, smiling, shook my head. "Don't be afraid. It's nothing to be ashamed of. Love is very pure." I let her go. Now, at last I understand.

After lunch I went back to my room and started reading the English translation of "Resurrection" that Chueh-min had just bought. Suddenly I grew frightened, and couldn't go on. I was afraid that book might become a portrait of me, even though its hero's circumstances are very different from mine. . . . Lately I've been daydreaming a lot, wondering how families like ours are going to end. . . .

I'm so lonely! Our home is like a desert, a narrow cage. I want activity, I want life. In our family I can't even find anyone I can talk to.

That book Grandfather gave me — "On Filial Piety and the Shunning of Lewdness" — was still on the table. I picked it up and skimmed through a few pages. The whole thing is nothing but lessons on how to behave like a slave. It's full of phrases like "The minister who is unwilling to die at his sovereign's command is not loyal; the son who is unwilling to die at his father's command is not filial," and "Of all crimes, lewdness is the worst; of all virtues, filial piety is the best." The more I read the angrier I became, until I got so mad I ripped the book to pieces. With one less copy of that book in the world, a few less people will be harmed by it.

I felt depressed and weighted down with all manner of unpleasant things. Everything in the room is so dull and tasteless; outside my window too, it's always so gloomy. I wished I could sprout wings and fly away, but the silent house engulfed me like a tomb. I threw myself on the bed and began to groan.

Many Chinese intellectual colleagues, and not a few leaders of the Communist Party, came from a very similar background.

Spring Silkworms is a collection of short stories — a dozen on the Japanese war period, and one regarding an ancient slave revolt. Mao Tun writes graphically about the little man — and woman — disrupted by cataclysmic forces beyond their control. The peasant, the shopkeeper, the office employee, the worker, the student, even the concubine of a local gangster, are wrenched out of the normal tenor of their lives. In *Epitome* the auther gives us a glimpse of the hell in which the mistress of an opium runner lived:

About eleven that night the Master finally returned, his face pale and splotchy. His bloodshot eyes looked smaller than usual. His head was steaming with sweat and he reeked of drink. He took out his pistol and thumped it down on the table. With palsied fingers Miss Ling helped him remove his clothing. Suddenly, laughing boisterously, he grabbed her, lifted her up and tossed her on to the bed. This had happened often before, but this time it was unexpected. Miss Ling couldn't tell what kind of a mood he was in; she lay motionless, not daring to stir. The Master strode up to her and angrily yanked open her garments, the black gleaming pistol clutched in his right hand. Miss Ling went weak with terror. She stared at him, her eyes large and distended. He stripped her and placed the icy muzzle of the pistol against her breast. Miss Ling was shivering so violently the whole bed creaked.

"I'll practise on you first," she heard the Master say. "Let's see how good my gun is."

There was a roaring in Miss Ling's ears. Tears coursed down her cheeks.

"Afraid to die, slut? Hah! Don't worry, I still want to play around with you for a while yet!"

Laughing cruelly, the Master flopped into bed, and instantly began to snore, deep in slumber.

Miss Ling huddled to one side of the bed. She was afraid to sleep, she was unable to sleep. If he had only pulled the trigger, she thought, my misery would have ended, quick and clean. Stealthily, she took the pistol, looked at it, then closed her eyes, her heart beating fast. But finally she put it down again. Life was bitter, but death was too frightening.

Most of the people fought back. Take Mr. Li the typesetter in Shanghai's prestigious Commercial Press. In Mao Tun's *Wartime,* he was at home with his wife and three children, hoping the war would go away, when the Japanese started their saturation bombing:

The three children had already eaten their fill. Holding on to a chair for support, the youngest was chattering animatedly in a language all his own. The two elder children were out playing in the courtyard, chasing things that flew like small black butterflies. As Mr. Li watched his three lively little youngsters, he was oppressed by the thought that this happy home which he had spent ten difficult years building might be blotted out in an instant by a shell or a bomb. Tears came to his eyes.

Suddenly, Mrs. Li came running out of the kitchen, a dish-cloth still in her hand.

"Do you know what happened? Do you know?" she cried, distraught. "The Commercial Press was bombed! The whole plant is in flames!"

"What! Then that big fire is at the Press? Who says so?"

"Hsiang's wife, next door!"

The seven-year-old boy bounded into the parlor with the little black things he had caught in the courtyard, his little sister right behind him. Mr. Li's eyes opened wide. Those black butterflies were bits of burnt paper! It was all clear to him now. His heart beat fast. The Japanese had smashed his livelihood, they had broken his rice bowl! Destroying China's biggest publishing house, they had broken the rice bowls of thousands of workers and employees! A savage laugh burst from Mr. Li's lips. His pale face became tinged with an angry purple.

"Those Japanese have gone too far!" he cried.

He forgot all about the danger of bombs. His "rice bowl" was broken. What more was there to fear! He rushed out of the door, why or where he had no idea, nor did he care.

Mrs. Li ran after him. "Don't go out!" she wailed. "Where are you going?" But the howls of all three kids bawling in unison pulled her back to the house.

Mr. Li ran to the entrance of the lane in one breath. Hsiang and another printing press worker were just coming in. Mr. Li greeted Hsiang like a long-lost friend.

"What's the fire like at the Press?"

"Dozens of big blazes!" Hsiang retorted angrily. He was in the uniform of the plant's fire-fighters. His clothing was half drenched, his face brick-red. On his head was a brass helmet. Wiping his mouth with the back of his hand, he said hotly:

"Japanese bombs fell like rain. Wherever they burst, fires started. There were fires all over the place. Our fire-fighting squad couldn't handle them all. And the Japanese wouldn't let fire-engines through from the concessions. The dirty bastards! I'm going to show those dogs a thing or two!"

"Plant Five is the only one left now," put in Hsiang's workmate, "but sooner or later the Japanese'll bomb that too!"

Mr. Li didn't know the man's name but recognized him as another typesetter. Mr. Li's heart was pounding hard. It seemed to grow bigger with each beat. Standing with these two valiants, Mr. Li felt like a new man.

There was no respite however for the Chinese people when the Japanese were finally defeated after eight years of savage fighting. Chiang Kai-shek, with four million troops equipped with billions of dollars worth of US arms and munitions, boasted in 1946 he would crush the relatively small People's Liberation Army in three to six months. But he was up against a new phenomenon in Asia — soldiers who knew precisely what they were fighting for, led by honest selfless men, and imbued by a burning desire to slough off the filth and corruption of the past once and for all.

Tu Peng-cheng's *Defend Yenan* depicts this new type of man in smashing prose:

> The battle raged far into the night. Tiger had only nine men left. Their ammunition was almost gone. Again the enemy attacked — this time from four sides.
>
> This is it! thought Tiger. Either the fish break the net or they die! He led his men in a bayonet charge to meet the oncoming enemy. White blades clashed in mortal combat.
>
> Ordinarily Tiger gave the impression of being stolid and rather clumsy. But now his movements were sharply agile. Like a whirlwind, he killed two of the enemy in an instant. Then something hit him, and he fell. He knew he was wounded but he didn't know where, nor did he care. Rising to a kneeling position, he threw his last four grenades. Then, mustering all his strength, he stood up and plunged into the smoke, slashing left and right with his bayonet, boldly lunging at the foe.
>
> His wild dash carried him up to a flame-spitting machine gun, terrifying the two enemy soldiers manning it. They turned to flee. With one kick he knocked the gun over, dispatched one man with his bayonet, brought the other down with his rifle butt. Threatening his frightened soldiers with a revolver, an enemy officer herded a dozen of them to surround Tiger. The PLA man had no more grenades or bullets. He faced a circle of bayonet points. With all the hatred that was in him, he whirled around, stabbed and hacked savagely.
>
> The enemy soldiers were afraid to come too near. They didn't dare shoot or use their grenades for fear of hitting one of their own men; any soldier Tiger pointed his bayonet at hastily drew back. The officer swore and fired his pistol into the air, but to no avail. His men didn't dare to close in.
>
> And so Tiger held the enemy at bay, his left leg flexed, his right leg straight, both hands gripping the rifle, its butt beneath his armpit. He stood like a man of iron.

In spite of the inadequacies of my translations, I felt that, aside from demonstrating the quality of modern Chinese writing, they served a useful purpose in presenting the real China to the world. They supplied the flesh and bone and sinew that many of our articles so sadly lacked. It seemed to me no ordinary person in another land could help but like and admire the Chinese once they got to know them as I did. Short of actually meeting face to face — very difficult in the existing "hate-China" atmosphere — the literary medium was probably the next best thing. I wondered whether the day would ever come when Chinese and Americans could mix in large numbers, not just on a literary level, but personally as well. The prospects didn't look very promising.

VIII

GATHERING STORM

1962-1965

The Three Bad Years, the increasingly vituperative attacks of the Khrushchov gang — China weathered them all. The realities proved again that Mao was right. The people strongly supported his policies. In the spring of 1962 Premier Chou En-lai announced that the country's economy had taken a turn for the better.

We could see it in our daily lives. Food and clothing became more plentiful and varied. Beef had been hard to buy, and pretty tough even when you could get it. Now we were eating fillets again. There was plenty of fruit and vegetables, and very cheap. Six communes in the outskirts specialized in supplying these to Peking. More factories went into production.

The "zeppelins" disappeared. When Khrushchov broke the commercial contracts with China in 1960, he stopped supplying gasoline. Bus service had to be sharply curtailed. But not for long. The next thing we knew, busses were rolling again, on schedule. They looked queer, for on their roofs lay huge floppy bags. These were filled with marsh gas which some clever people remembered was rising in abundance from outlying swamps. Piped into the big bags and fed into converted engines, the gas did the trick. The fact that the bags were now dispensed with meant that China was developing a respectable petroleum industry.

The crisis had passed but fresh problems were right around the corner. Chiang Kai-shek chose the first half of 1962 to launch a flurry of assaults and incursions against the mainland, aided and abetted by the US armed forces. They were squashed, of course, but still it was annoying. The Indians, who had been raiding China since 1959, made a large-scale invasion in October. In November, the Chinese army drove them out, chasing them all the way down to Assam, to the alarm of the

British tea plantation owners there, then turned around and came home.

In September 1962, at a meeting of the Central Committee, Mao stress-ed the need for vigilance against a capitalist comeback. He said that class contradictions still remained, that the struggle would be long and complex. Mao also noted that those seeking to overthrow a political power always laid the groundwork by first building public opinion in their favor.

In spite of shortcomings I was stimulated by life in new China. The Chinese people had conquered the Three Bad Years magnificently, in spite of Khrushchov's treachery, and were going on, cheerfully enthusias-tic, to build a country which had been backward and oppressed into a land of plenty. I was learning about their fabulous cultural heritage, their epochal revolution, their bold vision. I was coming to see Mao and his Communist Party as the true humanitarians, men and women to whom the ordinary folk were the source of all strength and creativeness, who worked with them, learned from them and taught them.

My Chinese friends and neighbors, most of my colleagues at the office, were warm, considerate, intelligent. In spite of individual shortcomings, they generally wanted a better China and a better world, and they worked toward that aim. I had a Chinese wife in the thick of intel-lectual ferment and a Chinese daughter who regaled me with insights on Peking teenagers.

I could and did read Chinese books, magazines, newspapers. My grasp of the language was pretty good. I could listen to the radio, see movies, go to the theater, chat with people, joke, laugh, discuss, argue. None of my intimates treated me as a foreigner, except to ask me occa-sionally for my views and interpretations of American events. I was flattered and embarrassed, for often they knew more of what was going on there than I did. Anyhow, I was accepted.

I was still very much the boy from Brooklyn, and everyone accepted that, too. I read the airmail editions of *Time* and *Newsweek,* listened to the Voice of America, kept up on the more important new books, talked with visitors from the old country, played a tape library ranging from Sophie Tucker to The Supremes. I missed a lot of things and places and a few people.

Yet swept along by the Chinese revolution, I was coming closer to socialism, at least in mental outlook. With my new understanding of the world and class struggle, I recalled my earlier concepts with wry amusement. These were, of course, a product of my personal history and environment, as well as of my subjective endeavors. I could see that better now, in retrospect.

Knowledge of my antecedents went back only as far as my grandparents. Both paternal and maternal grandparents arrived in America in the 1890's with the tide of refugees from the pogroms of czarist Russia. My father's people were from Kiev, dark-haired Ukrainians, former serfs. Grandma Shapiro was a milkmaid as a girl. Mom's parents were from Vilna — Vilnius in Roman times — blond, fair, northern Europeans. Grandpa was Samuel Samuelson, and this had been the name of his father, and his father before him — and of every first-born son back into family history — Samuel, son of Samuel. I was told that in Russia the Samuelsons had been "scholars", which meant, I suppose, that they had been literate, and hadn't had to work with their hands.

I had been only mildly curious about my European background. What little I heard of it sounded fusty and dreary. My grandparents had left Russia voluntarily, gladly, and had come to America with a dream of a new and better life. To a certain extent they found it. From the lower East Side of New York City, where they and many of their fellow refugees had settled, they worked their way up into the ranks of the lower middle class. It was the vibrant present that counted, not the past.

My own parents were not only disinterested in their European origins, they hated them, disowned them. They took pride in being Americans, they were fiercely patriotic, they laughed at neighbors who still hadn't shed their foreign ways, foreign accents.

It was this kind of environment in which I was raised. My father had satisfied the ideal of his immigrant parents, who at great financial sacrifice had put him through college, and had become a "professional man", a lawyer. My pretty mother, by the time I was born, was able to give up her job as a typist and devote herself fully to household chores and to me. She wrote me a touching letter on December 23, 1960, when I was already in China, telling me how I had come into the world.

"Forty-five years ago this afternoon," she said, "you first saw the light of a blizzard, for that is what happened that day. Should you have forgotten, the night before you were born the hospital on East Broadway, New York, telephoned me at midnight to come to the hospital at once. The Culver Line was running very infrequently from Boro Park in Brooklyn, where we lived. When Pop and I finally got to the Manhattan side of the old Brooklyn Bridge, we were told that the horse cars which ran along East Broadway had stopped at midnight. We had to walk in that snowstorm all the way to Montgomery Street and stop in doorways where I could catch my breath, and then continue on. (Cabs were not in use then.) We finally reached the hospital at 3 a.m., half dead, and found no beds available. I had to sit in the supply room with other women on stacks of linen until the following noon. You decided not to appear until 5 o'clock that afternoon. As I am telling you this it all seems as though it happened just yesterday. You were a red lobstery infant with long dark hair which eventually became very fair. You certainly were some baby!"

My mother was doting, yet efficient. She had to be, for in addition to her troubles with me (I managed to have all the childhood illnesses and two mastoid operations before I was six) she had to build up my father who was recovering from a bout of pulmonary tuberculosis, the "poor man's disease".

We continued to climb up the social scale and moved when I was ten, with my five-year-old sister Ruth, to the lotus land of Flatbush. Immigrant families living in the grime of New York City ghettoes longed to get to an area where there was greenery and fresh air, and Flatbush appeared the ultimate Nirvanah. That we could afford to make this move was a sign of real achievement. The mortgage on our one-family house was considerably heavier than its Spanish tile roof, and the streets were unpaved and had only temporary sewers which backed up when it rained and flooded to the top of the terrace on which we dwelt. But we had gardens front and rear, a garage for our new Buick, trees lining the road, and bushes and flowers everywhere.

At thirteen, in 1928, I had my first and last encounter with the ancient religion of my ancestors. Under strong parental pressure I learned enough Hebrew to make a brief Bar Mitzvah speech at a ceremony alleging that, in the traditional words, "Today I am a man." Hair on my upper lip, a breaking voice, and interesting developments in the pubic region had already led me to that suspicion. But this confirmed it, the speech in the temple being followed by a catered dinner given by the proud parents. Guests bestowed not only the usual cufflinks and fountain pens, but, no doubt stirred by the prevailing bullish optimism on Wall Street, stocks and bonds. In those days every small shopkeeper and pushcart pedlar was speculating in real estate or the market.

Then, in 1929, the bubble burst, stocks plummeted. According to a joke then going the rounds, whenever a well-dressed harried-looking man requested a room on an upper floor of a hotel, he was asked: "For sleeping or jumping?" Although I had the doubtful distinction of being wiped out in the market at the age of fourteen, I never was driven to such desperate measures.

Our fortunes declined in the depression that followed. I didn't feel any hardship during my high school and pre-law college years, though I supplemented family income slightly by delivering newspapers and selling eggs door to door from an uncle's farm in New Jersey.

But by the summer of 1934, my last vacation before law school, the future looked bleak. Unemployment was high. Men peddled pencils and apples on the streets. Shanty towns mushroomed on New York City's empty lots. My father enjoyed a brief flurry representing clients going down in bankruptcy and mortgage foreclosures.

Although I had enrolled for the autumn term in St. John's Law School, I didn't want to be a lawyer particularly. The stories I heard my father and his colleagues tell about the vagaries of their profession held little interest for me. The problem was I didn't know what I wanted. I was healthy, fairly good-looking and reasonably intelligent. I played ball with the boys, romanced the girls, and had no difficulty in getting good marks in school. Mothers held me up as an example for their sons to emulate, causing private snickers among my cronies. Things came to me easily, too easily, fanning the normal jauntiness of youth. Surely I could do better than sit in an office drawing legal documents?

But do what? Jobs were scarce and I had no special skills. At least as a lawyer I would be sure of a position in my father's office. I couldn't make up my mind. It was at this point I did something I was to do again when confronted by an apparently insoluble dilemma — I pulled up stakes and struck out for parts unknown.

While in college I had become friends with a classmate named Jerry Mann. Jerry also lived in Flatbush, and we knew people in common. What brought us closer together, however, was long and frequent philosophic discussion. Jerry was more advanced than I and had a rudimentary concept of class struggle. I saw it simplistically as a division between the haves and the have-nots, with the first callously trampling upon the second. My aim was to get into a position where no one could ever trample on me. I had no higher ideas than that.

Jerry, whose father was a cutter in the garment industry, was also restless. A tough boy, handy with his fists, he too was seeking a more exciting future than life as a lawyer. We decided to go out together and look, to hitch-hike across the country to California during our summer vacation. A friend of my father had settled there. On a visit to New York some years previous he had told us glowing tales of the wonders of the West. Jerry and I agreed if we could find better prospects there, we'd take them. If not, we'd return to law school in New York.

We set out one morning in late June, 1933, heading for Chicago. We arrived four days later, feeling ourselves already veterans in thumbing rides and cadging meals. In Chicago a World's Fair was welcoming visitors from all over the globe. On a strict economy budget, we paid our calls after closing time, skirting around the fence where it met Lake Michigan, having persuaded the Georgia red-neck guard that we weren't out to steal anything, only to sleep on the long well-upholstered seats of the excursion busses parked inside.

Reaching our next stop, Kansas City, proved more difficult. People seemed reluctant to give us rides. Was it our sprouting beards and increasingly unkempt appearance? We found the reason one afternoon when, after waiting hours in vain for a lift on the outskirts of a city, we glanced at the telephone pole behind us. On it was a poster which said: "Wanted, dead or alive, John Dillinger . . ." and went on to give a detailed description of the killer for whom the police of seven states were searching. No wonder drivers wouldn't pick us up!

Because we had only about fifty dollars apiece we tried to stretch our money by sleeping out in the open, weather permitting, and working for our meals. The well-to-do home owners and restaurant keepers we approached usually made us sweat for our suppers. But in the run-down dwellings our host or hostess would say: "Eat first, then we'll see." And when we'd finished, they'd laugh and say: "Forget it. We don't have enough to do around here ourselves."

Early one day we were on U.S. Route One, the Lincoln Highway, an asphalt swath over rolling plains which should have been covered with corn and wheat. Instead, only parched shoots stubbled the cracked soil, for there was a terrible drought. Homesteads were few and far between. We walked up to the nearest one and found the family at breakfast. They invited us to join them and plied us with eggs, milk, butter, homemade bread and deep-dish cherry pie. They told us they were having a disastrous year, even as they kept urging us to eat more. So strong is the tradition of American farm folk hospitality that it never occurred to them to let their hardships influence the treatment of guests at their table.

As the population thinned out, and with Dillinger on the loose, rides grew scarcer. When we finally reached Kansas City we decided to do what we had sworn to our families we never would — take to the freights.

We had thought originally that these were used mainly by hoboes. We met some of them, as well as gamblers, pimps, hustlers and con men. But in the summer of '33 — year of depression and drought — the bulk of the non-paying passengers on the railroads of America were migratory workers, men traveling from state to state harvesting crops, picking fruit.

They rode on top (freight trains haul few empties), sitting on the long three-plank catwalk, as the cars jerked and rattled along. Sometimes they were so thick up there it was hard to find a place to sit down. These men were very different from the slovenly hoboes. Lean, dignified, most of them carried a small cheap suitcase. On arriving at their destination, they would remove their smoke-grimed traveling clothes, wash thoroughly, shave, change into clean overalls, put the dirty garments into the case, and set out for their prospective jobs.

Jerry and I hit a "red ball" express freight out of Kansas City that brought us into Colorado Springs almost non-stop. We traveled right through the night and were riding, as usual, on top. We could rest only by turns in short naps, the one staying awake holding on to the sleeper with one hand and clutching the catwalk with the other. Not especially relaxing for either of us.

During a short stay in Colorado Springs I set out one night to climb Pike's Peak (elevation 14,000 feet). It's too hot in summer during the day. I went alone, since Jerry's shoes had worn through completely and he was housebound while having them repaired. Mercifully, I was dissuaded at the foot of the slope by local villagers. The temperature drops precipitously after midnight, they said. A party of mountaineers only the week before had been compelled to stop and light fires every half hour to keep from freezing to death. I was wearing only a thin sweater.

When Jerry and I resumed our journey a few days later, we once again were guests of the Atchison, Topeka and Santa Fe Railway. But then we were separated, running to catch a freight in New Mexico. I tripped over a switch, and by the time I got up, Jerry and the train were rolling off into the distance. The palms of my hands were lacerated and bleeding from my fall on the cindery roadbed. I wouldn't be able to grab any freight car ladders again for some time. Thoroughly disgusted with myself, I decided to return to New York and become a lawyer.

Jerry continued on and reached California. He was so charmed by it that he persuaded his whole family to move out. They went into business for themselves, and Jerry subsequently prospered. Would I also be in California today if I hadn't missed that freight?

After passing the New York State bar examination I went to serve my clerkship with a prominent firm of Jewish Wall Street lawyers. Because it was such a privilege to be allowed to work for them I was paid eight dollars per week instead of twelve — the usual rate in those depression days for gentlemen starvelings.

This limited my lunches to two nutted cheeseburgers (cream cheese on wholewheat bread studded with nuts) and a glass of orangeade, total price, twenty-five cents. After lunch I would loaf on the steps of the Sub Treasury Building at Broad and Wall and enjoy the sunshine, which was free.

Lounging there with me were hundreds of lesser employees of the New York stock exchange and various brokerage houses. Poorly paid, they were generally laid off shortly before Christmas, on the excuse that the market was slack, so that their employers wouldn't have to pay them any Christmas bonus. In imitation of the senior members of their firms they wore rolled-brim homburg hats, suits of charcoal gray, well-laundered shirts, and conservative ties. These were all cheap imitations, costing a fraction of the vestments of their idols.

Yet these young men were positive they would rise if only they convinced their bosses of their devotion and dedication. When an organizer got up on the pedestal of the statue of George Washington and urged them to join a white collar union of office workers, they hooted with superior laughter.

I was forming a different picture of the world. It seemed to me that neither diligence nor ability was any guarantee of success. I knew many people who worked hard all their lives, and were quite skilled at their jobs, who eked out only a marginal existence.

On the other hand, most of the senior partners in my Wall Street law firm were men of not more than average intelligence. One or two were rather stupid. Yet they drew enormous salaries. Why? They had wealthy clients. What mattered wasn't so much what you knew but who you knew. You could always hire bright young people to do the actual spade work.

Corporate law seemed so dull, and the people involved in high finance so narrow. Whatever was good for business they approved. My attorney employers were descendants of German Jews who had emigrated to America a century before, and represented scions of similar ancestry who owned corporations with large interests in southern turpentine. One afternoon several of the lawyers sat around our luxurious office listening to Adolph Hitler ranting over the radio.

"A great man. He's been excellent for the German economy," they said. "What a pity he has that one little flaw about Jews."

Hobnobbing with gentry such as these for the rest of my life seemed too great a price to pay for affluence and ease. I transferred my allegiance to another firm of attorneys.

Not so lofty, they also pulled down big fees, though more rarely, for they were negligence lawyers, better known as "ambulance chasers". They didn't do the chasing in person, but had a network of interns, policemen, safety inspectors, etc., who informed them promptly of any promising accidents, meanwhile praising them highly to the victim until they could rush down and get his or her signature on a retainer. They worked on a contingency basis — one third of whatever damages they recovered. Occasionally they demanded and got half.

Witnesses would be found, or created, and taught how to render the most damning kind of evidence against the defendant. Doctors or psychiatrists were hired for the medical testimony. Proceedings were instituted and preliminary hearings held. Then negotiations would start with the insurance company. Only insured defendants were sued, since few individuals had sufficient assets to pay the judgments my law firm hoped to get. And since they had a record of whopping recoveries in court, the insurance company adjustors were often willing to reach a pre-trial settlement. Sometimes they could be "persuaded" by means of a kickback.

If the case actually went to trial, then every gun in the arsenal was brought to bear. There was jubilation in the office whenever we won a big one, and open crowing over the smart tricks we had got away with.

I couldn't see this type of practice as my career. The firm was forever skating on the edge of, if not a breach of the law, then a violation of the legal profession's canon of ethics. Indeed, shortly after I left them, the senior partner was suspended from practice for several years for professional misconduct.

So, in spite of myself, I ended up doing what I had been trying to avoid — joining my father. Why had I been so set against it? He was a good lawyer, had a varied practice, was located right off Times Square, and was unencumbered with partners. He had told me a number of times I would be welcome. I suppose I had wanted to show that, after all the years of being raised and supported by my parents, I could make it on my own.

My political ideas were only beginning to form. I was a registered Democrat and voted in every election, but I could see many flaws in American democracy. We had a few criminal cases, which brought me into the precinct police stations, the courts and the prisons. There was a marked difference between the treatment of those with money and connections and those without. I discovered, too, that people were maimed or killed in accidents because landlords had been able to bribe municipal inspectors to overlook fire and safety hazards on their premises. I learned that the two major political parties which dominated the elections were machine-run, patronage-dispensing organizations, more responsive to their backers and free-spending lobbyists than to the interests of the average citizen.

On the international scene America was maintaining a policy of "neutrality" toward republican Spain while Nazi German air force planes were helping the Franco fascists pulverize cities and improving technique for the coming world war. At the same time the US government was permitting the sale of scrap steel from dismantled New York City elevators to the Japanese who were coldly slaughtering Chinese civilians, steel which would later return in the form of bullets in American boys' bodies.

I was generally dissatisfied with my own life, with what was happening in America and the world. Reading more, discussing more, I was groping for understanding, but not attaining much. Young Communists I knew tried to proselytize me, but I couldn't go along with their views. They uncritically praised anything that came out of the Soviet Union, including obviously poor films and inferior fiction. I had nothing against the Russians, in fact I admired the way they were building up their own country, and the position they took against the Nazis. What I couldn't stomach was the mindless weathervane spinning of the American Communist Party with every change of the Soviet wind.

Neither the Democrat nor Communist type of party appealed to me, yet I wasn't content to sit around bemoaning the state of affairs. I wanted to do something positive. An opportunity presented itself when I was approached by young composers and sketch writers who wanted to form an organization where their material could be centralized for presentation to prospective users — nightclubs, unions, and resort hotels — and which would see to it that they collected performance royalties.

I established the Review Writers Guild in 1941. The Japanese attacked Pearl Harbor in December of the same year, and America entered the war. It was a time of national unity, with nearly everyone rallying behind the war effort. Our Guild members wrote songs and skits in its support, as well as strongly pro-labor, pro-union material. With the rabid Right temporarily muted, there was a flowering of progressive creations.

Though stimulating, it was not very remunerative. I took only a small fraction of our members' modest royalties. Our law firm earned its fees in more mundane ways, though my father, I must say, had glamorous ideas. Regrettably, they never quite came off.

He was the lawyer for the shirt manufacturers of Allentown, Pennsylvania, and for the window cleaners union of New York City. In both cases gangsters moved in, and he moved out. He presided over the revival of "No, No, Nanette", an operetta. It fizzled back into obscurity after a short run in the old Orpheum. He introduced soccer to Madison Square Garden, using a slightly deflated ball. It aroused only mild interest.

By coincidence, we had two mental incompetancy proceedings in a row. Our clients in both instances were elderly men who had inherited life estates from extremely wealthy families which had founded railroads and the like. Because they were merry old rogues with expensive tastes in women and wine, the alarmed holders of the residual estates — the relatives who would get what was left when the old boys died — brought actions to have them committed to mental institutions as manic depressives, and to have themselves appointed guardians of their financial affairs. Manic depression is difficult to prove, since we all have our ups and downs — it's mainly a question of degree — and we managed to win both actions.

While they were pending, as the junior partner I had to do the running around, interviewing our clients, their mistresses and hangers-on, getting their signatures on legal documents. They were a peculiar lot, and I thought privately the aged lotharios were indeed abnormal. They made me uncomfortable, and I always came away feeling pretty depressive myself.

Nor was I exactly enchanted by the other people who sought our services. Just as doctors' patients are usually ill, people don't come to lawyers unless they are involved in some sort of unpleasantness. They want to draw a will in anticipation of death, or squabble over the spoils of someone else's will, they are being sued, or they want to sue, or keep out of jail. In nearly every instance they are motivated by fear or greed. I knew that was the way of the world, or at least as much of the world as I had encountered thus far. But I hated to think I would be spending my days in so grubby an atmosphere.

And so, when my draft number came up in November of 1942. I went off to the army with almost a feeling of relief. I was glad to get away from a dull life and uninspiring career. The army would be new, different, I thought, it held promise of adventure. Besides, I loathed the enemy for what they were doing in Europe and Asia, and considered them savage maniacs who had to be stopped. I was quite willing to help in stopping them.

My army service gave me little opportunity to contribute to the downfall of Hitler, Mussolini and Hirohito. It did, however, teach me the fundamentals of Chinese, and this proved to be the catalytic agent for the major change in my existence.

I returned to New York, early in 1946, a civilian. I spent the next year studying more Chinese at Columbia, then at Yale, still groping, still dissatisfied. I decided to go to China. Any change would be an improvement, I thought. In March 1947, I left New York.

It wasn't until some years later that I recognized that my delicate shudders at the sordidness of the American business world were half-genuine, half pious self-deception. They were genuine in that the sordidness was certainly there, and it was truly distasteful. Where the self-deception came in was that I used my revulsion as an excuse to run away, instead of staying and trying to change things.

By the time I attained this realization I had acquired legitimate reasons for remaining in China. It was edifying, nevertheless, if a bit painful, to be able to view myself honestly.

In any event, by the early sixties I knew that in China I had the kind of life I wanted most. I agreed with Chinese aims and policies, I liked the political atmosphere, the cultural and social life. I had a home, a family, Chinese and foreign friends. I felt that I could do more useful and satisfying work in Peking than in New York. In short, I decided that I wanted to remain permanently.

And so in 1963, I applied for Chinese citizenship. The proceedings were simple. I wrote out an application stating why I wanted to become a citizen of China. There were no forms, no interviews. A few months later I was asked to fill out a small form, giving my name, date and place of birth, country of origin and present occupation, and to submit three photographs. A week or two later I was issued a certificate of citizenship with the state seal on it and signed by Premier Chou En-lai. That was all. No ceremony, no oaths of allegiance.

From that day on, I could vote in the elections, travel anywhere in China without restriction, take part in political study and movements, hear confidential reports. My Chinese colleagues had always been friendly, but now there was a new intimacy, a closer rapport. I felt a heightened sense of responsibility toward my work and what was going on in China. I had stopped being an interested helper and became a full participant. It was good to know at last exactly where I was going.

I was somewhat troubled by the special privileges which the Chinese insisted that I retain. I drew the same relatively high pay as before, went on the annual free travel tours, still got a month's paid vacation, received complimentary tickets to the theater and sporting events, was invited to state banquets, had a place in the reviewing stands on national holidays. In short, my treatment remained that of foreign expert.

It didn't seem right to me having it both ways. During the next few years I tried sporadically to reject some of it. Chinese friends said I was wrong. They said it was Communist Party policy to respect the customs and habits of different nationalities. Didn't they have special kitchens for Chinese Muslims? Weren't the various racial groupings encouraged to wear their national dress, speak their national language? A person from a foreign country had more expenses than the Chinese. Foreign-style meals cost more, he might want to buy books and magazines from abroad, he sometimes was supporting dependants in his own country.

I let myself be persuaded. Most of the activities arranged for foreigners were useful for anyone who wanted to learn more about China. And having a place in the reviewing stands and attending state banquets couldn't do me any harm as long as I remembered I was there only because of the courtesy extended to foreigners and not because I had done anything particularly commendable. But I drew the line on the question of salary. I managed to cut it down a third, not because I was a flaming revolutionary, but because as a Chinese citizen I didn't want to live too far above the general average.

I wouldn't take more than 300 *yuan* of the 440 monthly salary to which I was entitled, but it was still too much. Phoenix was getting around 200, giving us a total of 500 *yuan*. Our rent was only seventeen-fifty a month. Food came to less than a hundred. Our cook and housekeeper, who slept in, received a monthly wage of thirty *yuan*. Even after sending a hundred or so to some of Phoenix's relatives, entertaining frequently and spending without stint on extras like fruit, liquor, candy and tobacco, we lived very comfortably indeed, in Chinese style in a Chinese household, and had a surplus of two or three hundred each month.

The stuff kept piling up and we didn't know how to get rid of it. To make matters worse the government, while indulging me in my request that I not be given more than 300 *yuan*, banked the rest in a special account, and frequently reminded me that I could have it whenever I wanted. Only when I went to the States in 1971 was I able to dent the bankroll a bit.

It took some adjusting, learning to be a "foreign" Chinese, but on the whole it was a fairly happy transition. The difficulties were mainly in my own mind and, eventually, I was able to work them out. I had my Western music, my Western books, my Western friends, as well as their Chinese counterparts. That was not only acceptable, it was useful to one translating Chinese literature for Western circulation. I had already been eating Chinese food and wearing Chinese cloth shoes in summer and tunics padded with silk floss in winter. That was because I preferred them, but whenever I felt like eating or dressing differently, nobody thought anything of it.

In any event the superficial trappings didn't mean anything to most Chinese. Foreign "super-revolutionaries" who wore old clothes and struck Spartan poses did not impress them. What mattered was your attitude toward your job and the people you worked with, your social behavior in your community. For an egocentric American from a high-pressure, impatient, materialistic society, it was an enlightening experience to start learning to be self-critical and think in long-range community and world terms.

To add to the excitement, a few months after I became a Chinese citizen, my mother came to visit us. We had been talking about getting together for years. I might have gone to New York, but my passport had long since expired, and what with the atmosphere of implacable hostility to China prevailing in Washington I wasn't sure that

I could get another one and be able to return to China. Besides, my
mother wanted to see my wife and daughter, see how we lived, see this
place which had so enchanted her darling boy that he was willing to
give up the joys of Brooklyn.

She was over seventy when she boarded a Northwest Airlines plane
at Kennedy airport, a brave venture for a lady who used to get seasick
on the Staten Island ferry and had never been on a plane in her life.
During our summer family tours when I was a child she was accustomed
to giving invaluable admonitions from the back seat to my father as he
drove the Buick through the New England mountains. On the plane,
after a first uneasy half-hour, she had no choice but to relax and let the
pilot drive the plane himself. To her surprise, they reached Anchorage
in one piece. By the time they arrived in Tokyo she was such a veteran
traveler that she didn't trouble to stay over and rest a few hours but
took the next available shuttle to Hongkong. There, a China Travel
Service man met her and took charge. The next day he delivered her
to the border at Shenchun, where Phoenix and I were waiting.

I recognized her immediately as she walked across the short iron
bridge linking China and the Territory of Hongkong. Older, but not
much grayer, and the same ramrod-straight back. She stared at me,
then threw herself into my arms. Later, she told me she thought for
a moment I was her brother Jerry. I looked more like him than the
much younger impression she had retained of me in her memory.

She and Phoenix were promptly enamored of each other. The
exchange of letters over the years had made them somewhat acquainted
but both were very pleased with what they found in person. The normal
courtesy and solicitude of the Chinese toward older people was, in
Phoenix's case, underscored by a strong warmth and affection that went
straight to Mom's heart.

We rode back to Canton on the comfortable air-conditioned train
which plies between the city and border, and drank fragrant tea. Mom,
like all in-coming travelers, was struck by the contrast with what she
had seen in Hongkong. "It's so clean here," she said. "And they're so
bright and fresh and darling," she added, indicating the pretty girl
attendants pouring tea and handing out scented washcloths.

She liked our hotel, too — a huge sprawling affair surrounded by
lawns and palm trees and lush tropical flowers. Everything was new,
everything was interesting — and very different from what she had been

led to believe. But her main interest was me and mine. So we strolled around a bit and the next day took the train for Peking.

The train was crowded and we shared our first-class compartment of four berths with a big, stocky Hunanese about the same age as my mother. He was obviously an army man. We knew this not only from the dark green trousers he wore with his plain white shirt, but because of the young orderly who came in and spoke to him from time to time.

We introduced ourselves and he told us his name. He said he was on his way to a meeting in Peking. I asked what sort of work he did.

"I'm a soldier," he replied, raising an imaginary rifle to his shoulder and pulling the trigger. Later we learned that he was the commanding general of the whole provincial border region and that the "meeting" he was attending was the National Congress, of which he was a member.

He knew half a dozen complicated card tricks which he patiently taught us, and a version of solitaire I hadn't seen before. We showed him a few American kinds. He wanted to hear all about us, and was as pleased as we that we could be reunited after so many years.

His own story, which he told at my urging, was laconic. In the twenties, he had worked in a weaving mill in Changsha. Conditions in Hunan Province were terrible, so the peasants staged a big uprising and the workers went on strike. Mao had led the peasant revolt. For a time, they were in control of a large part of the province. He himself had been a member of a workers' patrol. Then the reactionaries came back with modern weapons and artillery and slaughtered thousands. The people had only spears and knives.

"So what did you do?" I asked. "Head for the hills and fight on from there?"

"Oh, no. The enemy was too strong. I went back to work," he said. "But they treated us worse than ever at the mill. We couldn't live. So finally we had to go out and join the guerrillas."

People weren't really fired by romantic idealism, like it says in some novels, he explained. They revolted only when there was no alternative, when their backs were to the wall. Even then, their aims were limited and simple. A decent wage for the worker, a piece of land of his own for the peasant.

"I was very ignorant when I first joined the revolution," said the general. "I couldn't even read or write. Most of us were like that. We fought through many provinces. Gradually we came to see that it wasn't just this boss or that landlord who was at fault but the capitalist and landlord classes. They were the same everywhere we went. They had better weapons than we, but we were many and they were few. We took their guns away from them, and the poor people in their armies came over and joined us, and so we won and changed the social system."

We discovered that he had a very bad heart, and that he kept a small oxygen inhalator in his berth. The orderly was a medic, who was always within calling distance. But the old soldier was blithely unconcerned. He mentioned these things casually, in passing. He had installed himself in an upper berth, and we had a devil of a time getting him down. Only after repeatedly vowing that Phoenix and I both abhorred lowers, did he agree to change places. Our journey to Peking was very pleasant, and the general promised to come and see us.

Ya-mei and her grandmother were mutually delighted the moment they met. They could hardly speak a word at first, but they soon picked up enough in each other's language to enable them, adding gestures and drawings, to engage in long conversations. Both of Phoenix's parents were dead and Ya-mei keenly felt the lack of a grandmother. In her schoolmates' families the grandma often outdid even the grandpa in pampering the children. Coming from a similar tradition herself, Mom certainly didn't let Ya-mei down.

We gave Mom our room and borrowed a daybed for ourselves. She found our meals quite palatable, asking only for bread instead of rice. She spent hours in the kitchen with our housekeeper, who had not had the benefits of even a few weeks of "the English of southern England" which Ya-mei was then absorbing in her first year of junior high. Nevertheless, the ladies managed a fruitful exchange of recipes, beef in oyster sauce heading for Flatbush and potato pancakes with onion grated in passing into Chinese culinary lore.

Mom brought me up to date on the births and marriages and deaths among relatives and friends in the States, briefed me on the rise in prices and crime and the drop in moral standards. We did our best to explain what we could about China. But mainly we let Mom see for herself — in the stores, on the streets, in the residential lanes. We didn't make a Red out of her, but she agreed that it was a fine society "for the Chinese".

Our friends and colleagues — Chinese and foreign — were marvellous. Both Phoenix's office and mine gave dinners in Mom's honor. Chinese friends were constantly calling, presenting her with little gifts, showing her around. We were overwhelmed by their kindness. Mom had a whale of a good time.

A few things took a little getting used to, on both sides. Fresh from the land of the youth cult, she bridled a bit at their frequent reference to her "great age". We had to explain that this was said admiringly, that the term "venerable" was a mark of respect. Mom finally accepted this though only, I'm afraid, reluctantly.

To our Chinese friends, she was something of a phenomenon. Red — one of her favorite clothing colors — was worn in China mostly by young brides. They were puzzled, too, by smartly cut dresses, lipstick and permed hair on a woman of seventy. But they liked her honest modesty, her courage, her independent spirit. When they learned that she was a widow and had been working for a living until only recently, they paid her the highest accolade in urging me, her son, to "learn to be like her".

We had been separated for sixteen years. Mom confessed that she had frequently worried about me, wondering, in spite of my letters, whether I was "really" alright. Now she had come and seen that I was very much alright indeed, that my life and family were everything I had said they were.

But you couldn't deprive a mother and grandmother of her "worries". Having disposed of the Chinese branch of the family, she was able to concentrate her full attention on the American side. Could she be positive that they were getting along without her? There was no way to reassure her. After nine weeks in Peking she was burning to get back to New York.

Farewell dinners, some last minute shopping, then the return trek to Hongkong, Phoenix and I accompanying her to the border. We stopped over in Nanking, Shanghai and Hangchow, taking in ancient and revolutionary sites, communes and factories. Mom enjoyed it. She was impressed by things we had learned to take for granted.

"Isn't that wonderful," she said, when we visited the crèche of a Hangchow silk embroidery factory, where mothers had time off to nurse their infants. "They used to fire us when we got pregnant. In a lot of places you had to deny that you were even married if you wanted a job."

The border again, everyone being very tight-lipped until, half-way across the iron bridge, Mom turned and waved. Then I couldn't see her for my tears. Was this the last time we would meet? Very possibly.

A few hours later she phoned us in Canton from her hotel in Hongkong, and her brisk cheerful voice restored my optimism. In the long run our people were winning and the reactionaries were losing all over the world. Things were bound to improve, including Sino-American relations. Who knew? I might even get to the US. A wild thought in 1963.

Mom arrived in New York before Phoenix and I reached Peking. The gallant State Department canceled her passport, on the theory that she had violated some ruling of theirs against using a US passport to visit China. Actually China did not acknowledge American passports and refused to stamp them, issuing their visas separately. But the Hate China crowd was still strong in Washington, and any decent intelligent attitudes toward Peking had to be smothered.

In China, meanwhile, among certain philosophers it became fashionable to deny the dialectic principle that contradictions can only be solved when one side completely conquers the other. These gentlemen claimed that opposing factors could harmoniously and permanently blend into a single entity. Like Jonah and the whale, perhaps, or Mount Vesuvius and the people of Pompeii. Equal opprobrium was heaped upon the aggressor and the victim — "all wars are bad". Forget about exploiters and exploited they urged — "classes and class struggle no longer exist".

Again Mao warned: If class struggle was forgotten, if working class rule was abandoned, capitalism would make a comeback, the Chinese Communist Party would go revisionist, fascist, the country would "change color".

How could this be prevented? You had to have people who would carry on, who would keep the Party and government leadership in the hands of the revolutionaries, who would stick to Marxism, said Mao. You had to teach them to serve the people of China and the world. They had to learn how to unite with the majority, including those who disagreed with them — but not the phonies and opportunists. They had to be democratic, and listen to the masses as well as lead them. They had to be modest, self-critical, to admit and correct their mistakes. A man's ability to meet these requirements was judged by his behavior in the "great storms of revolution".

In the international arena the battle for men's hearts and minds also raged, with the Chinese and Soviet Parties both mapping very different courses to socialism and, ultimately, communism. They disagreed on every fundamental — the nature of revolution in capitalist countries, in

colonies, the continuation of class struggle and revolution within socialist countries, relationships between socialist and capitalist countries,
between socialist countries and people struggling for liberation, among
socialist countries, among communist parties, the nature of imperialism,
attitudes toward war, the atom bomb. . . .

The conflict, which had been flaring up sporadically ever since
Khrushchov's keynote speech at the 20th Congress of the Soviet Party in
1956, reached a climax in 1963 and 1964, when Khrushchov and his gang
launched a series of vituperative attacks on the Chinese Communist
Party. Every one of these was carried in full in China's *People's Daily*.

The Chinese did better than that. They published, in translation, the
complete works of Nikita Khrushchov, put them on public sale and
begged people to read them. These masterpieces were analysed and
solemnly discussed, along with the various denunciations in *Trud* and
Pravda, in China's millions of study groups. In my group we found
Nicky rough going. He was always windy and frequently incoherent.
Still, the nuggets of pure revisionism were worth the dredging. It was
so easy to take them apart.

At the same time, the Chinese Party replied with a series of articles
of it own, which came to be known as the Nine Polemics. In November
1964, China's *Red Flag* added a neat little coda: *Why Khrushchov Fell.*
In these lucid incisive documents we thought we detected more than a
little of the Mao touch.

None were published in Moscow. The Soviet people knew nothing
about them. They did get around, however, to many other parts of the
world. Their revelations of the degeneration within the Soviet Union
were more of a shock then than they would be today, when the situation is worse and more widely known. But their main value was that
they laid out the gut issues for those who claimed to be, or hoped to
become, revolutionaries. They showed the way the Soviet and other
revisionists were going, and the results. They stated what the Chinese
position was, and why, bolstered by common sense and plenty of facts.
Subsequent Soviet behavior and world developments further strengthened the Chinese case.

From then on, the die was cast. China no longer considered the
Soviet Union a socialist country. It was "social-imperialist" — an imperialist super-power with socialist trimmings, but imperialist nevertheless, with all the typical exploitative, chauvinistic, military-bases-abroad
characteristics. The Soviet Party was not communist, but revisionist —

building "socialism" on a bourgeois goulash basis, bringing back capitalism in disguise, selling out ordinary folk and sucking up to their
oppressors. . . .

To the high-minded Chinese, with their class-based humanitarian
ideals, such policies and conduct were utterly reprehensible. The breach
between the two Communist Parties which inevitably followed was
irreconcilable, for it went to the very heart of what a communist party,
a socialist country, was and should be.

In the summer of 1962 I was asked by the Peking Motion Picture
Studio to play in a film they were making about what was known as the
"executive headquarters" period of 1946. After the Japanese surrender
in 1945, fighting flared up between the Communist and Kuomintang
forces. American military representatives in Peking acted as "media-
tors", while American ships and planes were busily ferrying Kuomintang
troops to points of strategic importance.

At the same time America was trying to build a "third force" in
China of bourgeois intellectuals, hoping that these could form a government partial to the United States.

The only thing wrong with the idea was that the country was split
roughly into eighty-nine percent suffering oppressed humanity and ten
percent feudal fascist tyrants plus capitalist compradors. The other one
percent — if it was that much — was the bourgeois intellectuals, who
represented no one but themselves. Of course the whole concept was
absurd.

I was offered the role of an American academic who attempts to pull
Chinese intellectuals into the ranks of the "third force". The ham that
lurks in every man rose quickly to the surface. I couldn't resist the
temptation to immortalize my profile on celluloid, and graciously accepted. I was sure it would be a thrilling experience and very
glamorous.

It turned out to be anything but.

My first problem was with the make-up man. I relaxed and let him
have his way with what he thought an American dean of a Chinese
university should look like. I watched the mirror, intrigued, as he fitted
me with a bald head, mustache and goatee. It finally dawned on me
that he was turning me into the foreign intellectual whose image he knew
best — Lenin!

A hurried consultation with the director resulted in the removal of
the shrubbery. When exposure on the set to high voltage lamps in the

middle of August caused me to sweat so profusely under my rubber headpiece that all my make-up washed away, the baldy was also discarded. We settled for parting my hair in the middle and heavy horn-rimmed spectacles.

I found that movie-making is hard work, alternating with long boring periods when you do nothing. Before each shot in the Peking Studio there were a few practice run-throughs and endless fiddling with lights. For economy reasons they did only two actual takes. We merely mouthed our lines. The actors dubbed in their own voices later. The foreign stars were dubbed by Chinese professionals. Mine gave me a rather reedy tenor. Most of the time, you just hung around, waiting. In the intervals I had time to translate a whole book of modern Chinese poetry. Even observing the lovelies wasn't much fun. Their beauty was obscured by the heavy make-up they had to wear for the camera.

When the film began its nationwide run, theatrical friends who saw me on the screen said I looked very authentic — just like an American. They politely refrained from commenting on my acting. Phoenix, with wifely candor, pronounced it "vapid". I was reluctantly compelled to agree. I vowed I'd never set foot before a camera again. A dozen years passed before I broke my word.

The picture turned out to be pretty good in spite of me. It's called *After the Armistice*, and has recently been revived.

IX

CULTURAL REVOLUTION, FIRST HALF

1966-1972

For some years in certain areas of Chinese society feudal and bourgeois attitudes and methods had been growing. In the arts, for instance, a few quite decadent things appeared. Some educators tended to be conservative and stodgy, waspishly feuding among themselves as to which of their alma maters — be it Oxford or Cambridge or Harvard — was the most prestigious. . . .

Phoenix and I attended the graduation ceremonies of an English class in the Foreign Languages Institute. For a triumphal conclusion they put on an act from a British play — *The Importance of Being Earnest* by Oscar Wilde! The poor kids looked ridiculous in putty noses, crinoline skirts and top hats. What use nineteenth century English of the British upper class was supposed to be for them never seemed to have entered their teachers' minds.

How typical or widespread such phenomena were I had no idea. But the Central Committee of the Chinese Communist Party — which certainly was in a position to know — evidently considered the situation very serious. On the 8th of August, 1966, it promulgated its "Decision Concerning the Great Proletarian Cultural Revolution" — the famous "Sixteen Points" which set the guidelines:

> Although the bourgeoisie has been overthrown, it is still trying to use the old ideas, culture, customs and habits of the exploiting classes to corrupt the masses, capture their minds and stage a come-back. The proletariat must do the exact opposite: it must meet head-on every challenge of the bourgeoisie in the ideological field and use the new ideas, culture, customs and habits of the proletariat to change the mental outlook of the whole society. At present, our objective is to struggle against and overthrow those persons in power taking the

224

capitalist road, to criticize and repudiate the bourgeois reactionary academic 'authorities' and the ideology of the bourgeoisie and all other exploiting classes and to transform education, literature and art and all other parts of the superstructure not in correspondence with the socialist economic base, so as to facilitate the consolidation and development of the socialist system.

Today, there is some question as to whether the tone of the statement was not excessive, whether the degree of danger wasn't overrated. The manner in which the campaign was subsequently conducted was certainly extreme.

I participated, directly or indirectly, in several aspects of the Cultural Revolution at the same time, joining a "battle team" in *Chinese Literature* and, later, a "revolutionary" group formed by foreigners. I had missed the very beginning at the Foreign Languages Press because I was holed up in the Friendship Hostel rushing out a translation of a new novel. By the time I moved back home again, Peking was a different city. Walls were plastered with big character posters, with fresh ones going up at all hours of the day and night, accusing and defending Party leaders at various levels and excoriating manifestations of the backward and reactionary left over from the old society.

"Red Guard" organizations — teenage groups — were raiding the homes of former bigwigs and digging up the most amazing things. Before Liberation many of the rich absentee landlords and bureaucrat capitalists and top Kuomintang officials had their homes in Peking, living in genteel leisure, far from the sources of their harshly accumulated wealth. These ladies and gentlemen, even before the details of their pasts became known, were invariably the most hated people on the block. For although a new society had been established, they rarely changed their insolent manners and avaricious habits. During the Cultural Revolution the Red Guards made for them with unerring instinct.

In the compound across the lane from us was a retired businessman who got his original capital from extensive land rents, a common thing in the old society. Though only about sixty and in vigorous health, he had himself pushed around in a wheelchair of shining tubular aluminum, because he liked his comfort. He and his wife, a fat, pasty-faced woman, never spoke to any of the neighbors — mostly working people, with a sprinkling of office staffers, who heartily returned their antipathy. When the Red Guards went in, they found trunks filled with old ceremonial Kuomintang uniforms — reminders of the old boy's days of glory, and some outlandish ancient costumes — burial clothes which would enable them to join their ancestors in swank feudal style.

I went to view some of the treasures unearthed by Peking's Red Guards in the first stage of the Cultural Revolution. They filled two galleries in the city's Exhibition Hall. There was money, pots of it, gold and silver coins and solid gold bars, illegally hoarded. There was memorabilia of the days when they were riding high — tricolored hats, fringed epaulette uniforms, medals, decorations, autographed pictures of Chiang Kai-shek. Weapons galore, from sword canes to submachine guns. Several radio transmitters. Kuomintang flags. Carefully cherished were title deeds, originals — though one cautious chap had his photostated as well — and pre-Liberation account books, neatly listing every debtor and exactly what he owed, capital plus compound interest. The old regime crowd were apparently all set. Just waiting for Chiang to make his come-back.

As we now see it, these people were merely a bit of fuzz on a miniscule lunatic fringe. But at the time you had the feeling that fiendish counter-revolutionaries were lurking everywhere, and this added several degrees of temperature to the already over-heated atmosphere.

Red Guard raids didn't help. While the kids' antipathy to musty remnants of China's feudal past was understandable, they did considerable damage, smashing and defacing cultural relics, confiscating "reactionary" private library collections. Friends of our still haven't been able to track down their books.

But worst of all it seems to me, the Red Guards, spurred by inflammatory slogans from above, set a pattern of lawlessness. According to the ground rules laid down by the Sixteen Points, the Cultural Revolution was to be conducted by means of wall posters and large open debates. Searches and seizures violated the Sixteen Points, to say nothing of China's Constitution. But in the ten years that followed they became a widespread and accepted practice, not just among adolescent hot-heads but in mature groupings as well — all in the name of "revolution".

Ya-mei and most of her schoolmates were members of the Red Guards. I was interested to observe their reactions. Problems were coming up all the time. Some kids took a stand, some wouldn't stick their necks out, some tried to play both ends against the middle — just like their parents. The majority — depending on their own position — formed opinions and drew conclusions. They were learning to separate the wheat from the chaff, not on the basis of the usual childish petty squabbles and jealousies, but in their relation to the political strife of the adult world.

This sudden broadening of vision made them hungry for more. All of China was in ferment, and the kids wanted to see for themselves. They began traveling — in groups of tens, hundreds, thousands — to schools, factories, to other cities, other provinces. They simply swarmed on to trains and went. When a government regulation proclaimed that they could travel without charge it was only confirming a *fait accompli*.

Millions came to Peking. Mao received them — en masse — on eight different occasions at Tien An Men Square. The Peking kids traveled to other parts of the country. It was very casual. Ya-mei went up to Talien (Dairen) because the train to Chungking — where she had planned to go with a dozen of the girls from her school — was too crowded that day. Of course it raised hob with the nation's transport facilities, and local authorities went mad trying to amass enough food and water and accommodations for unpredictable numbers of kids daily descending upon them without notice. Ya-mei slept on a high school gymnasium floor in Talien and paid a few cents a day for her meals. She said everyone was "very nice", accepting it all quite as a matter of course. The local teachers looked after them.

The brakes were not applied to this great children's crusade for many months. The Red Guards helped spread the Cultural Revolution and learned a lot from the experiences of others. In old China most people spent their lives within a few miles' radius of their little village. It was good for youngsters to break out and see something of the world. But their travels disrupted other passenger and freight traffic. A few kids got uppity and tried to tell people how to run their local struggles. Gradually, they were channeled off the trains and on to "Long Marches" in the tradition of the old Red Army. Wherever they stopped, whether in communes or in factories, they worked and earned their keep, in addition to discussing developments of the Cultural Revolution. Finally it was felt there had been enough cross-fertiliza-tion and everyone — workers, students, commune members — was urged to concentrate on solving the problems of his or her own organization.

The influence of the anarchistic manner in which the children behaved was deep and persistent. They had got out of the habit of going to school, of studying. They had become accustomed to being a law unto themselves. Discipline, application to their books, examinations, respect for elders — were not "revolutionary". Even after the Cultural Revolution ended, it was several years before the smashing of schoolroom windows and insolence to teachers could be halted, and some semblance of normality restored to the process of learning.

In the Foreign Languages Press, the battles were intense, the walls of our office corridors were papered with big character posters immediately after the universities and colleges put up theirs. Then "work teams" were sent in to "guide" the movement, and the youngsters who had dared to speak up — most of them were young cadres — were cross-examined, accused of being "anti-Party" or even "counter-revolutionary". The big character posters dwindled to the vanishing point.

Mao followed with his blast against these suppressive tactics and said, in effect: "Fire away at anybody, however high, who has been putting a spoke in the wheels of socialism." Unfortunately each person interpreted this edict in his own way, and many good leaders were extravagantly attacked in a flood of big character posters. Now the walls in the Press weren't enough. Two strings were run the length of the hallways with posters hanging from each of them, on both sides. The dining room was co-opted as well. You couldn't walk — you literally had to plow your way through big character posters from one room to another. Arguments and debates raged in every office, heated and straight from the shoulder.

Young men and women — the girls were very active in the Cultural Revolution — would get up and speak before audiences of hundreds, sometimes thousands, and calmly and effectively make their points. I wondered what had happened to the traditional Chinese reticence. It was a healthy change from the feudal habit among intellectuals of indirection and circumlocution.

Power in the Press was seized first by one side, then the other. There was some violence and a small Army group — unarmed — came in to sort out the differences and get the arguments back on a reasoning and debate level. Eventually a leadership group was formed, consisting of a few Army men and representatives from both sides. The work of the Press — turning out books and periodicals in foreign languages — never stopped all during the Cultural Revolution. But due to the bitter factional strife we were often late, and quality dropped. While the factional differences didn't end automatically with the creating of a leadership group, production was able to proceed more smoothly.

Meanwhile, all over China extremists who called themselves "revolutionaries" began to appear. Lin Piao had set in motion a "suspect everyone, down with everything" campaign. He was vigorously supported by Chiang Ching and other influential figures who were later to become known as part of her Gang of Four organization. The slogan misled millions of ardent young people, and perverted the Cultural Revolution, for a time, into a kind of witch hunt.

Chairman Mao had said that the "Party persons in power taking the capitalist road" — the targets of the Cultural Revolution — were a "mere handful" of whom "only a few are absolutely unrepentant", that is, actual class enemies. But the response evoked by the extremists at the top caused attacks on almost every leader, whether a Communist or not. A friend of ours was accused of being a "non-Party person in power taking the capitalist road"!

Equally important as targets of the Cultural Revolution were decadent ideas, culture, customs and habits — hangovers from centuries of a repressive social system, which provided the environment for a recrudescence of exploitation and tyranny. But "suspect everyone, down with everything" encouraged a strengthening of the very attitudes and concepts Mao was battling to change.

A fanatic "othodoxy" developed that had distinct Confucian overtones. Some young men of worker or peasant background described themselves as having been "born Red" and claimed that they were the only true revolutionaries. Everyone else was suspect ... Chairman Mao had indicated that the main stress in the arts should be on contemporary Chinese life. The extremists wanted to ban Chinese classics and foreign arts completely ... Chairman Mao thought the education system needed reform. Some fanatics wanted to eliminate teachers and let the students teach themselves ... Egged on by Lin Piao and the Gang of Four, who utilized and manipulated them, they carried everything to its ultimate absurdity.

Throughout the country they formed new "revolutionary" teams and regiments. Bigoted and highly factional, their members behaved like brothers in a feudal robbers band, and bickered riotously with rival groups.

In many places extremists temporarily seized power. For forty-eight hours they held the Foreign Office, sending out cables giving orders to embassies. Their adherents burned the British Mission in Peking. They raided the Chinese Foreign Office and broke into the Secret Archives. The influence of their ideas created absurdities in the periodicals sent abroad — categorical condemnations of Shakespeare, Beethoven, "jazz", a plethora of stories about heroes, all of whom died, some needlessly, red flags and pictures of Mao on covers and throughout the magazine.

Meanwhile, in the name of "defending" Mao, they sniped at the tried and true Communists around him — from high Party leaders down to solid, hard-working county Party secretaries — inventing "material" about them, slandering, spreading rumors, trying to undermine and topple the best in the Communist Party structure so as to facilitate obtaining complete control. The very methods of oppression applied by the extremists were feudal, medieval — and this was painfully apparent in spite of all attempts to wrap them in a "revolutionary" aura.

Almost every person in authority in the Foreign Languages Press was accused of "taking the capitalist road", and almost all were suspended from their duties. They were compelled to write detailed summaries of their pasts and analyse their "mistakes". Some were not allowed to go home and lived under guard in a special section known as the "monsters' enclosure". These naturally did not include the few who supported the extremist crowd, or were their secret backers and instigators.

The prisoners, in the early stages, were loaded on open trucks, placards stating their "crimes" hung around their necks, and "paraded" through the streets — an old feudal custom for those accused of capital offenses — somewhat to the puzzlement of the local populace. Each morning they were assembled in the meeting hall before a large portrait of Mao, where they bowed and recited passages from the Chairman's works regarding lenient treatment of counter-revolutionaries who made a clean breast of things.

They were also required to perform various menial tasks, like scrubbing the toilets. Each had turns of being questioned and lectured by various "struggle groups". Most of the time they sat at improvised desks in dim office hallways, interminably writing "confessions" and "exposures".

I found all this confusing, and a bit nauseating, and most of my Chinese colleagues felt the same. True, there were wall posters up about the detainees, alleging all sorts of misdeeds in their past and while in office. But these were only claims. I was raised on the tenet that a man is innocent until proven guilty. Why should people be denied their freedom before any legal proof was produced? Investigations were going on, but these took months, even years.

I didn't like the bowing before the portraits, and the incantations. It was straight out of old Chinese mysticism, exactly the sort of thing Mao furiously opposed. Nor did I care for the enforced dirty jobs routine. Chairman Mao affirmed the dignity of labor. He said it was good for intellectuals to work with their hands since it enabled them to appreciate the vital contribution made by workers and peasants. But it was necessary for everyone to participate. To impose it as a punishment on a minority of pre-judged pariahs bespoke a contempt for labor, not a respect.

Why didn't those of us who disapproved of these practices protest against them? I think it was partly a lack of courage, and partly because those doing the detaining were the group which had seized power and which had been given the seal of approval by the Army team then overseeing Cultural Revolution activities in the Press. You couldn't help wondering, under the circumstances, whether there might not really be something in at least some of the charges. In that case, might it not be better to let matters take their course for a while?

I felt sure, moreover, that the highest Party leadership was firmly in control of the situation and that, sooner or later, they would straighten out any temporary injustices. Actually, control in a few sectors, like the media and the arts, was already in the grasp of the extremists, and they were working feverishly to grab the whole thing. There were several very rotten apples quite near the top of the barrel.

The going was increasingly rough. What had the most immediate impact on me was the incarceration of Phoenix. In the Dramatists Association, where she worked as an editor on one of the magazines, she was accused of being a participant in the "evil" arts of the Thirties. This sweeping condemnation of an entire era is something Chiang Ching dreamed up in 1966 when, in collaboration with Lin Piao, she conducted a conference with army people working in the arts. Since the accomplishments of writers and artists in this period had earlier been hailed by Mao Tsetung, it seems astonishing that no one spoke up in their defense. Perhaps the explanation is that several of the leading figures in those days were currently under attack for various other "crimes", and people hesitated to come forward, even indirectly, as their champions.

Then, early in 1969, Phoenix was told she could not come home, but would have to live in the office, and continue her "study" there. No explanation was given. We were mystified. I visited her almost every evening. The first few times a guard — usually some young woman colleague we knew well — dutifully remained within earshot. But gradually she grew bored and wandered out, and we could talk freely.

Phoenix said she was informed her history was being investigated. We tried in vain to guess what this might mean. Since student days in Shanghai she had worked under the leadership of the Communist underground. In Chungking, during the Kuomintang-Communist co-operation period of the anti-Japanese War, she had been one of the many people in the arts receiving direct guidance from Chou En-lai, who was there as the Communist representative.

I queried the members of the workers and army teams which had been sent in to supervise the "movement", as well as the "revolutionary" colleagues who were conducting the proceedings in the Dramatists Association. None of them could shed any light. They knew simply that instructions had come from "higher up".

Only after the downfall of the Gang of Four did we hear that the order was issued by Chiang Ching as part of her campaign to smear anyone who might have some knowledge of her unsavory past. Phoenix had never met her, but both were playing on the stages of Shanghai in the Thirties, and Chiang Ching was no doubt nervous about what Phoenix had heard. Out of respect for Chairman Mao veteran theater people never gossiped about Chiang Ching. But during the Cultural Revolution she was gambling for top stakes, and this was her way of discrediting possible detractors in advance.

In early 1969 we didn't realize this. Phoenix, an emotional, active person, fretted under the restraint. I was worried about her health. We spoke of other things, and reassured each other that all would turn out well in the end, and to "trust the Party and the masses". Had we realized to what extent high Party leadership was infiltrated by traitors and renegades, and what ruthless fascists Chiang Ching and her Gang of Four organization were, we would have been a lot more frightened than we were.

On the lower working levels, the Party as an organization ceased to function. The encouragement, or at least tacit approval, from above of a review of the records of all Party functionaries — during which they were suspended from office — had created a power vacuum. This inevitably engendered rival factions, all attempting to take over the running of the day-to-day affairs in their respective units. Their concern was justified, for the various offices, factories, farms and schools were floundering.

Most of the members of the "battle teams" and "revolutionary regiments" then formed were sincere. But they also included a small number of rogues and criminals who saw the chaotic situation as an opportunity to gain power for themselves. Those and the "revolutionary" units which they soon controlled provided ready-made "troops" for the big wheels operating behind the scenes. The Lin Piao-Gang of Four crowd could and did utilize such organizations to ruthlessly crush their opponents, or even those they merely disliked.

Hundreds of persons in the arts who had for the most part followed Mao's line, and had matured politically and artistically under Chou's guidance, were confined on various trumped up charges issuing from Chiang Ching's headquarters. There were many mysterious deaths among these — scores in Shanghai alone. Famous writer Lao Sheh was alleged to have "killed himself" in Peking. Peasant novelist Chao Shu-li was proclaimed a "suicide" in Shansi. . . .

We got only occasional odd bits of news. Rumors were so rife we tended to scoff at the more lurid tales. Moreover, the "revolutionary comrades" exercising the detention in Phoenix's office mainly were people who had worked with her for years, and liked and respected her. They were quite pleasant, and obviously sincere. Their treatment of her was generally considerate, often kindly. Once, when a group of rampaging teenage "revolutionaries" broke into the Dramatists Association looking for "reactionaries" to parade through the streets, Phoenix's people hid her and others in the cellar until they were gone.

Then, at the end of 1969, she and her entire organization moved to a "May Seventh Cadre School" in the country. People who work in offices tend to lose touch with the vast majority who produce the machines and food and daily necessities, and Chairman Mao had proposed, on May 7, 1969, that they should put in periodic stints in field and factory. Outfits like the Dramatists Association created their own small rural settlements, and these came to be known as "May Seventh Cadre Schools". Since the Association abandoned all activities during the Cultural Revolution, instead of individual members going by turns for a few months as Mao envisaged, the whole organization remained at the "School" until 1975.

They moved twice in the course of this period, ending up in a lowlands between Peking and Tientsin where they raised meager rice crops on sandy alkaline soil. As it turned out, they had little to do with the neighboring communes, and consequently not much opportunity to "learn from the laboring masses". But they did learn to do their own labor — making bricks, building their own houses, tilling, planting, harvesting. . . .

Phoenix enjoyed the physical part. They didn't let her do much, but she liked the *gung ho* spirit, and working in the fresh air. She insisted on going along on the morning jogs, from which she was exempt, and wrote proudly that she could run half a mile and had slimmed down nicely. The problem was that when the others came home on periodic holidays, she was not allowed to leave the "School". She was miserably homesick, and increasingly depressed by the long time it was taking to finish "investigating" her. She developed heart flutters and had fainting spells. Although psychosomatic, they were none the less dangerous. Several times she had to be given oxygen.

I was very concerned. We didn't think it wise for me to visit her in the prevailing extremist atmosphere, but Ya-mei went once, remaining a week or so. She said her mother was for the most part well-treated and tried to appear cheerful, but she clearly was unhappy. Phoenix was permitted to come to Peking to see me off when I left for the States in 1971, and when I returned a few months later early in 1972.

At home I was coping, but lonely and bored. Ya-mei, on finishing middle school in 1969, had been assigned to a paper mill about fifty miles from Peking in Tung Hsien, the former terminus of the old Grand Canal. She came home only on weekends. I rode my bike to the office every morning, and returned every evening to an empty house. Except for our *paomu* housekeeper, I was alone. Since my own needs were simple, and no one was doing any entertaining, I let her go, too.

Foreigners working in government organizations and schools, stirred by the Cultural Revolution, were eager to take part, but there were differences of opinion as to how. Some wanted to be treated exactly the same as the Chinese. One passionate fellow who objected to the comforts of the Friendship Hostel where most of the foreign experts lived, wrote a big character poster which he hung in the dining room alleging that the place ought to be "burned down". To the bottom of this proclamation some joker sarcastically tacked a packet of matches. Some wanted to criticize the Foreign Experts Bureau. Others were mainly interested in the units in which they worked. Everyone wanted to be kept informed of the over-all developments.

A meeting of foreigners working in Peking was called in January, 1967, and was addressed by Chen Yi, then Minister of Foreign Affairs. He said they could participate in all Cultural Revolution meetings, read and write posters if they wished, criticize and exchange views with their Chinese colleagues. If some wanted to live more simply, that was up to them. The foreigners came from sixty different countries. They had their own ideologies, their own opinions, their own life-style. Under no circumstances would China try to impose the Chinese viewpoint on them. Those who wanted to take part in the Cultural Revolution could form their own rebel organizations or join existing Chinese ones. About a hundred of us joined a foreigners' group called "Bethune-Yenan".

It was beset from the start with special difficulties. The Chinese rebel groups functioned mainly within their own schools and places of work, and dealt with people and problems with which they were familiar. The foreigners worked in various organizations. Most of them were unable to speak or read Chinese and could act only on second-hand information, which was frequently unreliable. "Bethune-Yenan" had to grope half-blind in a very fast Chinese ballgame. Still, the experience was a useful one. We certainly learned a lot about class struggle in China, and among ourselves, and the Chinese gained a better understanding of the foreigners in their midst.

It was Mao's opinion that revolutionary changes were taking place not only in China but all over the world. A poem he wrote in 1963 expresses beautifully his lofty scorn for pipsqueaks like Khrushchov who thought they could stop China, and his own conviction that the surge of global revolution is irresistible. My favorite translation reads as follows:

REPLY TO COMRADE KUO MO-JO

On our small globe a few flies
Bump against the wall,
Droning, groaning,
Shrilling, moaning.
To ants a locust tree appears
A land of vast enormity,
Do midges really dare imagine
They can shake a mighty tree?
The west wind showers leaves on Changan
And whistling arrows fly.
Many things are urgent,
The earth turns, days fleet by,
Ten thousand years is much too long,
The time is nigh.
Mid boiling seas, 'neath angry skies,
The five continents stir tempestuously,
All vermin shall be swept away,
All, inevitably.

Changan — today, Sian — was the ancient capital. Autumn Changan, deluged with enemy arrows, was on the verge of collapse. A simile for the Soviet revisionists? For the old order throughout the world? Mao never explains his poems.

In spite of the emergence of negative, and even dangerous, aspects, Chinese society over-all was continuing its march forward. A new morality on a grass-roots level was evolving. On a tour through the south in 1970 I saw something of this. In a triple intersection in Shanghai there is a busy store which sells all kinds of oddments from buttons to snacks and soda pop. Calling itself *The Spark* (after Mao's line "A single spark can start a prairie fire"), in 1968 it extended its hours so as to better "serve the people". The eight men and women working in the store felt quite pleased with themselves.

"We ought to stay open nights, too," one of them suggested.

"Oh, no," another replied. "It's the working people we're catering to, and they're too tired to shop at night."

They decided to ask the customers. Factory workers on the day shift said: "You open when we go on shift, but you're closed when we come home." Commune members said: "We bring vegetables into the city in the wee hours of the morning to feed you fellows and we're pretty hungry by the time we get here. But your store is always dark."

The argument continued, with those unwilling to work nights rationalizing against it. Those in favor said that all around the store were factories, hospitals, markets, and a railway station which were busy day and night. The store should keep pace.

"We don't have enough staff," was another objection. "The electricity would cost too much. We wouldn't be able to meet our expenses."

"We're not in this just for profit," was the reply. "If people can get a bit to eat when they want it, they'll do their job better, and that will be better for the country as a whole."

There was no answer to that. The store changed its name to *The Spark Day and Night 24 Hour Emporium*. Business doubled in the first month. In the next two years volume rose to eight times the original figure. Profits also increased. More people were added to the staff. Everyone praised them.

"It went to our heads a little," the manager told me with a grin. I was chatting with some of *The Spark* people in the back room of the store. "But then that business with the bicycle pump straightened us out."

"What do you mean?" I asked.

"Well, a lot of people ride bikes to work. One day a fellow with a low tire asked if we had a pump. We didn't, of course, and at our regular meeting at the end of the day we discussed whether we ought to get one. Some said who ever heard of a snack bar with a bicycle pump? But most said what's the difference? If it will help serve the people, we ought to buy one, so we did.

"A month or so later a man tried to firm up his tire and found that the pump was out of order. He mentioned it to our day shift chief, and rode on. A few days later, the same thing happened, with the same man, and then a third time, a week after that. The man pointed to a *Serve the People* motto we had hanging on the wall. 'Hadn't you better take that down?' he asked drily.

"Our day shift chief was very indignant when he told us about it. 'There's no pleasing some people,' he said. 'Here we are, a snack bar, and we spend money to buy a bicycle pump. Just because something goes wrong with it, that fellow has the nerve to complain!'

"We talked it over and decided the day shift chief was wrong. If you serve the people you have to do it thoroughly. Going through the motions isn't enough. We had the pump repaired and bought another one in addition."

There was no holding *The Spark* after that. They had a lot of out-of-town customers coming from the nearby railway station, so they made up a list of all the hotels and inns, with their rates for accommodation, and directions of how to get there. They also printed maps of the principal bus and trolley lines and major points of interest.

"Would you believe it? That girl," said the manager, indicating a pretty young miss sitting opposite," took a man nearly twice her weight to the hospital. Tell it yourself, Lan," he urged. The girl blushed and looked away. The manager laughed. "We can never get her to talk about it. Lan was on duty one afternoon when a little girl came in, scared and weeping. She said her grandpa had fallen down and couldn't get up. All the neighbors were out. Lan ran home with the child —she only lived around the corner — and found the old man on the floor, dizzy with high blood pressure. He was a big husky chap, a retired shipyard worker, but Lan somehow got him down two flights of stairs and over to the hospital. There she registered him, had him treated and given a bed. Then she left. The hospital people thought she was his daughter. It wasn't till the old man came around to the store a few weeks later, accompanied by his son and daughter-in-law, to thank Lan, that we knew anything about it."

I looked at Lan, who was pink with embarrassment. She couldn't have weighed more than a hundred pounds. The manager pointed to a man about forty.

"Chang here isn't quite so shy. He can tell you his story. It happened only recently."

"There isn't much to tell," said Chang. "I was on night shift when a man from the vegetable commune in the suburbs came by on his bicycle cart with a load for the market. He had cut his foot and asked whether we had a first aid kit. I put some iodine on and bandaged his foot, but I couldn't stop the bleeding. The cut was too deep. The hospital is only down the block so I took him there, had the cut fixed, and brought him back to the store. He was weak and pale from loss of blood. 'Take it easy,' I said. 'Rest,' I gave him a drink of water. 'Can't,' he said. 'Got to get those vegetables to market.'

"It was on the tip of my tongue to say I'd do it for him, but then I thought — I'm tired. It's four in the morning. The market's on the other side of the city and I've never pedalled a bicycle cart. But the next thing I thought was — you talk a lot about serving the people, but if it's a little trouble, you've got all kinds of excuses. People will be waiting to buy those vegetables in a couple of hours.

"So off I went. It was tricky riding and I sweated a lot but I made it. By the time I got back the sun was up, and some fellows from the commune took the man home. That's all there was to it."

"You really serve the people," I said admiringly to Chang. "That was fine."

"Fine, nothing." Chang said dejectedly. "After all these weeks I still haven't found time to go out and see how he is."

A quarter of a century before, when I first arrived in Shanghai, good hearted folk like Lan and Chang, seeing people starving on the streets, could only stare helplessly and walk on. Now, with a new social system, the ordinary man and woman were able to give full rein to their natural kindness. Since the establishment of the People's Republic the quality of human relationships had been raised to a higher level — among colleagues, between leaders and the led, teacher and student, husband and wife, parent and child. Violence, except in self-defence against a class enemy, was bad. Principles, reason, were good.

These concepts have carried over into China's international relations. Her army, navy and airforce are purely defensive. China possesses both the atom and the hydrogen bombs, but she has publicly stated she will never be the first to use them, in fact she proposes not just a limitation on testing but the destruction of all nuclear weapons.

All of the larger population centers are honeycombed with tunnels, deep enough to be effective against atomic blasts. I visited a few in Peking that are quite elaborate. The one beneath the school near the People's Market has small classrooms. Outside Chienmen (Front Gate) the big tunnel has kitchens, medical clinics, telephones and electric light. Of course these underground networks are defensive in nature. As

Chairman Mao humourously pointed out, it's pretty hard to attack anyone from inside a tunnel.

To developing nations China extends loans, at very low interest or interest-free, and makes outright gifts. No political strings attached. She deals with all countries, regardless of social system, diplomatically and commercially, on a basis of equality. She supports the weaker nations against exploitation by the super-powers. She gives moral and material support to revolutionaries in certain countries, but makes sure that they represent the people and not simply another oppressor faction. Even in hostile nations she seeks friends, people-to-people.

In the autumn of 1971 we became aware that strange things were going on. The annual National Day parade in Peking on October first had suddenly been called off. For several weeks the name of Lin Piao did not appear in the press. All kinds of rumors were circulating. The Western media said that a plane from China had crashed in Outer Mongolia, but that the bodies had been charred beyond recognition.

When Lin Piao was named as Mao's successor in the new Communist Party Constitution in 1969 many of us were puzzled. It didn't sound like something the Chairman would agree to. Mao was still healthy and mentally keen. How could you be sure that a "successor" would not change in political nature? Why couldn't the Party select a new Chairman when the need arose? Later, we learned of serious errors committed by Lin Piao in the past, for which Chairman Mao had criticized him. With so many fine members of the Communist Party why, even if you had to choose a successor in advance, pick Lin Piao and not someone else? These questions troubled me then, and still do today.

Lin Piao had a shrewd Machiavellian angle. Mao, he said, was divine. Like all divinities he had to be unquestioningly obeyed. "Carry out the Chairman's directives whether you understand them or not," said Lin. "Mao Tsetung Thought is the pinnacle of Marxism."

Subtle. Mao is undoubtedly one of the great men of history. But as a Marxist he has always maintained that there is no "pinnacle", that man's understanding of the world, the universe, continues ever to grow as his experience and knowledge increases. To attempt to petrify Mao Tsetung thought was to attack its very essence.

Further, Lin's call for blind obedience contained the implication that Mao's ideas were mystic, obtuse, in need of interpretation. And who would be better suited for this task than Lin Piao the man who, according to the Party Constitution, "consistently held high the great red banner of Mao Tsetung Thought", who was the "sincerest and most dedicated of all in carrying out and defending the proletarian revolutionary line of Comrade Mao Tsetung", who was Chairman Mao's "close companion in arms" and designated as his successor?

When Mao came under attack there had been a strong emotional public reaction which took the form of people by the millions wearing Mao badges, buying busts and pictures of Mao, putting up statues in his honor. Lin Piao saw this as an opportunity to deify and mysticise Mao for his own purposes, and spurred it on to extremes. Lin affixed the titles "Great Teacher, Great Leader, Great Supreme Commander, Great Helmsman". All four appellations had to be appended every time Mao was mentioned. No meeting could open or close without everyone standing and facing a portrait of Chairman Mao and wishing him "long life". At the same time, it also became the custom to wish "good health to Vice-Chairman Lin Piao". Lin's words of wisdom were frequently quoted in speeches and in the press. To question Lin Piao was deemed equivalent to questioning Mao Tsetung himself.

All of Lin's private inclinations drew him toward the Soviet revisionists — military "co-operation" with Moscow, soft living for a small elite — though publicly he adopted the pose of the dedicated Spartan. In 1966, after America stepped up the war in Vietnam, certain leaders had proposed that China send a delegation to the 23rd Congress of the Soviet Party to restore the alliance between the two parties. Mao had refused. A self-reliant, united China, fighting a people's war, he said, could cope with both US imperialism and Soviet social-imperialism. The majority of the Party leadership had supported Mao. So Lin had kept his opinions to himself.

In August 1970, at a meeting of the Central Committee, he proposed that the post of Chairman of the People's Republic, equivalent to that of President, be restored. He claimed that he wanted Mao to occupy this position, in addition to the chairmanship of the Communist Party, knowing full well that the burdens would be too heavy for one man, and figuring that he, Lin Piao, would therefore surely get the chief executive command. This proposal was rejected by the Central Committee, after being attacked by Chairman Mao.

Lin didn't have much string left to his bow when the Nixon visit was announced in 1971. He couldn't drum up any real support in the army, which was overwhelmingly loyal to Mao. His attempt to build a rank-and-file fascist corps — May Sixteenth — had failed. Lin was desperate.

He decided to assassinate Mao, frame "evidence" against Mao's strongest supporters, rush in, weeping copiously, as the named "successor", and proceed to "restore order".

The scheme was discovered and he fled, frantically, with a few of his closest associates. In the mad scramble they didn't take on enough fuel, and their plane crashed in Outer Mongolia, in September, 1971, killing all on board.

Although the Soviet Union was not mentioned by name, the Chinese press accused that country of complicity with Lin Piao. "Plots against the Party are not isolated or fortuitous. They have their international connections . . . Domestic and international class struggles must be regarded together." No facts were given, but the direction in which Lin was heading when his plane went down was obvious.

The revelation of the story to the general public was, of course, a shock, in view of Lin's position as the successor to Mao. How could a man so trusted, who voiced "revolutionary" sentiments so often and so loudly, turn out to be a traitor plotting to bring back a bourgeois regime? How could this happen in socialist China? The net effect was to make the Chinese more wary of demagogues. They proved to be less susceptible to flag-wavers and tub-thumpers when the Gang of Four came out into the open only a few years later.

China's growing strength at home and abroad, political and economic problems within the big countries, the contradictions among them, cracked the wall of antagonism Washington had erected to isolate Peking. More visitors came from America. Among them, in 1971, was a Chinese professor who had obtained American citizenship and who had returned to see his aged mother in Shanghai. A Chinese colleague spotted the news item first.

"If a Chinese who's an American citizen can visit his mother in China, why can't an American who's a Chinese citizen visit his mother in America?" he asked.

I hadn't given the matter much thought in years. Without diplomatic relations, it hadn't seemed possible. There were still no formal relations, but clearly things were changing. I talked it over with my Chinese family. Phoenix was busy with the Cultural Revolution, and Ya-mei was finishing her three years in the paper mill and intending to apply for medical school, but they urged me to go, if I could. My office fully agreed. Then it was announced that Nixon would visit

China. If ever the atmosphere was conducive, this was the time. I applied for and obtained a Chinese passport with no difficulty.

But so far as Washington was concerned, I was now a "foreigner". I would need a visa to get into the States. For that I would have to make application at a US embassy or consulate, and there was no assurance they would grant it. I decided to apply in Canada. If I couldn't get into America, at least my family could drive up and see me. The Canadian Embassy in Peking granted me a visa and I was ready to go.

China was stable when I left for America in November 1971. My wife and daughter and a few friends saw me off at the Peking airport in properly reserved Chinese style — no tears, no embraces. I was to be the first New Yorker to visit New York as a Chinese from Peking.

The cultural shocks began when I boarded the Air France plane the next day in Shanghai. Softly piped Parisian jazz, the perfumed cabin, chic short-skirted hostesses — I had forgotten this world, it had slipped into some recess of my mind. The transition wasn't too abrupt, for the majority of the passengers were Chinese — heading all over the world on diplomatic and trade and technical missions — and I was still talking more Chinese than English by the time we reached Paris. Here I parted company with the most distinguished of the passengers — China's delegation to the United Nations.

They were going to New York and I was heading for Montreal first, and then Ottawa, to apply for an American visa. I was switched to a Canadian Airlines plane at Orly, having missed the Air France connection. Our Shanghai-Paris flight had been late. Dignitaries appearing at every stop along the way to greet the Chinese UN delegation had tended to be long-winded.

The huge 747 was more than half empty. I don't remember too much about the flight. I slept most of the time, worn out from twenty-one hours on the Shanghai-Paris leg, with touchdowns in Rangoon, Karachi, Cairo and Athens. Between dozes I watched a John Wayne movie about the Civil War. I felt pretty nauseous. It could have been the bumpy air off Labrador.

Immigration at the Montreal Airport was brief and friendly. Customs just waved me through. "Wanna look at this stuff?" I asked the inspector, indicating my smart Chinese zip bags. He was chomping a cigar and had a pistol belt around his bulging middle. It must have been my Brooklyn accent, which seemed to have come back automatically. He barely glanced at me. "Nah. Go ahead, buddy." I was "home".

I spent the next ten days with a Canadian friend, whom I had met at the Trade Fair in Canton, where he was buying corduroy eight years before. He had invited me to stay with him if I ever came to Canada. I never thought I would take him up on it. He and his wife lived comfortably in the pleasant West Montreal section. Their pretty teenaged daughter was finishing high school. Their twenty-year-old son, a good-looking boy with rather a lot of hair, was in college. He was sarcastic about the social order and thought the future looked bleak.

Several of my host's business acquaintances, whom I met in the next few days, were also pessimistic. All of Canada's major industries were controlled or owned outright by the Americans. Inflation was rising, the cost of living was high. Drug use was spreading among the youth, though crime was not as rampant as it was in the States. There was trouble with the French-speaking population, a depressed minority with the usual syndrome of low-paying jobs, therefore less opportunity for a good education, qualifying therefore only for low-paying jobs. Unemployment among them was much higher than in the English-speaking communities.

The Canadians I met were warm-hearted, intelligent, I liked their clean, well-lighted subways, their beautiful shopping centers. They were a talented people. It seemed a pity that their social gains hadn't kept up with their technological progress.

Actually, I didn't see much of Canada. Besides Montreal, the only other place I visited was Ottawa, where I was given a glorious Szechuan luncheon at the Chinese Embassy. At the American Embassy I applied for a visa. They were a bit startled, but polite and helpful. It came through in a little over a week, and I picked it up in the US Consulate in Montreal.

I had telephoned my mother as soon as I arrived in Canada, and she and my sister Ruth and her husband Jack had come tearing up the next day in their car with a carton of lox and bagel, positive, and rightly so, that nothing could compare with the genuine Flatbush variety. They stayed one day, then rushed off again to prepare for my homecoming while I awaited my visa.

We used to spend all day driving from New York to Montreal when I was a kid. Today, what with the super-highways and super-cars, it was only six hours. Everything had speeded up. I, the sophisticated New Yorker who used to weave through Times Square traffic with the ease and grace of an All-American fullback, found myself leaping wildly to avoid being smeared by the rapid-acceleration monsters from Detroit.

You go through US Immigration and Customs in the Montreal Airport. All you have to do, on landing in New York three quarters of an hour later, is pick up your bags and go. It was dark when I arrived, and I remember only walking dazedly to a huge parking lot with my mother, sister and brother-in-law, then whisking along a broad highway for twenty minutes or so and pulling up before a one-family house on a quiet tree-shaded street. Here Ruth and Jack lived, directly in back of James Madison, my old high school, and a few blocks from where I had grown up as a child.

We went in. A large Boxer dog flung himself on me in a frenzy of welcome and licked my nose with a slobbery tongue. My mother sat down on a sofa and tried not to look exhausted. She was eighty, but insisted on living alone in an apartment nearby. Jack showed me to my room. All the kids were away and there were three empty bedrooms. Ruth made some coffee and sliced a deep-dish blueberry cake. We ate at the kitchen table, with the dog wheedling for scraps, just like the old days. Twenty-five years. Incredible.

A lot had changed, as I discovered in the succeeding weeks. Some of it I liked — good music on stereo FM radio, small inexpensive TV sets, fast travel by super-highways and on planes, cheap useful gadgets for the house, clothing of synthetic knits and fabrics, lively imaginative styles, convenient super-markets, handsome new office buildings.

Most of all I liked the young people. Americans were always outspoken, but now they seemed particularly articulate. There was nothing "beat" about the kids I met. They were very critical of the social order and those running it. They wanted new concepts, new values, though few had any clear idea of what this new America should be like, or how to bring it about. Still they were questing, discussing, organizing, summing up past experiences, trying to evolve new programs. I had the feeling that strong positive forces were starting to take shape in America.

Some of the youngsters were on hard drugs — I saw a few ashen, dull teenagers in Union Square Park one morning — and almost everyone smoked pot. But most of the dulled minds I encountered were among the hard-core Old Left, who clung to the faded charms of the Soviet Communist Party, and the starry-eyed liberals, still hoping for a knight in shining gray flannel to come riding up and bring them the best of both worlds. The Chinese in feudal times had a wish-fulfilment figure they called the "clean official". He was the high-minded gent, within the Establishment of course, who would dispense even-handed justice to rich and poor, and bring peace and prosperity. After vainly waiting two thousand years for this messiah to appear, they decided to try something else.

I watched TV, went to the theater, saw as many movies as I could, and thought how sad that such artistry should not be devoted to a better cause. The pornography was overwhelming. Breasts and back-sides were thrust at you from film screens and news stands in indiscriminate abundance. People were becoming bored with public sex, and Hollywood was turning to cruel and bloody violence in an attempt to prop up the sagging box office.

I spent two weeks with a friend who had "made it", as a manu-facturer of ladies' sportswear, and lived in Hollywood Hills. He had a beautiful home, and telephone extentions with long lines that could be dragged out to the side of the kidney-shape swimming pool, a Phil-ippine houseboy who cooked, and no pictures on the walls. My friend shared the place with a film producer, who was actually making a picture. Only three major studios remained of the original dozen. Both men were divorced, had no children. They were intelligent, troubled by the way America was going, but too "practical", or spiritually weary, to try and change things.

Intellectuals generally, particularly those with social consciousness, or artistic ability, were fed up, with their jobs and way of life. A few of the older generation were fighting back, but not many. Some had reconciled themselves to finding what pleasures they could. One or two of the braver ones were talking about leaving. A well-paid TV writer in New York told me he was seriously thinking of moving to Paris with his whole family — they had a big apartment on Central Park West — and opening a delicatessen.

These were mostly well-to-do middle class liberals, a relative mi-nority. The vast majority of the people were as I remembered them —

riding crowded subways in the morning to tend a machine all day or do some mindless office job, then coming home tired in the rush hour to an "economy" meal and sitting before the synthetic excitement of TV until bed time. The unemployed and semi-employed lived in vermin-infested leaky flats, nursing their hatred of slum-lords who stalled or refused repairs until misery and frustration impelled the inevitable blow-off. I saw the burnt-out hulks in Brownsville and Bedford-Stuyvesant.

There was new life in the city, thanks to large infusions of new blood — mainly Black and Puerto Rican. Dark-skinned kids seemed to comprise about a third of the student body of my old high school, James Madison. The subways were crowded with them, traveling to and from various schools, bright, lively, talkative. A hush fell whenever one of the teams of policemen, who patrolled the subways day and night, entered the car. Half of the kids usually got off quickly at the next stop. Experience had taught them to hate and fear the cops. Blacks and Puerto Ricans were moving into the city as whites moved toward the suburbs. They would make or break New York, depending on how they were treated. Racial tension was high, not a good omen for the city's future.

I had the feeling that the whole society, not just the poor, was hemmed in, restricted. Kids couldn't learn much in school that "related" to them and their problems. The country's leaders were pursuing the same dreary futile policies. Jobs were dull and hard to find. The average man was revolted by American-made carnage — in Vietnam, and on the streets at home.

People had to live behind double- and triple-locked doors, and it was wise to keep a dog. You couldn't stroll in the park at night. Old ladies were fearful in apartment house corridors and elevators. Girls had to be careful anywhere, any time. Even if you had a car — once the magic carpet to open spaces — you couldn't use it much. There were just too many of them. Highways were crowded, there were frequent traffic jams, parking was expensive and distant from places of work. Most people left their cars at home during the week in front of the house. The fancy tin on front and tail made them too long to cram into the old garages.

There was little in the way of intellectual fare. Movies were so awful that people stopped going. Several friends told me they hadn't seen a movie in, literally, years. Neighborhood theaters which used to run continuous performances twelve hours a day were now open only a few hours in the evening, and on weekends. Theatrical fare was generally inane. I saw one off-Broadway show which breathlessly announced the discovery that the Vietnamese were human, like the rest of us. That left only TV, which did ball-games beautifully, was great on "funny" shows, and had brought the afternoon tear-jerkers intact from radio without breaking a soap bubble. Who needed religion as "the opiate of the people" when you had TV?

The greatest inhibitor was inflation, high prices. No decent apartment for anything under a hundred and fifty a month for two rooms. Five dollars for a haircut that used to cost fifty cents, thirty-five cents for the nickel subway ride, half a dollar for a ten cent hamburger — and they didn't even toast the roll. It was less a question of keeping up with the Joneses than of keeping your nose above water. The ordinary American dared not lose his job. He had to toe the line. Within his "free" society he was compelled to lead a cautious narrow existence.

I found useful gadgets and technological marvels in America after twenty-five years, but not much joy.

With this was a widespread, intensely introspective mood. Millions — not just the pundits — were asking "Where has America gone wrong?" Her financial and military pre-eminence was crumbling. Especially since Vietnam, people all over the world regarded America with loathing. Internally, the moral structure was a shambles. More Americans were taking a good look at their government. They had learned to be sceptical about news emanating from Washington.

They realized that they had been had on the China story. In anticipation of Mr. Nixon's visit to Peking a new kind of China coverage was appearing in the press. The mindless "blue ants" now turned out to be civilized, efficient, likeable people who had pulled their country up by its bootstraps and were making remarkable progress. With the removal of the restrictions from above, the inherent long-standing friendliness of Americans toward China overflowed. There was a China craze. Chinese blue denim work clothes and fishing baskets sold in department stores for ridiculous prices. High school and college students snapped up copies of the Little Red Book. Anyone who had been to China, however briefly, wrote articles, or a book, and appeared on TV. China was the "in" thing.

I basked in the reflected glory. Coming straight from Peking at such a time, I was bombarded with questions, most of them thoughtful, sincere, on every conceivable topic. They ranged from China's internal policies to her international relations, from Mao's philosophic concepts to people's everyday life. I did the best I could, within the limitations of my knowledge and ability. In general, the majority of my listeners accepted without demur the purely factual information I had to offer — that life in China was good and moving forward, that China had no aggressive intentions but would fight in self-defence. A few of the Old Left wanted to know about China's differences with the Soviet revisionists, a few Zionists wanted to know about China's "hostility" to Israel, a few young people were worried about China's "friendliness" to Nixon. Though I couldn't always satisfy the questioners, I think in the process I satisfied most everyone else.

My greatest difficulty, and where I was least successful, was in persuading Americans that the average Chinese worked mainly to serve the people, and had no particular interest in making a lot of money or becoming famous. To most Americans I talked with, this was inconceivable. As China's prosperity grew, people would surely become more acquisitive. It was human nature to be selfish. You could never change that, they assured me.

The Chinese don't agree, I said. They're trying to end selfishness. But I admitted it would take some years yet to see whether it really could be done. Usually, we left it at that, with many wishing China well for the sake of the future of mankind. The older idealists reserved judgment. They had been burned too badly by the recrudescence of "human nature" in the Soviet Party.

I ran into several China detractors. The main plaint of these gentlemen — bourgeois intellectuals who posed as liberals — was that in China there was no "freedom" for bourgeois intellectuals who posed as liberals. Could you write and speak as you pleased? Were you free to travel? Often, before I had a chance to open my mouth, others in the audience would jump up and sound off about how little real creative freedom there was in America. As to freedom to travel, they said, that needed money, first of all, and if the State Department didn't like your ideas or where you wanted to go, it could and did frequently refuse to issue a passport.

My reply was that in Chinese society, as in every other existing society, a distinction is drawn between liberty and licence. Thirty-five years before I had learned in St. John's Law School in Brooklyn that freedom of speech did not include the right to shout "Fire!" in a crowded theater. In China violence and the advocation or causation of violence against the people and their government are prohibited. Other than that, any one is free to say or write what he likes. If his ideas run counter to the foundations of Chinese society — the transition to socialism, people's democratic dictatorship, leadership of the Communist Party — as intellectual convictions, and not as active planned measures against those foundations, they may be aired. At the same time the rest of the society, the masses, are free to refute his ideas and use the written and spoken word to take him intellectually to pieces. That was the policy though not always fully implemented.

As to travel abroad, there isn't much interest in it. It's expensive, time-consuming, and just would never occur to the average Chinese, any more than it would have occurred to the average American, say, fifty years ago. If he has the urge to travel, a Chinese would prefer to do it in China where there are thousands of fascinating places to visit and no language problems. Provinces of fifty and sixty million are bigger than many European countries. Chinese are free to travel outside the country, but so far the demand seems to be limited.

What made the biggest impression on the Americans I spoke to were things the Chinese today take for granted — nearly full employment, women's liberation, universal education, guaranteed care for the elderly, low cost of living, low cost medicare, a low crime rate, virtually no drug or v.d. problems, or sexual depravity, or racial or religious discrimination, no foreign bases in China, no Chinese bases abroad, no foreign wars, no conscription, no national debt, no inflation, no personal income tax. . . .

Young Americans — and their parents — thought a recent change in the Chinese education system was good. I told them that in most places when youngsters graduate from high school they are assigned to jobs. What is available in the way of openings changes annually. The kids can list their first three choices in order of preference, and the authorities try to satisfy them. But it could be anything — farming in a commune, tending a machine in a factory, sweeping streets, cutting hair, selling at a counter. Young people are taught that all work in honorable. There is no high or low, only a division of labor.

The Chinese have found that a few years of work helps a lot in teenagers. It settles them, they gain confidence, become more practical, more mature. They learn not only technique but character and political stand from the older people with whom they work. It gives them a chance to "find themselves".

I saw it happen in my own daughter. After three years in a paper mill, she changed from a child to an adult. As a kid she had been an indifferent student, interested mainly in play. But living and working with older serious-minded folk, seeing how useful practice was to theory and knowledge, she gained a new concept of education. She began studying English and math in her spare time, and preparing for possible return to school.

At that time working youngsters, besides needing the approval of their peers, also had to be endorsed by the leaders of their place of work. This latter requirement no long exists, since it was found that it led to favoritism. College entrance exams, formerly dispensed with, now must be passed. Anyone under twenty-five, whether still in school or already at work, can take them. Ultra-"left" extremists had promoted the theory that the ideologically sound would inevitably succeed technically or professionally. This went against Mao's call to be "Red and expert", a dialectical combination of both.

In China the working girl and boy learn to be servants of the people, to see themselves in relation to the whole society. They go to school not to "better" themselves — a doctor earns no more than a good factory technician — but to become better equipped for service to the community. When they finish their schooling they may be sent back to their original unit, they may be assigned elsewhere.

"I wouldn't mind living there myself," a New York friend said, laughing. He wasn't altogether kidding. China still has plenty of problems and short-comings, but the Chinese are convinced they're on the right track, and they're pushing ahead. While it is wrong to romanticise about China, it is impossible to close one's eyes to her accomplishments.

America to me was still an exciting place. All the bad things the pundits and analysts had been saying were true — about crime, poverty, corruption, decadence, oppression, exploitation. But the people were the salt of the earth, and more and more of them were beginning to figure out what was really wrong. Some were thinking in terms of thorough-going change. Although that was in the future, the force of events within the country and on a global scale was clearly impelling America on a collision course between the haves and the have-nots, and my bets were on the quiet, ordinary men and women whose ancestors had warned the tyrants: "Don't tread on me."

At last it was time to go. It was the end of January, 1972, and I wanted to make a brief stop-over in London and be back in Peking in time to witness Nixon's arrival on February 21st. My parting with my family at Kennedy was not solemn. We all felt now that the ice had been broken there would be more coming and going between China and America, and the chances of our meeting again were good.

I flew to London where I spent a pleasant two weeks, visiting friends, seeing the sights, taking in a few shows and concerts. I also paid a courtesy call at the Chinese Charge d'Affaires Office. (It's now an Embassy.) A few days later they telephoned and said that Edgar Snow was dying in Geneva. Did I want to go? I said yes, of course. They helped me get a Swiss visa and booked my passage.

I dashed off as soon as the arrangements were made, but Ed was already gone by the time I arrived. He had terminal cancer. Although the Chinese had flown in their best doctors and nurses from Peking and from Algiers, where they were setting up a hospital for the Algerians, they couldn't save him.

Ed was a fabulous guy. As American as apple pie, yet with a deep feeling for the Chinese people and a perceptive understanding of the aims and methods of their driving force — Mao Tsetung and the Communist Party. As a result of his first trip to the Northwest in 1936 and lengthy interviews with Mao in Pao An, Ed wrote his classic *Red Star Over China,* stating with remarkable clarity, though he himself was never a Communist, what the Chinese "Reds" were doing and where they were heading. I met him on his first return to China in 1960, and again on subsequent visits in 1964 and 1970. It was a pleasure talking with Ed. He probed and dug away at every little thing, but he was so modest and relaxed no one minded.

Head and shoulders above ninety percent of the journalists writing on China, Ed Snow was maligned and boycotted by the "respectable" press in America for twenty years. Even after his long talks with Mao in December 1970, when the Chairman's comment that he would be happy to discuss Sino-American problems with Nixon led to the momentous international break-throughs in the Far East, Ed's offer to do a series of articles was turned down by a leading New York paper. They were ultimately published in the Italian journal *Epoca.*

Ed never flagged in his admiration of the new Chinese and the new China. He recognized and pointed out short-comings, but the warmth and friendliness of his approach was keenly appreciated by the Chinese. Chou En-lai cabled a message as Ed lay dying, and Huang Hua, another old friend, now China's Minister of Foreign Affairs, flew in from New York. Mao sent Lois Wheeler Snow, Ed's wife, a letter of condolence. "His memory will live forever in the hearts of the Chinese people," wrote Mao.

Ed's passing was more than a personal loss to those who knew and loved him. It was a departure from the scene of one of the most articulate proponents of friendship between the Chinese and American people. But Ed had done his work well. It must have been a source of great satisfaction to him, in those final days, to hear the news of Nixon's impending visit to Peking and to feel the balance of the American press swinging toward that cordial and appreciative appraisal of New China for which Ed had labored so mightily and well.

After the memorial service ended and friends who had flown in from all over the world had gone, I stayed on with Dr. George Hatem (Ma Hai-teh to the Chinese) to keep Lois company for a couple of weeks. George and Ed had gone to the Red Areas together in 1937, when they were both young men in their twenties, and they had remained close friends over the years. George had rushed to Geneva when Ed fell ill and had been working feverishly ever since — as liaison between the Chinese and Swiss medical people, coping with the press, meeting visitors, doing a million and one things. Lois and Ed's children — the boy Chris and the girl Sian — were there, as well as Lois' able sister Kashin. But we thought it might be good to help take Lois' mind off things a bit now that the tension had relaxed. And so we gladly agreed to her proposal that we all go up to a friend's chalet in the Swiss Alps.

I spent about ten days with them, high amid magnificent mountains covered with snow. It was rugged country but the accommodations weren't exactly austere. Our two-level house, beneath its cuckoo clock trim, was steam-heated by an oil burner furnace and had piping hot water all day long. In the nearby "center" shops sold all the blessings of civilization at prices to suit the altitude. The kids skied every day, while we older folks went staggering through the drifts or rode to the top of impossible peaks in cable cars. Everyone was glad to collapse before the fireplace in the evening and muse on world affairs.

In Geneva we had watched on TV Mr. Nixon's almost silent entry into Peking. The visit and its significance was the main topic of conversation. There was a division of opinion as to where this move was leading. Some were afraid that receiving him in the Chinese capital would improve his chance of re-election and hurt the anti-war forces in the West.

Those of us familiar with the ways of the Chinese Party advised them to keep their shirts on. There was more than one way to skin a cat, we said. In Asia the underlying long-term contradiction was between the drive toward socialism — as represented by the socialist countries and the people's movements there — and the attempts of the imperialists to maintain and extend their grasp. But there was also an acute global contradiction between the two major imperialist powers — America and the Soviet Union, the last having earned the label both by its internal policies and its foreign military and economic incursions. A dialogue was possible between China and America because people's war had made the American position in Asia untenable, and it was the. Americans who had to make the concessions.

These were mainly an acceptance of the inevitable. The US military had to get out of Vietnam, Laos and Cambodia as rapidly and with as much grace as they could muster. This had first priority. Taiwan and the Chiang Kai-shek crew had gradually to be abandoned. No further impediments should be placed in the way of trade and diplomatic relations between China and Japan. Sato and his *bushido* warriors had to go. Washington should stop interfering with the urgent desire of the Koreans north and south, to reunify their homeland.

In the months which followed we saw China continuing adamant in her support of the three small Indo-Chinese countries. American planes no longer attacked from the convenient proximity of Taiwan. Korean troops began withdrawing from Vietnam. The fall of Sato and his war gang signalled large public demonstrations in Japan against the manufacture of arms for the US invaders and interference with their shipment. The new Japanese government placed restrictions on American use of bases and port facilities.

Japan established diplomatic relations with China, Australia and New Zealand elected labor governments which did the same. Since calm fruitful discussions were obviously possible with Peking, America's main theoretical prop for the invasion of Southeast Asia — "the need to contain China" — was knocked out from under.

All this followed the Peking visit, and was of considerable encouragement to anti-Vietnam war forces the world over. It could hardly have helped Nixon in his election campaign since his trip to China was recognized as an admission of the failure of US Far Eastern policy. Moreover, the American people were still judging him on how quickly he ended the war in Vietnam, and that he showed no sign of doing, merely switching from ground attacks to massive bombings.

Most of these events had not yet transpired when we armchair analysts were batting around the possible effects of the Peking meeting in our Swiss chalet. Arguments waxed hot and heavy, both sides lacking facts to back their contentions. Now we know.

Lois was in fairly good spirits. She was talking about going to New York later in the year to put the finishing touches on Ed's book and getting out one of her own — on the Chinese theater. George and Kashin and the kids were staying on for a while, but I had to get back. I was already several weeks over my planned leave.

They drove me down the misty snowy mountain into the sunny valley below and put me on the train. From then on everything happened fast. In a few hours I was in Geneva. The next day I went by car to Berne. The following noon I was at the Zurich airport with Dr. Huang Kuo-chun, the cancer expert who had tended Ed. The flight to Paris took one hour. From there to Shanghai was another seventeen. We changed planes and landed in Peking at nine o'clock that evening. The drive home from the airport, where I was met by cheering wife, daughter, and a few friends from the office, was thirty minutes.

I dispensed the delicious Swiss chocolates and cheeses with which I had crammed my luggage to the limit of my weight allowance, assured everyone that I wasn't a bit tired, washed, got into bed and slept, on and off, for the next two days. When I came out of my stupor I was briefed on family affairs. Phoenix's Dramatists Association was still awaiting reorganization, but Ya-mei was about to start medical school — a three and half year course in Western and Chinese traditional medicine. We were all very excited about that.

It was no effort for me getting back into the swing of things. I was a Chinese. Peking was my home. But I was told to "rest". So for the next couple of weeks — it was already the middle of March — I rattled around, chatting with friends, popping into the office, wandering through shopping centers and along the streets. I was in great demand as a speaker on "America Today".

When I could stand it no longer I went back to work. The morning of April 1, 1972, twenty-five years to the day of my arrival in Shanghai, found me on my trusty Conventry Eagle, pedalling leisurely down the lane on my regular half-hour ride from house to office. Sunlight, filtering through the morning mist, gilded the tiled roofs rising behind the compound walls. Three old men were sweeping the lane with big bamboo brooms. The air was fresh, trees were beginning to bud.

Phoenix had been granted leave from her May Seventh School to greet my return. She had to go back again in two weeks, and 1972 was a troublesome year for both of us. In writing to family in America I said nothing about her true situation, but it was difficult to explain to foreign friends in Peking, or to visitors from abroad, why my wife was never around.

That summer I was transferred from *Chinese Literature* to *China Pictorial,* though I continued to spend most of my time translating novels.

X

CULTURAL REVOLUTION CONCLUDES
A NEW ERA COMMENCES

1973-1979

Things began to change in 1973. In January Phoenix was allowed home for the Spring Festival. At the end of April she came again for two weeks. After sampling my cooking, she promptly hired a new *paomu*. In August she returned on a sick leave that extended until April 1974. Only two months later, in June, she came again, and never went back. Her trunks in the School were packed by colleagues still there in January 1975 and shipped home. She was assigned to a special study group for the "old, infirm, and ill" with homes in Peking.

That same month, on Chairman Mao's proposal, Teng Hsiao-ping was appointed Vice-Chairman of the Party Central Committee, Vice-Premier of the State Council, Vice-Chairman of the Military Commission of the Central Committee, and Chief of the General Staff of China's Armed Forces. Mao had been calling for a restoration of unity and calm. It was possible in this new environment to reach a more rational appraisal of persons and events.

In June 1975 the result of the investigation into Phoenix's past was formally announced. She was completely exonerated of all charges.

At long last our life was returning to normal. Ya-mei finished med school in 1975 and was assigned to the Peking Traditional Medicine Hospital, only a fifteen-minute bike ride from the house. She was put into the Growths and Tumors Department, which treats both benign and malignant growths by the combined application of Western and traditional technics. She married a classmate, Kuo Tai-ping, from Shanghai. After a year in a mountain hospital in Honan he was assigned to the Drum Tower Clinic in Peking, actually a small hospital, to work as a surgeon. They live with us in a bungalow in the rear garden. Ya-mei gave birth to a little girl named Hsiang, or Fragrance, in May 1977. On my last visit to the Old Country I returned laden with the latest models in New York and Hollywood infant wear, much of them gifts from enthusiastic friends and relations. Fragrance looked cute as the dickens in them.

Phoenix was working again, this time as an editor of a film magazine. Friends we hadn't seen in years, many of whom had been under attack by the Gang of Four "purists" — more of this later — called to see us. They too had resumed their careers in Peking, in Shanghai, as writers, actors, directors, administrators.

I visited the States again in 1974 and 1977. Happily, I found my mother still thriving at eighty-five, my sister and family doing well, most of my old friends still around.

It seemed to me that America was continuing to slide downward. Unemployment was higher, particularly among young Blacks and other ethnics. No one seemed able to stem the inflation. The thirty-five cent New York subway fare which had so aroused my indignation in 1971 was now half a dollar. The value of US currency was falling on the world market. Crime was worse, moral disintegration seemed to be accelerating. I was in New York during the blackout that summer evening in 1977. I watched TV films, after power was restored, of thousands of poor people looting stores, cheerfully and matter-of-factly. Why not, since corruption was so widespread, and extended to the highest offices in the land.

Yet in China, too, we were conscious of a slackening of ethical standards. Nothing like America, but serious for a country which had been so clean. By the end of 1975 it was very apparent. Ya-mei and her girl friends stopped skating on our nearby lake because boys were deliberately bumping into people and knocking them down. A friend's son was badly cut on the forehead because, when waylaid by a gang who demanded his fur hat, he didn't hand it over quick enough. Purse snatching and burglary were more frequent. There was some murder and rape. Children sassed teachers, broke windows, went to school only when they felt like it. Sales people were surly. Even the bright young waiters and waitresses in the Peking Hotel where foreign tourists stayed were inattentive and rude.

Living standards also declined. There were all sorts of shortages. Coal, which ninety percent of the Peking population used to heat their houses, was difficult to get. Power shut-offs were frequent. Friends who visited family in their old homes in the provinces returned with stories of real privation.

Nor was the situation in the arts any better. For nearly thirty years I had specialized in translating contemporary Chinese fiction into English. Now there were virtually no new creations. The few that were written were contrived and dull. On the stage we had only the "model operas" — traditional Peking opera with modern themes. Their stories were intrinsically good, but little else was performed. People got tired of seeing the same thing over and over again. Painting appeared limited to posed, photographic-type oils. Musical composition was repetitious, trite.

What was going on? We couldn't understand it. China seemed beset by countless problems. There was a pervading sense of uneasiness. Articles and editorials in the press didn't help. They railed against veteran cadres, claiming they were "empiricists" and "bourgeois" and relied too much on practical experience. Their worst sin, thundered the editorials, was that they pushed production — or scientific research, or study, or artistic creativity — when every true Marxist knew that all you had to do was stress "political revolution" and the other things would take care of themselves. It was the duty of the arts to attack those "capitalist-roaders". This should be the "sole specialization" in education. Anyone in a factory who did an honest day's work was only helping the "capitalist-roaders". Above all, the press exhorted, be "revolutionary" — "Better a socialist train which is late than a capitalist train which runs on time." "An illiterate proletarian is superior to an educated bourgeois."

The result was great confusion. In the name of "revolution", college students, regardless of their major, spent six to eight months of the year on farms, "learning from the former poor peasants". Library sections containing foreign books were locked. You risked being called "a slave to foreign culture" if you persisted in a demand for access. Ancient Chinese writings were branded as "feudal" or "Confucian", and were also taboo. In several parts of the country trains stopped running when vociferous factions brawled and vilified their "capitalist-roader" leaders. Similar strife paralyzed local government organizations, right down to the county level, badly disrupting agriculture. Steel and other industrial output dropped sharply.

It gradually became evident that the extremists who called themselves "revolutionaries" had regrouped their forces and were again on the offensive. We weren't sure who was heading the ultras' clique, though Chiang Ching, the Chairman's wife, was a prime suspect, primarily because we had been exposed to her strange mentality in our work.

She had a thing about pianos. Quite early in the Cultural Revolution she announced that the piano had always been the instrument of the bourgeoisie and that she, Chiang Ching, was going to see to it that it be made available to the broad masses. It would be brought to them "down in the country and up in the mountains". I could just picture fourteen men heaving and straining and hauling a piano up some summit and delivering it to an astonished woodcutter.

Another of her brilliant innovations was the principle of the "Three Stresses". This demanded that in any artistic creation the positive be stressed, and within that the heroic, and within that the most heroic. The net effect was that you had a hero or heroine of sheer cardboard who, already being most heroic, had no room for development. All the other positive characters could serve only as foils and echoes, and under no circumstances surpass the main protagonist.

As for the villains, they got the opposite treatment. On stage they often wore make-up of a bilious green. For the cinema, the camera usually panned down on them from a height to make them look smaller. To stress their murky natures they were filmed in such dim light it was difficult to discern their features. They skulked around in the sinister manner of the baddies in old-fashioned melodramas, their wickedness immediately apparent to everyone in the audience. But it took the "most heroic characters" a full three or four acts to see through them, which made you wonder whether the author was trying to equate nobility of spirit with thickness of wit.

Then there was Chiang Ching's attack on Beethoven, out of a clear blue sky. It came not long after she had welcomed Eugene Ormandy and the Philadelphia Orchestra and complimented them on their performance. Their program had featured the music of — guess who — Beethoven!

But she was not just a screwball, she was an unprincipled egomaniac. The "new" model opera and ballets for which she claimed credit were vehicles which had been on the boards for from ten to twenty years.

She simply hijacked them, made a few trifling changes, often for the worse, and prohibited any mention of the original creators. Feature films and TV versions of these were also made, again crediting Chiang Ching with the adaptation.

Friends in the theater said she was impossible to work with. She would fly into a rage when crossed, and think nothing of insulting the offender publicly. Five minutes later she'd be all solicitude and sweetness to her poor victim — after having shocked everyone into submission.

Those who obeyed her and built up her image she rewarded handsomely. The troupes which put on "her" operas and ballets got special treatment. A niece of ours, a ballet dancer in another company, complained that they couldn't get replacements for their worn out practice slippers. Chiang Ching's pets, she said, not only had slippers to spare, but were fed excellent after-show suppers, had plenty of chocolate and other quick energy pick-me-ups, and were constantly going on tour, both in China and abroad.

Hao Liang, who sang the male lead in the model opera *Red Lantern* became, on Chiang Ching's recommendation, a Vice-Minister of Culture. Liu Ching-tang danced the role of the hero in *Red Detachment of Women,* a model ballet. He was raised to a similar post and put in charge of China's film industry, about which he knew next to nothing. That didn't stop him from throwing his weight around and promoting the movies Chiang Ching and her gang wanted, and squelching those they disapproved of.

I had only one encounter with Liu Ching-tang, and that was enough. Joris Ivens in 1976 had just completed his epic documentary on new China and was returning to Paris. Phoenix and I were among those seeing him off at the Peking airport. In the small reception room, besides a number of Chinese dignitaries, there were several foreign friends. As the Chinese arrived, two or three of whom were veteran revolutionaries high in the government, they shook hands with each of us, whether they knew us or not.

But when Liu came in he completely ignored not only the foreigners but the veteran leaders as well. He headed straight for Joris, to whom he offered awkward remarks until plane time, which was mercifully soon. The arrogance of tyros like Liu Ching-tang was a sorry contrast to the courteous friendliness of the old timers. As we were to learn, it was typical of the "rocket" (because they rose so fast) cadres fostered by Chiang Ching.

Phoenix and I were at the Changchun Motion Picture Studio in the Northeast in July 1975, where I was continuing my illustrious career as a movie star. Again I was an American villain — this time an Air

Force general in the Korean War. For the sake of our family reputation as thespians, Phoenix insisted on coaching me personally. While we were shooting, the Studio received a written comment by Chairman Mao on *Pioneers*, a film they had made about the Taching Oilfield. Chiang Ching had assailed it viciously, listing ten "flaws" and demanding that it be suppressed. Mao said there was nothing seriously wrong with the film and approved its release. He indicated that nit-picking criticism hampered creativity.

The Studio's reaction was ecstatic. A mass meeting was called which Phoenix and I were permitted to attend. Everyone turned out, beating drums and gongs and carrying big banners. When Chairman Mao's rebuke to Chiang Ching was read, the audience cheered. It was not only because this particular film was vindicated. What mattered was that the erratic virago who had been raising such hell in the arts was at last being publicly ticked off. Surely this signaled a turn in the tide?

But when we returned to Peking we were amazed to find that no one knew anything about Chairman Mao's blast. Chiang Ching had managed to prevent it from being circulated. Yu Hui-yung, then the Minister of Culture, was subsequently revealed to be her man.

We heard through the grapevine that Chairman Mao also said: "People are afraid to write articles or plays. There is nothing in the way of novels or poetry. People come under fire for the slightest fault. No one is allowed to offer any opinion. That's no good."

In spite of this, Chiang Ching continued to ride high. We didn't know then about the other three in her Gang of Four (Chang Chun-chiao, Yao Wen-yuan and Wang Hung-wen), but we were very much aware of the lady herself and the damage she was doing in the arts. Chiang Ching was pressing for plays and scenarios attacking "capitalist-roaders" — meaning actually the tried and true Party leaders — and very few writers were responding. How could she flagrantly oppose Chairman Mao's policies and remain in a position of power? Was her backing so strong? Did it mean that Chairman Mao and the veteran revolutionaries were losing control? We were growing concerned.

The tension accelerated. Chairman Mao's health was plainly deteriorating. He looked weak and haggard when we saw him on TV. To make matters worse, Premier Chou En-lai was in the hospital, gravely ill. In January 1976, he died.

It was a staggering blow. Chou En-lai, whose remarkable talents had been devoted totally to implementing Mao's policies for fifty years, whose selfless drive and warmth and gayety had endeared him to millions as the ideal revolutionary, was gone, at the very moment Mao, and China, needed him more than ever. What was going to happen? We soon found out. Letters from friends in Shanghai said posters had been put up attacking Teng Hsiao-ping, who had been chosen Vice-Premier in 1975, and demanding that Chang Chun-chiao be appointed Premier. Mao responded swiftly, with all of his old fire. On his proposal the Party Central Committee named Hua Kuo-feng as Acting Premier. Stories were already circulating that Chang Chun-chiao was part of a "Shanghai Mafia" in which Chiang Ching was also involved, so Chang's defeat was welcome news. Hua Kuo-feng was not yet a familiar figure nationally, but Chairman Mao's endorsement reassured us.

The next clash came in April. In 1976 Clear and Bright, the traditional day for remembering the dead, fell on April 4. People were angry at what they considered inadequate funeral services for their beloved Premier Chou En-lai, and their hatred of Chiang Ching had intensified when they saw her, on TV, standing by his bier with her hat on. In a surge of emotion that swept all of China they began preparing wreaths and poems of eulogy days in advance. The Monument of the Martyrs in the center of Tien An Men Square would be the natural focal point in the capital.

Late in the day of April 3 an order was issued by the Peking municipal authorities: "Stay away from Tien An Men Squate tomorrow."

I never saw such a combination of grief and cold fury as gripped the people of Peking. The following morning they poured into the Square by the millions, on foot, in trucks, in many instances led by their local Communist Party secretary. They bore large wreaths of paper flowers, beautifully and lovingly made by themselves, and marched solemnly to lay them at the foot of the Monument of the Martyrs.

The wreaths soon overflowed into the Square. Groups stood in silence, tears coursing down their cheeks, some raising a clenched right fist in Communist salute as their spokesman read a statement, or recited a poem.

My whole office turned out. I went by in a car that afternoon, and we stopped for a few minutes. I noticed plain clothesmen jotting down license numbers. We ignored them and gazed at the stupendous scene.

The evergreens and hedges forming the background to the Monument looked as if they were covered with snow. White paper carnations with wire stems are also symbols of mourning in China, and thousand of people had attached theirs to branches as small personal tributes.

These were expressions of homage to a great statesman and dear friend, pledges to carry on the cause of Chairman Mao for which Chou had so valiantly fought, and thinly veiled defiance of Chiang Ching and her gang. Many poems reviling them by innuendo were also put up.

Processions were still arriving, endlessly, as we drove slowly away, our own eyes wet.

The trouble came the next day, April 5. Someone had ordered that the wreaths be removed. But as they were being carted away, new ones were being delivered. One mill brought a wreath of solid steel weighing several tons on a flatbed truck and lowered it carefully into the Square. "Let's see those bastards move that!" said one of the steelmen grimly.

Tempers flared, a clash occurred, and suddenly "militiamen" swinging truncheons tore into the crowd. The fighting spread, many were hurt. There were, it was rumored, some deaths. Scores were arrested.

"A counter-revolutionary incident," cried the Gang of Four the next day in their controlled press. "Teng Hsiao-ping is behind it!" Praise was heaped on the militia, which Wang Hung-wen directed.

But the Tien An Men disturbance was a fatal blunder for the Gang. While previously many had been confused by their "revolutionary" pose, the venomous treatment of people who wanted to pay respects to the memory of Chou En-lai was something everyone understood. If the Four were against Chairman Mao's most loyal and dedicated supporter, they surely were bad. Public opinion crystallized against them.

Again Chairman Mao acted. He recommended that Hua Kuo-feng be appointed Premier and "First Vice-Chairman" of the Chinese Communist Party. This ensured that Hua, and not anyone from the Gang of Four, would lead the country and the Party in the event of Mao's illness or death. At the same time, Teng Hsiao-ping was removed from office. Had the Chairman been misinformed about him? Was it a tactical maneuver in the battle against Chiang Ching and her faction? We still don't know.

Though the Gang had won a small victory in having Teng, one of their most outspoken critics, expelled, they had suffered a stunning defeat when Mao destroyed any chance they may have had for a legal take-over. They retaliated by intensifying their efforts to pin "capitalist-roader" labels on all leaders, high and low, who adhered to Mao's principles.

Everyone in the Ministry of Culture, to which Phoenix was attached though not yet assigned to a specific job, was subjected to interrogation: "Did you go to Tien An Men Square on Clear and Bright? What did you see? Did you copy any of the poems? Did you see anyone there you knew? What were they doing? Have you heard any rumors circulating against Comrade Chiang Ching?"

This last because word of Mao's stringent criticism of the lady had leaked out and was being happily spread. No one was foolish enough to answer directly. The usual response was an innocent expression and the counter-query: "What rumors?"

I too was involved in a brush with the Gang of Four. Foreign Languages Press had been translating Chairman Mao's poems for publication and circulation abroad. Late in 1974 I had participated in a discussion of a draft translation with very perfunctory footnotes. A number of us had pointed out that all of Mao's poems, through literary or folk allusions, commented on specific persons, places and events, and that foreign readers would not be able to appreciate them fully without detailed explanations.

Now, at a second meeting in 1976, we were shown a final version, in page proof, with no comments or footnotes at all. I and one or two others really ripped into the editors. Why invite us to discussions if you don't heed our advice? we said. Don't you want people to understand Mao's meaning?

Behind all this was Chiang Ching. One of the poems praised Yang Kai-hui, to whom Mao had been married and who was killed by the Kuomintang in 1930. Chiang Ching didn't want the world to think of anyone but herself as Mao's wife. To delete only the footnote to Yang Kai-hui would be too obvious an exposure of her own jealousy. She found a simpler device. She compelled the editors to omit all footnotes and amplifications.

Our strenuous objections angered the lady. There were dark hints of reprisals. A few persons at the meeting, who had not been introduced, had assiduously taken notes. Later, I heard they demanded the names of those who had criticized, and asked why the Foreign Languages Press was "using foreigners to attack Chinese"?

This was disquieting at a time when some Chinese friends, appraising the general situation, were gloomily forecasting that "heads will roll." I remembered Mao had warned that under certain circumstances it was not impossible for China to go fascist.

Certainly the attacks by the Gang of Four (though most of us still didn't know them by that name, or as an organized faction) were becoming more open, yet we could see no counter-measures to restrain them. Among our friends, the concensus was that there must be a split in the highest echelons. No one was sure which way the struggle would go. Would all the blood and sweat of the previous decades prove to have been in vain? Was China to be plunged into another civil war? We were very worried.

Chairman Mao passed away on September 9, 1976. For at least a year we knew he was dying. Yet, when it finally happened, we were shocked. Who could imagine new China without Chairman Mao? He had conceived it, raised it to maturity, guided it through shoals and storms. Not for nothing was he revered as the teacher and helmsman. What would we do without him, particularly now, when China was in such dire straits?

Even while the Chairman's body was lying in state, Chiang Ching was demanding his papers. The Party custodian refused her. The Gang of Four stepped up the pressure. They notified local Party and government units to take orders from the "Wang Hung-wen Office" of the Central Committee, rather than the regular Office of the Central Committee. Wang had his "official photograph" taken. Chang Chun-chiao wrote a memo proposing "executions" and the "suppression of counter-revolutionaries". More arms and munitions were handed out to the Shanghai militia, which was put on battle alert.

On October 4 the Gang published an article in the *Guangming Daily* threatening Hua Kuo-feng and other top leaders of the Central Committee. Implying that the Four were in possession of a "testament" left by Chairman Mao recommending that government and Party control be given to them, the article said: "Any revisionist chieftain who dares to tamper with the principles laid down by Chairman Mao will come to no good end!"

That was it — an open declaration of war against the Party. On October 6, the Four were arrested. Their chief lieutenants were rounded up the same evening. Strongholds such as Shanghai, and Tsinghua and Peking Universities, were taken over in the days that followed.

Relief was universal. Huge celebrations were held all over China. Foreign newspaper correspondents noted their obvious spontaneity and genuineness. We could breathe again.

From various parts of the country reports began coming in of the depredations of the Gang of Four. It added up to a pretty horrendous picture. They had used their power and position to build a coterie of the worst elements in China and tried to wreck the existing structure of society by persecuting the people and their veteran leaders. As part of their attempt to discredit these leaders they sabotaged the economy. Between 1974 and 1976 industrial output dropped in value by one hundred billion *yuan* (about 62 billion US dollars), steel fell by twenty-eight million tons, forty billion *yuan* worth of state revenues were lost. China's economy was on the brink of collapse. Where the Gang was able to put their cronies in, production ground to a halt.

They disrupted administration in the rural areas so badly that many communes quit farming. Szechuan, once known as "China's Rice Bowl" because of its bounteous harvests and annual surpluses, couldn't feed its own population.

Higher education and scientific research stopped. There was virtually no creativity in the arts. Ancient Chinese classics and foreign cultural fare were banned.

The groundwork for these machinations was laid in 1966 when Chiang Ching, in collaboration with Lin Piao, published a critique which claimed that a bourgeois revisionist line predominated in the arts from the very inception of the People's Republic. The Gang later extended this smear into every field of endeavor — agriculture, industry, the armed forces, education, health, the media, science, security, the judiciary, foreign trade, even foreign affairs. On this basis, they could, and did, set aside many leaders who had been implementing Chairman Mao's policies, and blew their errors and inadequacies into major proportions.

Their scenario was simple. If they could persuade the country that Mao's policies had never been properly carried out, that the havoc which they themselves were creating was due to the failures of the existing Party leadership, they could then pose as the only true defenders of Mao's line and modestly offer themselves for the highest Party and government posts in the land. Naturally their organization would participate in the take-over at every level.

The designation of Lin Piao as Mao's successor and the appointment of Chiang Ching to the Politbureau and to the Cultural Revolution Committee had been interpreted by some as an endorsement of their extremist policies. Because of this, many people — myself included — for a time were fooled by their ultra-"left" sloganeering. But eventually most of us realized they were talking rot. Moreover the general public was disgusted by the Gang and their methods. When the Four were arrested, there was wild rejoicing.

In 1977, after eleven years, the Cultural Revolution came to an end. But due to the disruptions of Lin Piao and the Gang of Four it had lasted too long and at times extremist elements had got out of hand. It will be some years before historians can make a comprehensive appraisal. Among our Chinese friends the feeling seems to be that all of the facts have not yet been revealed, that more information may yet be forthcoming. We'll just have to wait.

Certainly some good came of the Cultural Revolution. While the turmoil bubbled all the scum to the surface — class enemies, sycophants, opportunists, cowards — the honest, the courageous, the dedicated also showed their colors in overwhelming number. For millions of young people who never experienced exploitation in the old society it proved graphically what class struggle is all about.

China indeed had class enemies, only they were Lin Piao, the Gang of Four, Chen Po-ta, and perhaps others yet unnamed — not, in the vast majority of cases, those originally accused of being "Party persons in power taking the capitalist road".

The People and the leadership have learned that, while no one can guarantee that no demagogues will ever again appear in China, they can make it impossible for them to remain undetected for any length of time. For this the formula, as Teng Hsiao-ping recently indicated, is democracy, mass line, and an atmosphere in which all the people, in the Party and out, can raise questions, voice opinions, criticize defects, and supervise the work of the leadership.

As if these momentous events weren't enough, nature joined in with an earthquake in July of 1976 that killed hundreds of thousands. Its epicenter was the industrial city of Tangshan, only about a hundred miles from Peking.

I was awakened before four in the morning by the violent shaking of our bed and Phoenix yelling: "Earthquake! Earthquake!" Still half asleep, I clumsily dressed and staggered into the front garden. Everyone was present and accounted for — our *paomu,* our next-door neighbors and their kids. Ya-mei was honeymooning in Shanghai with Young Kuo. The house seemed intact. Later we found a big crack, right through the foot-thick wall, running from ceiling to floor.

Others didn't get off so lightly. Many of Peking's picturesque buildings have plastered-over walls of rubble and mud. Quite a number collapsed under the initial tremor — nearly 8 on the Richter scale at Tangshan, 6 or 7 around Peking. Casualties were higher in Tientsin and towns in the earthquake zone, where people rushed out into narrow crowded streets and were killed by flying bricks and tiles. In traditional style homes, where pillars and beams support the roof, it was relatively safer indoors. The walls are only to ward off the weather, and tend to fall outward during quakes. Prefabricated tall modern dwellings were the most dangerous. The huge cement slabs which form the floors and ceilings came down flat, directly, crushing all beneath.

We learned these things, and other quake lore, in the next few days. The unthinkable had happened. Centuries before, Peking had been chosen as the capital partly because it had been free of the serious quakes which periodically rocked other parts of North China. We should have been warned, according to the stories going round. The seismographic instruments had recorded suspicious signs. Moreover, snakes and burrowing animals had come out of their holes, horses had refused to enter their stalls, domestic fowl had roosted high in trees. But certain officials had been lulled by a false sense of security — or had been criminally negligent.

Recriminations were no use. The situation had to be met. Immediately, the Chinese genius for organization and self-discipline swung into action. Food and medical care were rushed to Tangshan and other badly stricken areas. Teams began clearing away the rubble and erecting shelters.

In Peking, the parks and playgrounds were filled with makeshift shacks of every description. They lined the sides of the broad avenues, and mushroomed in gardens and on campuses. It was feared there might be another quake. Indeed, the ground never stopped trembling, and there were minor shocks every few days. Many homes were destroyed. Of those still standing, several needed only one more good shake to bring them down as well. For about a week everyone was urged to stay out of all buildings, regardless of condition, except where absolutely necessary.

Fortunately, the water supply in Peking was not disrupted. Electricity, which had been cut, was restored for certain hours of the day. Trams and busses ran. Most work resumed. But vigilance was constant. Ya-mei, who had hurried back with Young Kuo from Shanghai, was among the doctors on duty in the hundreds of first-aid stations set up all over the city.

With our next-door neighbors, we erected a temporary shelter in our common front garden. We built it of poles — supplied by our respective offices, tar paper, matting and plastic sheeting. Our beds were planks laid on benches and chairs. We all slept there at night. There had been a little looting — which was severely punished. But the main danger was a new tremor, and someone at night had to hear the shouted warnings, and listen for a possible ringing of the phone, which was in the house.

I rather enjoyed my shifts. Peking was very beautiful in the summer moonlight. The stillness was almost absolute, broken only by the occasional wail of a far-off train. You could feel beneath your feet the solidity of a city which for a thousand years had been a major center of civilization. It would take more than an earthquake to destroy Peking.

Gradually, as the weeks went by, those who could began moving back into their homes. Outdoor living was too inconvenient, and the nights were turning cold. Remembering my army training, I dug a drainage ditch around the shelter, but when it rained the inside of our flimsy structure was damp from leaks and drips.

For a time, after returning to the house, we continued to be cautious. Chinese beds are simply a mattress on a board platform. We, being more effete, had managed to buy a boxspring affair, but still had the board platform of our old bed. We suspended it above us by tying it to the bedposts in the pious hope that this would protect us should the ceiling fall in the night. Similar contraptions were erected for the rest of the household. But we kept banging our heads, and finally decided repeated concussions might prove more injurious than what, by then, seemed a highly unlikely collapse. We dismantled the thing and resumed more or less normal living.

That was the state we were in when Joan and Doug arrived in early October of 1976. Joan is my sister Ruth's daughter and Doug is her husband. Both are young lawyers, practicing separately in Chicago. Joan is a pretty girl who some kind Chinese friend said looks like me. Doug's face was so covered with the then fashionable American youth whiskers it was difficult to tell who he looked like — unless it was Santa Claus in his twenties. They got to Peking shortly after the Gang of Four had been nabbed, and all China was in a mood of exultant celebration. We had a hard time trying to answer their whys and wherefores about things we understood only imperfectly ourselves.

My *China Pictorial* office was more than generous in extending hospitality. Although the kids paid their own fares and hotel bills, we provided the "interpreter" — actually the man in charge of our English section. The head of our Foreign Affairs section, a very competent woman, also accompanied us on our subsequent tour of south China. Phoenix and I helped show them around Peking — street committees, factories, the Great Wall, the Ming Tombs. . . .

We had them over to the house a number of times. They sampled Chinese home cooking and met some of our Chinese friends. Ya-mei was in the nauseous stage of early pregnancy, which didn't add much appeal to my suggestion to Joan and Doug they ought to consider starting a family. (Something must have persuaded them, because they had a little girl in 1978.) Ya-mei and Young Kuo were roughly the same age as our visitors, and the two couples were mutually intrigued with each other. They exchanged information on how they lived, what they thought, what they hoped for.

Phoenix couldn't get away, but I went with Joan and Doug and my two colleagues on their swing through the south. We visited Nanking, Shanghai, Yangchow and Canton. The streets of the first two were jammed with demonstrators, joyously celebrating the downfall of the Gang of Four. These cities were strongholds of the Gang, and their persecution of opponents had been brutal.

In Shanghai we stayed at the Peace Hotel, formerly Sassoon House, a great Victorian pile on the Bund. We each had a big room with twin beds, a curtained alcove containing a couch, a large closet with timed light switch, and a bathroom with pure brass plumbing fixtures bearing the trade mark "Crapper & Sons, Ltd." (etymologists please note). Not exactly a simple proletarian life-style, but that's where they put us.

Right on the corner, where Nanking Road meets the river-front drive known as the Bund, is a wide strip of park backed by a huge billboard. Plastering the board were cartoons in lurid colors exposing the machinations of the Gang in strongly uncomplimentary terms. We could see them from our hotel windows, but Joan and Doug wanted to take pictures and know what they said. So we went down for a closer look.

As I translated the captions aloud into English, we were soon surrounded by a crowd of thousands. They were smiling and friendly. Some understood English, or maybe they just liked the idea of us laughing at lampoons of their hated oppressors. But they were pressing so tightly, the kids were having difficulty in taking notes. We decided to move on.

Everywhere it was the same. Marchers pounding enormous kettle-drums on open trucks, young men in colorful turbans rhythmically beating waist drums, girls with streaming broad ribbons tied around their middles dancing the vigorous *yangko* — all heading for the Shanghai Municipal Government headquarters on the Bund to present pledges of support from their factory, their farm commune, their office, their school . . . and denunciations of the local henchmen of the Gang of Four. Knots of people gathered in front of cartoons and posters on walls in many parts of the city.

There wasn't nearly so much visible evidence of the reaction in Canton. The persecution hadn't been so bad — though there was plenty. Besides, the annual autumn international trade fair was in session, and the city was bursting at the seams with businessmen from all over the world. We were in another posh hotel, with semi-tropical gardens, opposite the fair grounds.

At Joan and Doug's request a meeting was arranged with a few officials from the local judiciary. It was not a very satisfactory session. Some of their answers to the kids' questions were evasive and vague. One man in particular struck me as a likely sympathizer, at least, with the Gang of Four network.

Nevertheless, on the whole our young visitors were pleased and impressed by their tour. They had seen a lot that was positive. They also had hours of opportunity to quiz my poor colleagues who, out of their years of experience, were able to provide them with honest comprehensive information on a great number of topics. They were going back via Hongkong and when we saw them off at the Canton railway station they were effusive in their thanks. Doug dashed out of the train at the last minute to present us, on the platform, with Frisbees they had brought from America to give to Chinese children but had forgotten.

Both had taken hundreds of pictures. They wrote later to say they were kept busy giving slide shows and talking about their trip. Doug became active in the Chicago chapter of the US-China People's Friendship Association.

My colleagues and I spent another two somewhat less hectic days in Canton, then returned by plane to Peking.

Reconstruction was under way in all fields of endeavor. Some had been merely fractured by the Gang of Four syndicate, others were virtually shattered. The question you heard most frequently was — how could such a pack of scoundrels, obviously inept and unsavory, gain such high positions and hold them for so long? No one I knew had a satisfactory answer. It didn't come, to me at any rate, until January 1979, when an article in the *People's Daily* by a "Special Commentator" — meaning a top-ranking leader in the Chinese Communist Party — gave the frankest and most convincing explanation I have seen to date.

He indicated that some of the causes originated in the 1958 to 1962 period. Fifty-eight was the year of the Big Leap Forward and the formation of the people's communes. Fifty-nine through '61 was a time of floods and droughts and severe shortages in China's food supply. The Soviet Union chose '60 to pull out their experts, with blueprints, and cancel contracts for over a hundred major engineering projects.

"Our socialist construction suffered heavy setbacks and the national economy developed great difficulties," said Commentator. "This situation was due to many subjective as well as objective factors. Among the more important was the abnormality of democratic life within the Party and the sabotage of the principle of democratic centralism. Certain leading cadres cast aside the practice of investigation and research, the factual approach, and gave orders blindly. They wouldn't listen to contrary opinions, they rejected criticism, and crushed (dissenters) with horrific labels. As a result, it was impossible to correct certain errors and failures in our work which originally were not difficult of solution. In fact it made them increasingly serious."

He went on to say how, after a brief interval of relative democracy, Lin Piao and the Gang of Four plunged the country into near anarchy.

People want to know, he said, "how such a great Chinese Communist Party could permit (them) to run amok for more than ten years? Our tens of millions of Communists, especially our many old cadres —

veterans of hundreds of battles — could handle the Kuomintang reactionaries, could cope with the imperialists. Why were they so helpless in the face of a few petty clowns like Lin Piao and the Gang of Four? There is only one answer: For years political life within the Party was extremely abnormal and undemocratic. In consequence, our society was undemocratic as well."

It was a bitter and costly lesson, and today democracy is fostered and encouraged. Critical letters are written to and carried in the press. Instances of corruption, inefficiency, bureaucracy, injustice are published and followed up by a special editorial investigative staff. Replies are elicited and printed — usually containing an apology and solution.

While still accentuating the positive and publicizing accomplishments, the news itself also includes criticisms and outspoken comment. During the latest Communist Party Central Committee meeting at the end of 1978, the drive for modernization by the end of the century was announced and stress was placed upon the restoration of democracy and legality and the correction of errors committed by the leadership during the Cultural Revolution and before. Many people were interviewed and asked for their reactions. Workers in a Lanchow plant were particularly blunt. I read their remarks in the *People's Daily*.

"Whenever the economy made a little progress, whenever our livelihood improved a bit," said one man, "we'd be hit by another 'movement' and they'd go smash."

Another worker expressed the wish that the impracticabilities and wild boasts of the Big Leap Forward would not be repeated. "No matter what, we mustn't run our Four Modernizations program like 1958. This time we must be strictly objective," he said.

Though strongly in favor of modernizing China, he cautioned: "You can't do it without democracy. In the past we didn't encourage democracy very much and we were always getting into trouble. It's not surprising that people couldn't liberate their thinking. Before each 'movement' we were told we could speak frankly. But when we did, we were blasted and labeled and picked on. We hope this time we'll have real democracy, not some watered-down version, and that people, no matter what their ideas, will be able to say whatever they please. History proves that when the Party Central Committee listens to the voice of the working people it makes fewer mistakes."

In addition to the daily newspapers, China has its wall posters, in which citizens can and do express themselves freely. You see them on walls all over Peking. Many express legitimate complaints, but you get a few crackpots. One gentleman wrote indignantly that the Army had rejected his marvellous military invention, and demanded that he be allowed to send it to Sweden so that he could win a Nobel Prize.

Convinced now that democracy is here to stay, people are digging into their jobs and professions, being more innovative. A return to the socialist principle of "from each according to his ability, to each according to his work" has brought pay raises and bonuses, and this is further stimulating enthusiasm. A modern industry, agriculture, military and science and technology by the year 2000 is an audacious goal for a backward country like China. But there are already signs that we very likely will attain it. Factories and farms are producing again. The department stores are jammed with shoppers. Schools and scientific institutes are functioning and expanding. Foreign trade, technology, credit, culture are welcomed.

The changes became quickly apparent in our own fields. During the Cultural Revolution not only was I compelled to participate in sending abroad in our periodicals material I knew was utter bilge, but almost all twenty of the major contemporary novels I had translated over the years were condemned for alleged ideological impurities in themselves or in their authors. Now, one by one, the writers were being rehabilitated and the books reprinted.

One accidental good which came to me out of the Cultural Revolution was that since few writers dared touch pen to paper, and since therefore no new novels of any merit had appeared, I was given a classic to translate — *Outlaws of the Marsh*. Written in the fourteenth century, it is a fictional dramatization of twelfth-century Sung dynasty events. Over a hundred men — and women — are forced by a harsh feudal officialdom to take to the hills. They band together and ingeniously defeat every attempt of the government troops to quell them. Within this framework we find intrigue, murder, sex, mystery, warfare, adventure . . . in a connected series of fascinating individual tales, recounted in the suspenseful manner of the traditional storyteller. It's a smashing yarn, a kind of Chinese Robin Hood — but definitely not for the kiddies.

China's Foreign Languages Press is putting it out in three volumes, the first of which is ready for distribution. The illustrations are Ming dynasty woodcuts, made specially for the novel in the fifteenth century.

But writers are writing again, in fact one or two never stopped. During his enforced idleness while being "investigated" a friend of ours knocked out a novel, a trilogy, of a million words. In addition to a few interesting novels there is a large number of first-rate new short stories. The literary journals are back in business. They sell out as soon as they hit the stands.

Phoenix is once again editor of the magazine *Playscript*. She says they have more excellent dramas than they can possibly print, with contributions pouring in daily. Television and the arts are lively. Only the film industry is still limping along. Their recent stuff is artificial — I like their pre-Cultural Revolution products better. It's their feature films that are poor. They make very good documentaries.

In the spring of 1978 Phoenix and I went on a tour with a group of foreign experts working for *China Pictorial* and several Chinese colleagues. For nearly three weeks we traveled through the south, visiting Nanning in Kwangsi and Kunming in Yunnan. But the highlight of our junket was a fabulous little town called Chinghung on the Lantsang River, which becomes the famous Mekong after crossing the Chinese border not very far to the south.

A small plane from Kunming brushed the tops of mountains to set us down in a prefectural center called Szemao. From there we went by station wagon on a dizzying ride along a winding road through steep mountains densely covered by semi-tropical trees and vegetation. Suddenly, stretched before us was a large flat valley bordering on a river and, surprisingly, modern buildings and broad paved streets. In so remote an area I had expected something much more primitive.

We had arrived in Chinghung, capital of the Hsishuang Panna Tai Autonomous Prefecture, which embraces the counties of Chinghung, Menghai and Mengla. It covers an area of 25,000 square kilometers, fifty-five percent of which is mountain forests. Thirty percent of its 620,000 population are Tais, but there are also settlements of other racial minorities scattered mainly in the heights.

It is a mountainous country, and even the valley basins, called "badz", run 500 to 1,300 meters high. They have only two seasons, a dry and a wet, with around 1,400 mm. of rainfall per year. Temperature averages a pleasant 22 degrees Centigrade. Rice is grown in the "badz". The slopes are planted with corn, cash crops and tropical fruits. We were told that occasional tigers and elephants can be found in the interior, but fortunately we didn't meet any of these face to face.

Hsishuang Panna means "Twelve Districts". Chinghung means "Town of the Dawn" — and thereby hangs a tale. According to folk legend, a long, long time ago, a demon king, impressed by the fertility of the Chinghung "badz", appropriated it, and took seven beautiful Tai maidens to be his wives. The people hated him, and the maidens tried to think of how to get rid of him. One day, wife number seven hit on an idea. She plied him with drink and flattered him outrageously.

"What a remarkable demon you are," she cooed. "You must be absolutely invulnerable."

"Well I am," he boasted, "more or less. The only thing that can kill me is a hair from my own head, twisted around my neck."

Soon he was snoring in drunken slumber. The girl pulled out a hair, wrapped it around his neck, and yanked. The demon's head rolled across the floor. Because he was a fire demon, whatever it touched burst into flame. The seven wives, and all the people, quickly sloshed water and extinguished the blaze. They threw the head into the Lantsang River and a new day dawned in Chinghung. Thus, the name — "Town of the Dawn". Every year in the centuries which followed, the Tai people have been celebrating with a Water Splashing Festival their destruction of the Fire Demon.

We arrived just in time to join in the holiday. Though Tai in origin, it is celebrated by all the minority people, as well as by the numerous Hans (they comprise the majority of China's millions) who have settled in the Tai communities. The festival lasts for three days and marks the Tai New Year.

The first day, we trouped down to a high bank along the Lantsang. On the slope, and for about a mile along the broad sandy flat between the bank and the river, were some thirty thousand national minority people, all decked out in their beautiful folk garb. They had come to watch the Dragon Boat Races and the Rocket Contest, to see the dancing and just wander about enjoying the color and merriment.

A cannon's boom signaled the start of the races. Each Dragon Boat, so named because of the dragon's head carved upon its prow, is paddled by sixty to eighty men, or girls, half on each side of the craft. One person wields the rudder in the stern, two or three more stand pumping with their legs on the prow to give the boat added impetus.

They shoved off, in heats of four, from the opposite side of the Lantsang, angled against the swift current. Various parts of the crowd moved toward the river's edge as contestants from their commune brigades, or militia units, competed. The winners marched, dancing and singing, to a special stand where each was rewarded with a traditional tot of the potent local rice wine. It wasn't enough to get any of the paddlers drunk, but the poor county head, who had to imbibe with each set of victors, was pretty glassy-eyed before the morning was over. I don't know who won the finals. Nobody seemed to care. The fun of the thing was all that mattered.

In the meantime, the rocket competition was proceeding full blast (no pun intended) further down the bank. The idea was to see whose homemade rocket could fly the highest and the farthest. The Chinese invented rockets centuries ago, and most of them soared off swiftly. A few seemed to have booster devices that shot them even higher.

The crowds were fluid, drifting after the sword-play demonstrators, dragon manipulators, peacock dancers, and performers of Tai and Hani dances. The national minority costumes were a dream. Together with their ornaments they are fairly expensive, but obviously the girls can afford them.

The second day of the holiday was the water splashing carnival itself. We went well into the countryside to Manting, a village production team of a Tai commune. All gathered in a large open square, equipped with small basins of water.

Then the dancing began. Half a dozen youths, heads bound by strips of mauve silk tied in the back, wove through the crowd in a large circle, dancing and rhythmically beating their elephant foot drums.

Everybody joined in, the Han and foreign visitors trying awkwardly to imitate the graceful gestures of the dancer's hands. Villagers splashed cadres and local army personnel, who laughingly returned the compliment. Water flew madly in all directions, regardless of race, regardless of rank. I and our entire visiting group were soaked from head to foot. I can't remember when I had a more hilarious time.

General merrymaking was the item on the agenda for the third and closing day of the festival. For this we went to Manchinghung, a commune headquarters village. Here too the people were predominantly Tai, but many Hanis lived among them, plus a goodly number of young Hans from other parts of China who had been assigned here on finishing school. There was considerable intermarriage among the races.

We strolled down the village street, where they were having market day, as they do on every Sunday. The shops were crowded with colorfully dressed minority folk, buying everything from toothpaste to small transistor radios. Outside, on both sides of the street, village women sat selling tomatoes and peppers they had raised in their own gardens, and hot chilli sauce and cold drinks. They can fix their own prices, which are sometimes higher, but often lower, than the government shops'.

Young men wheeled their bikes slowly along, looking for marriage mates. Finding sweethearts during the festival is an old custom. If a girl answers when a boy stops and speaks to her, it means she considers him a possible suitor. At the end of the day when darkness falls he comes looking for her again, with a flashlight instead of a flaming torch, as was the ancient custom. If she is still there, and willing, he takes her to her home, sitting side-saddle on the rear rack of his bike, and meets her parents.

The Tais themselves, who are relatively numerous, are promoting marriages in the mid-twenties and family planning, just like the Hans. For racial minorities whose numbers are small, no limitations exist.

Phoenix and I had lunch that day in the platform home of a young Tai couple. Formerly, these buildings were of bamboo and thatch, but now everyone uses the stronger timber and tile. The picturesque style remains the same.

We met their two children, sturdy boys of three and eight. The older lad was in school, as are ninety-six percent of all school-age Tai kids. Classes are conducted in Tai, and reading and writing is taught in that language. At the request of the Tais, the children also learn standard Han. Education and medicare are free for national minority people. Malaria is down to 0.006. Smallpox and cholera have been wiped out.

The husband could speak Han a bit. He said both he and his wife worked in the fields, and had about a hundred and fifty *yuan* left to put in the bank each year after all their expenses were paid.

Bananas, mango, papaya, oil palms, fine timber trees, and the like, abound throughout the prefecture. Folk handicrafts are superb. At the moment the absence of a railway prevents these from getting to market in any real number. But the transportation problem will be solved in the near future.

"Visit us again in five years," said our hosts in Chinghung as we were leaving. "We'll have a lot to show you."

On the return leg we spent a few days in Kunming, visiting ancient landmarks and temples that didn't interest me much. But in their museum they have two thousand-year-old bronzes recently unearthed, cast by a people called the Tien who had a kingdom which then ruled that region. Detailed etchings on their bronze vessels show them to have been remarkably like the South American Incas, in dress, in weapons, even facially. They raised humpbacked steers which no longer exist in China, and buried bronze models of them with their dead. There are several in the museum. I bought a replica of one, also of fine Yunnan bronze, and brought it home with me on the plane.

In the months that followed there were momentous developments in foreign affairs. The first big breakthrough occurred in October 1978, when Teng Hsiao-ping, representing China, went to Tokyo to sign a Treaty of Peace and Friendship with Japan. It contained the much debated anti-hegemony clause, to the fury of the Soviet Union. It also paved the way for vastly expanded trade between the two countries.

Next came an even bigger thunderclap. On December 15th, Chairman Hua Kuo-feng and President Jimmy Carter simultaneously announced the establishment of formal diplomatic relations between the People's Republic of China and the United States of America as of January 1, 1979, and the opening of embassies on the first of March. America's defense pact with Taiwan would not terminate until the end of 1979, and China did not renounce the use of force to liberate the island. But subsequently the US declared a cessation of arms sales during the final year of the pact, and China ended its shelling of the off-shore islands, pulled its navy out of the Taiwan Straits and offered to negotiate with "Mr. Chiang Ching-kuo". The Hua-Carter announcement also inveighed against the attempt by any country to impose hegemony "in the Asia-Pacific region or in any other region of the world".

The rapport was expected sooner or later, but none of us thought it would happen so quickly. Clearly, the atmosphere was improving. The Canton Motion Picture Studio sounded me out about playing the role of a "good" American — the friend of Wen Yi-tuo the liberal professor in Southwest University who was murdered by Kuomintang gunmen for supporting student protesters.

Peking Hotel was thronged with American tourists and businessmen. I met quite a few — everyone wanted interpretations of what was going on. I had no special wisdom, but at least I could figure out what was bugging them and talk in words they understood. Many of them found it difficult to communicate with their hosts, due not so much to language as to their very different backgrounds.

For me personally formal Sino-American relations is a heartening development. China is my home, America is my roots. My wife, my daughter, my grand-daughter, my dearest friends, and I myself, are Chinese — in principles to which we are dedicated, in our attitudes and way of life. At the same time, in the States I have family I love and friends I'm enormously fond of. I recall with nostalgia all manner of American places and things. For thirty years these two aspects of my existence were kept pretty much apart. The blending of the best of both has now commenced.

Only a few nights ago Phoenix and I were invited to a banquet given in the Great Hall of the People by China's Association for Friendship with Foreign Countries to celebrate the new relationship. Attending were Leonard Woodcock and members of the American Liaison Office — soon to become an embassy, four visiting US senators, and various Americans living in Peking. An orchestra played Chinese tunes and *America the Beautiful* and *Home on the Range*.

A new era has begun, not just for me and mine, but for all the people of both countries. We have much to offer each other. My own experience tells me that Chinese and American can be a very happy combination.

About the Author:

SIDNEY SHAPIRO was born in New York's Lower East Side in 1915, raised in Brooklyn, and graduated from St. John's Law School in the midst of the Depression. He began work with a prestigious Wall Street law firm, but after serving in the army during World War II, chose to pursue his growing interest in China by seeking work as a lawyer in Shanghai in 1947. Married to a Chinese woman, he remained in China after the Communist regime took control of the country, subsequently raised a child, and in 1963 applied for and was granted Chinese citizenship. He has enjoyed an acclaimed career as a translator of Chinese fiction, both classic and modern, his most recent achievement being a notable English rendering of the classic Chinese epic, *Outlaws of the Marsh.*